A
ROCK
BAZAAR

TWENTY-MINUTE FANDANGOS

AND FOREVER CHANGES

A
ROCK
BAZAAR

EDITED BY

JONATHAN EISEN

VINTAGE  BOOKS

A DIVISION OF RANDOM HOUSE | NEW YORK

FIRST VINTAGE BOOKS EDITION   November, 1971

Copyright © 1971   by Jonathan Eisen

All rights reserved under International and Pan-American Copyright Conventions. Published in the United States by Random
House, Inc., New York. Distributed in Canada by Random House
of Canada Limited, Toronto. Originally published by Random
House, Inc., in 1971.

ISBN: 0-394-71120-3

Library of Congress Catalog Card Number: 71-159342

Acknowledgment is gratefully extended to the National Enquirer
for permission to reprint "How To Tell If Your Child Is a
Potential Hippie and What You Can Do About It" (October 4,
1970). Copyright © National Enquirer, Englewood Cliffs, New
Jersey.

"The Mike Curb Story," by Howard Smith, is reprinted by permission of The Village Voice. Copyright © 1970 by The Village
Voice, Inc.

Manufactured in the United States of America by
H. Wolff Book Co., N.Y.

PREFACE

Greetings! Here are some other titles. In them you may find some clues. The first letters of each, arranged in a certain way, may spell out a word or saying. See what you can do. (Don't give up except if you feel like it.) *No More Hazards Monday, Flood Scenarios Played Backwards, First Person Plural Found Dead, Tablets for Tomorrow, Soup Stain Anguish, Smegma's Revenge, Tympanic Ecstasy or Something Else, Eustachia: The Rise of Twentieth Century Lather, Albion Your Witness, Tiptoe Warts Illusion, Salamander Greaseball Tourney, Colophons for Cleveland, Secret Anderson Parlour Raquets, Cauliflower Consciousness, Outwardly Bulbous (As Told to Frank Edwards).*

Just like in the old John Cage books, you can start anywhere. Yes, that means you don't have to start at the beginning. As an experiment several copies of this printing have been specially perforated so that the true anti-structure partisans can search them out in bookstores, separate the pages and shuffle the book around to their own liking. Perhaps this very book is perforated! If so, just follow the simple instructions that may be enclosed in a special envelope affixed herein.

Many people have actually asked me (they have said): "Jon, what is this book about? You have edited *The Age of Rock* and its sequel and cousin, *The Age of Rock 2*, and now this. Is this really *The Age of Rock 3* in disguise? Is there something you're not telling us?" In response, I smile laconically, the faintest hint of a knowing line curls my lip on the left side. I say, "No, and yet it is in some ways the responsibility of rock music." Notice, I don't say "product of." Or, "about," without the "of." I ask them to look at the galleys and give me their opinion. We discuss the culture long into the small hours of the morning.

J.E.

CONTENTS

A
ROCK
BAZAAR

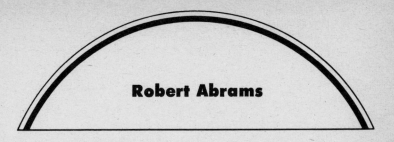

Robert Abrams

SCRIPT FOR THE CATACLYSM

America is a strange land in a strange time. Its history is not as pretty as its landscapes; its heroic past is caked with blood. The first settlers were Puritans, seeking religious freedom, and their first actions were to create a repressive environment. Witch-hunting was the first blood sport (animals and fowl were slaughtered for food) and the slave trade, which was to flourish for nearly three hundred years, helped America grow prosperous. Consequently, the McCarthy era and Vietnam cannot be looked upon as alien barbarities, new inhuman follies; they are but extensions of our earliest traditions and customs.

Many have tried to capture the elusive American psyche, so filled with rich contradictions. In 1835 Alexis de Tocqueville did a good job on us in his *Democracy in America*. He had the advantage of being an objective visitor. But Mark Twain and Melville, full-blooded Americans and carrying all of the national genes—cynicism, humor, cruelty, compassion, superstition—spoke out succinctly, fluently. Brooks Adams, looking back from the early 1900s, also made a cogent analysis:

> In every civilization there are, as Saint Paul pointed out, two principles in conflict—the law, or the moral principle, and the flesh, or the evil principle; and the flesh is, in a general way, incarnated in the principle of competition, which, rooted in the passions of greed, avarice, and cruelty, is apt to prevail to an unendurable degree unless restrained by law. And it is to regulate and restrain competition that human laws have been and are still devised.

And still the American measurement and summary goes on. In the 1960s foreign film makers were avidly making the analyzing trip. Godard filmed the Jefferson Airplane as part of the Youth Revolution; Antonioni did *Zabriskie Point*, a collage motif of American ways. This is the story of another attempt to capture the representative American posture.

"Well, Roman, baby, what do you think?"

The man in the well-furnished, rather plush office thought back to his childhood. As a small boy in his native Czechoslovakia, he had always wanted to make films. Finally one day that dream was realized in that land of unlimited dreams, the United States of America. And now he was being asked to make a film about this abundant land. He was to have as much freedom as he needed to convey his impressions; his producer just had a few ideas to "keep audience interest," as he put it.

"I think you should include some sex, perhaps a rape or two, and some killings, a lot of crime, a lot of perverted hippies, dope, stuff like that, maybe even some witchcraft."

Charles Manson was born at the end of the Depression. His mother, fifteen at the time, was unmarried. From the time he was eight, young Charlie was in a variety of reform schools. Finally, he wound up at Plainfield, Indiana, the toughest school in the Midwest. By his own count, he escaped twenty-seven times, which is even a couple more times than Dylan claims to have run away from home.

He was not released until he was twenty-one. He was out about six months when he was arrested and convicted of larceny for an automobile theft. He received a sentence of three years. After his release, he was back in the can soon after on a "ten twenty-one," a bum check rap.

In the year 1970, Roman Polanski was on top of the world. His young bride, the prominent starlet, Sharon Tate, was pregnant with his child. He had recently celebrated the success of *Rosemary's Baby* and he was being approached to do some far-out scripts.

While Charles Manson's parents were migrating westward, from Oklahoma to California, they met another Okie, Woody Guthrie. Perhaps it is this association that encouraged young Chuck to become a folksinger.

He started out about the time Joan Baez was becoming a big star and sang mostly the traditional songs of the hill folk. Soon, though, he found he had more to say than he could within the framework of the Child ballads. His songs were rather exotic— tunes like "My Quasar Laser," "Omphalos," "Dulce Domum," "Ode to Idomemeus" and the by now quasi-classic, "Readywhip up Your Cunt." It was while playing the troub that he began to meet personalities who would emerge during the sixties as impressive people.

The first person to take an interest in his career was Peter Fonda. You may or may not recall, but at this time Peter had just finished making *Tammy and the Doctor*. Peter really talked up Manson's career to all the pop heroes that he knew, so that's maybe why you never heard of Chuck. But somehow word reached Terry Melcher, Doris Day's son and producer of the Byrds, that there was this enormous talent on the Strip.

One night at Fort Ord in California a certain young girl became stage-struck. In an amateur-hour contest, she had sung "Soldier Boy" and won. (The fact that her father was the fort's commanding officer didn't hurt.) From that time on, she dreamed only of the day when she would appear before millions on the silver screen.

Los Angeles is not so much a geographical location as a state of mind, similar to the Woodstock Nation and the Haight. As such, one continually experiences the environment. Most trends, fads, etc., have gotten their start in this city. The smog and the climate combine to provide a sameness about the weather that other areas do not possess; hence, anything that changes the boredom level is permissible.

The latest large-screen scene in this scene-setting capital is an interest in the occult arts. We live in an age when people want desperately to find something to believe in, having rejected the traditional beliefs. And so we are now calling upon the traditional heresies, such as drugs, sex and Satanism. And, indeed, drugs and sex abound in the worship of the Devil.

"Well, J.B., the basic idea of the plot is to have a pregnant, young, beautiful jet-setter murdered. I think we can call into play a lot of different fantasies about America. She should be a newly-wed, from an impoverished background."

"How about Sharon for the leading lady?"

"That's a good idea, 'cause we can get actual footage of her during pregnancy."

"Great idea, boss. I'll phone you later as we get more of this down on paper."

Charles Manson was an honor student at Fairfax High in Los Angeles. Although he was generally well-liked, people got uptight about some of his rather eccentric behavior and peculiar talents. Like when things were misplaced, he had an uncanny ability to find the lost items, and at parties, he would tell fortunes that more often than not came true. And he had a way of looking at you—it was downright stone weird, man.

Later, after graduation, Manson didn't go on to college like the rest of us; he babbled something about wanting to go to India because of some books he had read, stuff like *The Razor's Edge* and *Siddhartha*. I wonder what ever became of him? I'm sure he wound up doing something kookie.

☞ BOY TELLS OF CHAINING BY CULTISTS

Indo, Calif., Oct. 30 (UPI)—Anthony Saul Gibbons, 6, sitting on a pillow on the witness stand so he could be seen, testified Wednesday he was burned with matches and imprisoned in a packing crate in a desert commune for starting a fire.

The small boy was barely audible as he related the events that led to his being chained inside the sweltering box for 56 days during the summer on the farm commune operated by a cult called Ordi Templar Orientalis.

Eleven members of the commune, including the child's mother, are on trial for child abuse, a felony.

Anthony, now a ward of the court, said his fingers were burned with matches after he started the fire which destroyed a house and injured a group of goats June 20.

The boy was questioned repeatedly before he took the oath as Defense Attorney Keith Blazer attempted to establish if the boy knew what a lie was. The boy said he understood that he would be punished if he told a lie.

After Anthony testified, the prosecution rested its case.

"Okay, J.B., for the murderer we'll have some hippie type who's head of a communal group. He'll have to be totally handsome, and irresistible to women—all women. Furthermore, he'll be knowledgeable in all sorts of arcane cult lore. Like, he should be able to manufacture drugs and lead black masses and heal the lepers. You know, maybe some overt Christ symbolism wouldn't be bad. I mean, that seems to be popular with the young. And yeah, the locale is Southern California."

Many are the stories told of Charles Manson's fabled instrument of pleasure. Some claim it is three-pronged, like the trident of Neptune, and capable of supporting a series of different activities. I am told that often he engages in vaginal intercourse, rectal intercourse and oral intercourse simultaneously. Others tell of its legendary length, accurately measured by the Bureau of Standards and determined to be 58.42 centimeters long when erect. An Angel I knew claimed that his glans was punctured and that he wore a gold earring dangling from the head.

The first time I met the Princess she was dancing. But not just dancing . . . I mean dancing! The barely restrained lust of the Wife of Bath.

She is covered by black feathers, except for bare breasts. Her skin is chalk-white, a complexion obtained by bleaching with arsenic.

The bizarreness of her dress is nothing compared to the bizarreness of her residence, the place where we next met. The castle of

the Princess Leda Amun Ra is as legendary as she. Its location way
up in the hills over Hollywood makes it appear to float and hover,
much like a spaceship in a sci-fi movie. Inside are hand-carved
shutters, and outside, in the driveway, there is a silver Packard
with black curtains. No moat, no crocodiles, but other animals,
and a huge statue of Satan's head in the back.

The bedroom is occupied by the largest bed imaginable, covered
with a black canopy. In the middle lies the Princess, resplendently
naked, legs spread a country mile. The smell of woman open is
dominant in the air, yet one sees no visible companion. And then,
as we near, we see a black form between her thighs. On closer
inspection, one sees, held at arm's length, a black swan, which the
Princess is plunging into her femininity.

"I will conceive" is the only sound in the room.

"When they find the killer, they'll find him to be a doper and a
hellhound."

"How about having the F.B.I. involved? That way we'll get in
from both sides. The guy is a hippie pig, so neither side can hate
him. And to make it further out, we'll have him be part of a super-
secret death squad. That should appeal to the paranoia prevalent
in America."

"Don't you think that's a bit heavy?"

Sharon Tate used to visit Princess Leda, and she would come
with the worst degenerate homicidal homosexual in the country.

A favorite composition in the Polanski household has always
been Berlioz' *Symphonie Fantastique*, Opus 14.

California itself is a strange place. It somehow seems fitting
that, according to prophecy, its destiny is to fall into the ocean à la
the land of Atlantis. New York may be amphetamized, but California is strung out on downs. The effect of no seasonal change
makes time disappear.

It's not a cultural center and yet it sets the style for the culture

in this country. And everyone is so goddamned physically healthy
—probably the healthiest needle freaks in the universe. Yet in this
atmosphere, death is an ever-present constant. Driving down the
coast road from San Francisco to Los Angeles, one is struck by the
attractiveness of suicide, of merely going over the cliffs into
the welcoming waters far below, or perhaps around a curve into
the canyon.

NUDE HIPPIES FOUND STREWN IN WEEDS

On the sixth of August, the Manson family attempted to score
some dope. In a deal involving sixty-three keys at a good price,
which no one tested, the group wound up with 126 pounds of pure-
dynamite oregano.

Charles Manson was friendly with Dennis Wilson, one of the
Beach Boys. Through him he met Terry Melcher, perhaps the best
producer in rock. In one way or another, a misunderstanding arose
in which Manson claimed Melcher had promised to get him a
contract. When things didn't work out, Manson resorted to the
ancient code of the West and ordered Melcher offed. Unbe-
knownst to the hippie cult-leader, Melcher had rented his Hollywood mansion to Roman Polanski.

DEATH TO THE PIGS!

"Roman, I have some bad news for you—your wife has just been
murdered."

Charles Manson was arrested and accused of the murder of
Sharon Tate and her guests on the night of August 8. The only
evidence against him is the confession of Susan Atkins, and indications are she will repudiate her confession.

It is a known fact that the police have been after Manson for a
while, since he is such a vulnerable target. And the fact that the
press has found him guilty is indicative only of the polarization
that is prevalent in our society.

At one time, I felt this to be a mere murder, the kind that takes place every day, only this time it involved some people into some heavy L.A. things. And maybe because it's precisely that they were into heavy L.A. things that such an obvious frame is being attempted. I don't think that Manson exists as an entity, and hence he is neither guilty nor innocent. He is only what you want to believe—we will never be allowed to know more.

"Well, Roman, that sounds like a dynamite outasight plot. What are you going to call this film?"

Live freaky, die freaky.

Steve Sidorsky

TONGUE-RAPE SUFFOCATION:
THE DEATH OF ROCK

I don't have to tell you about the tongue, known or unknown. If you don't know what it is by now, forget it, go on to something else 'cause the tongue is past, it's over; and if you knew it in its heyday you're all the better for it, but now everybody talks about tongues and it just doesn't mean so much any more.

So lemme tell you about the death of rock as a result of over-intensified tongue-suffocation-burnout. Ya see, there's this principle involved here (too painful for most to accept) which says that once a tongue becomes a tongue (is recognized as such and nominally identified), it ceases to be a tongue per se and is transformed into a tongue-in-retrospect via nostalgic trivialization. (You know that.)[1] Meaning that a tongue is a tongue, a real *mindfuck* tongue, only *once*, either as a result of intellectual

---

[1] One of the greatest (real-hall-of-fame-material) examples of this conceptual/perceptual transformation is in Dylan's *Nashville Skyline*, when he and Johnny Cash sing "Girl from the North Country." Remember the first time you heard it, especially the end of the last verse: "She was once . . . a true . . . luv . . . uh-of . . . mine . . . mm . . . mm . . ." etc.? Weren't sure they'd make it, were you? Well, they did and now you can't hear the song any other way, right? Well, this isn't necessarily a tongue (it is, but it's irrelevant). Well, all right, if you must know, it's a C & W diluted ready-made, extracted from R. Charles's definitive primal unknown tongue in "I Got a Woman" (but it's not nearly as simple as that). But like I say, it doesn't matter because it's the *form* that's important here (as opposed to content, like in high school compositions), the principle of the thing, the transformation of tongue per se to tongue-in-retrospect. Ya see?

gymnastics involving sudden structural and/or experiential transition, musical awe and/or any other awe (which leaves you feeling quite satisfied) or through a quasi-DMT taxonomic urgency flash (which also leaves you satisfied, but so spaced you don't even realize it).[2] And while tongues-in-retrospect can be indexed, schematized, discussed and whatnot, their intrinsic nature as second-level paraparticipatory audience involvement modifiers renders them irrelevant. O.K.

Now this was fine and dandy as long as it remained a secret, as long as tongue production and consumption were at an unconscious level, or better, a preconscious level (like in "It sounds far-out!" etc.). Your average tongue was short, to the point and, most important, spontaneous; there was none of your aural objectification of the will involved, and this is why rock was such great stuff in the old days—it got you into important things like hair and clothes and balling and dope. But once people began inserting tongues into records (or searching for them), instead of letting them merely (!) happen, it was downhill all the way. Our primary interest levels changed and now it's art, culture, revolution and, of all things, meaning.

The reasons for this are numerous, but too mundane to elaborate on here. O.K., there's your media overfuck, your postlinear consciousness revision (both cause and effect and thus new cause), your Establishment co-option cum institutionalized legitimization move, etc. And the Indo-Chinese police action.

In short, we got into real trouble, and the only possible escape was to render the whole thing ineffectual before it destroyed us. So . . .

So out of the chosen few who were hip to the crisis there arose but a single group able to function at a sufficiently effective level, and they created an album which not only contained the most sophisticated and most varied smorgasbord of tongues imaginable, but an album which was, in itself, a tongue, a kind of supra-tongue, beyond which it was simply impossible to progress. I mean, like after you win the Triple Crown and the MVP award,

[2] It also makes it (almost) impossible to ever listen to the record again, except for a few people. Think on that.

what else is there to do? Either you stay there and enjoy it, or you kill yourself.[3] There's no going back, no halfway point.[4] And (as if you didn't know) it was the Beatles, of all people (of all people), who worked this thing out, and they managed it on the most neglected (and rightly so) of all their albums, the redoubtable *Abbey Road*.[5, 6]

Now lemme backtrack some. Ya see, there now exists an entire rock aesthetic, as expounded by R. Meltzer, Memphis Sam Pearlman[7] and all the other members of the Stony Brook-Fusion renaissance, and it's this massive psychopathic body of thought which took like six years (and that's longer than your average all-nighter) to finally get down on paper. And now, all rock music and related areas are judged (or not judged) according to a certain set of standards (or what have you) depending on your point of view (or quality of dope, or old lady or old man, etc.) on that particular day.

But the fuck-up is that once a body of art or an artistic movement adopts a set of theories and/or guiding principles (your Surrealist Manifesto, for example, or your Futurist Movement), it immediately or eventually tends to lose that vitality and originality and somewhat raving insanity which deemed it significant (and thus worthy of a set of theories and/or guiding principles[8]).[9] So today, instead of declaring a rock artifact (song, group, album cover) "heavy" or "groovy" or "far-out," we perceive it in terms of tongues, moves, ready-mades, etc., etc. And the importance of

[3] They sorta did both.

[4] Like, ya can't be a *little bit pregnant*, hmmm?

[5] Yeah, redoubtable. Like the redoubtable Babe Ruth or the redoubtable Georgia Peach (Ty Cobb).

[6] O.K. Here are some *Abbey Road* tongues: aquatic (known and unknown) tongues, academic beef tongue, Columbus tongue, instrumental-move-cum-tongue, San Francisco rock renaissance tongue, intra- and extra-quotation/reference tongues, hesitation/silence tongues, etc. There's more, but you find 'em.

[7] Who took the Fugs to the Liberty Diner at 7 A.M. that morning.

[8] See Pearlman's paradox of unpredictable inevitability or inevitable unpredictability, which won't make it any clearer, but it's a righteous piece o' writin'.

[9] I somehow feel greatly fulfilled after writing this section.

Abbey Road in the rock continuum is its (almost) perfect formal revelation of the most essential postulates of your rock aesthetic. And this is nice. Except that it reveals them to such a degree that its (this is *Abbey Road* we're talking about) very existence destroys this foundation. (Which is O.K. if that's what you want.)

So listen. If you've done your homework and read your R. Meltzer, you know about rock's intrinsic quality as, preeminently, a self-destructive creation. And from all the other shit flyin' around (*Partisan Review*, educational television, etc.), you're aware of its (rock's) being the most energetic and significant artistic movement of the twentieth century, blah, blah, blah. This is accepted now, like a postulate from high school geometry, that kinda thing. And the two most important means to this end (end?) are, of course, the tongue and, by no means a poor second (actually a dead heat), the trivialization by reflexive afterthought scheme of which the Beatles (and to a lesser extent, the Stones) are acknowledged and unacknowledged masters.

Well, here's the big move.[10] *Abbey Road* (especially the awesome second side, "the quiet side," as some call it) not only is loaded with tongues, but *is* a tongue in itself. (Just wanted to remind you.) Self-referential tongue density is a main reason for this. The transition tongue following George's S.F. rock renaissance quotation meta-tongue, which follows "Carry That Weight," is nothing less than ingenious as a vehicle for bringing the tongue principle of static kineticism and kinetic stasis to crystal perfection. And this quality (auto-tongue self-conception) allows it (the album) to build upon itself, musically and otherwise, becoming the most remarkable verse ever recorded in the history of (recorded) music. Its quasi-religious humanistic work ethic and multidimensional extratemporal tongue-enforcement motif puts it head and shoulders above any other lines in rock.

> And in the end,
> the love you take
> is equal to the
> love you make.

[10] If I start to sound sentimental, I am. I feel as if I'm somehow about to give birth.

Extraordinary! It's been more than a year, but it's not unusual for it still to evoke chills in the listener, because beyond anything else, this verse says everything on every level that everyone's been trying to say for the past decade: your civil-rights movement, your flower-power-cum-love ethic, your communes qua alternate society moves, etc., etc. It's like the single unarguable, unimpeachable statement on human (i.e., postlinear) existence.[11]

But, true to form and function, the boys refuse to stop here, and what ensues is the second most extraordinary move in music history. The ever-extended mood-imprint-via-silence technique which follows is *too long* merely to signal the end of the record and consequently develops a high-energy, panic-by-lack-of-foreknowledge field, which threatens to extend to infinity, and this scares you shitless since the previous rushes (the love, hope, peace, etc.) are beginning to recede through abstraction-by-cerebral-diffusion. This plane of opposing responses is one of the Beatles' finest creations, one of their most laudable tongues, indeed. And they still refuse to rest on their laurels because the gestalt has to be completed, the tension relieved, and the drama concluded.

And so to fulfill all of this, the lads insert a deranged, jangling, dissonant chord and make their death move with

> Her majesty's a pretty nice girl
> But she doesn't have a lot to say.
> Her majesty's a pretty nice girl
> But she changes day by day.
>
> I want to tell her
> That I love her a lot
> But I gotta get a bellyful o' wine.
> Her majesty's a pretty nice girl,
> Someday I'm gonna make her mine.
> Oh, yeah, someday I'm gonna make her mine.

What do these lines *mean*? And what do they have to do with the economics of love? It's the mind-boggling simplicity and crush-

[11] This is the dramatic juncture in the (my) narrative—where your basic postulates (tongue and trivialization scheme) begin to unite, the ol' pre-Socratic one-and-the-many move.

ing triviality of these lines that complete the trivialization-by-reflexive-afterthought death move and cause the ruination of all that precedes it on the album. And it's nothing less than the apotheosis of self-destruction and *the ultimate concretization of the heretofore (merely) abstract principle of all rock music.* Yessir.

No wonder this was the last album the Beatles (really) made together.[12] Their (and rock's) greatest creation could only result in self-destruction. And here's why.

To repeat, the first basic principle of rock is that its end result must be some form of reflexive trivialization, resulting from, oh, trivialization qua self-depreciation, trivialization qua trivialization, etc., etc. The success of any rock effort is determined by its failure to say anything significant, and any *apparent* success (at significance) is in reality a failure because of its failure to fail. *Abbey Road* was a success in that it *did* ultimately destroy anything that was meaningful within itself, but this success was so successful that ultimately it resulted in failure because of this success. And since the measure of success is the ability to fail, their apparent successful failure at failing was in the end a failure since they failed to fail to succeed by the their success. Far-out!![13]

Heh, heh. But there's more. Because if the Beatles had stopped here, we would still be left in the same realm (reality, thought-system, whatever you like) as when we began, only at the highest rung of the ladder.[14] They had still to take that giant step, that leap of faith, and make it not only bigger and better, but *different.* And while there are many trivialization schemes in many albums, only the Fab Four were able to create a scheme which was *extra-album*; and this is about where we're ready to hit the fifth dimension—strawberry fields forever.

Ya see, just as *Abbey Road* renders itself trivial by reflexive

[12] See footnote four (4).

[13] "She knows there's no success like failure/And that failure's no success at all." Aha!!

[14] As with your moral/immoral, love/hate and rational/irrational (etc.) dichotomies—they're essentially the same, just at different ends of the pole. Likewise your tongue, anti-tongue, supra-tongue, etc., progression and great or small trivialization schemes. It's a matter only of degree and in this case *Abbey Road* is like an advanced Ph.D.

afterthought (and thereby succeeds within itself but fails through its ultimate failure to fail because of this success in the larger context—the long view, as some call it), so *the entire album as an album* (an album qua album, if you will) *is itself rendered trivial, is downright ignored as a result of the concurrent world-wide Paul McCartney-is-dead publicity-by-rumor-mongering move!!* All the running around, checking album covers, playing this song backward and that song upside down, and talking to barbers and gypsy handwriting analysts—all this activity completely and totally overshadowed the stuff on the album itself.

Here, then, is your trivialization scheme operating at a total optimum efficiency level—not *in* rock as a self-referential art object, but *on* rock itself as a cultural phenomenon. It could very well be the biggest move of the last century (except maybe for when O'Malley took the Dodgers to Los Angeles).

And it all brings us to the question that maybe rock really isn't dead, because the Beatles' *aesthetic* success at *extra-musical* success was so overpowering that it forced us to overlook this aesthetic success (failure). And since extra-musical success is O.K. in rock,[15] it's not unrealistic to believe that we're right back where we started from.

And since everyone's into country music now anyway, it probably doesn't even matter.

Doo-wah.

[15] Gold records, per capita groupies, *Rolling Stone-Life* magazine interview ratios, busts, etc.

WE THINK THE AVERAGE PARENT SHOULD KNOW AS MUCH ABOUT DRUGS AS THE AVERAGE PUSHER

*Sometime soon you'll want to talk with your
teen-agers about drugs. The sooner the better.
We hope these pages give you something to start
talking about. Because we want you to get to your
kids before somebody else does.*

☛ OPIATES

When most people refer to "narcotics" this group of drugs is what they are talking about. Opiates are used medically as painkillers. On the street they cause pain for the user and society in general.

OPIUM a white powder from the unripe seeds of the poppy plant. Opium can be eaten, but it is usually smoked in an opium pipe.

MORPHINE extracted from opium. It is one of the strongest medically used painkillers, and is strongly addictive.

HEROIN strongly addictive drug prepared from morphine. Outlawed even from medical use, heroin is the most commonly used drug among addicts. It can be sniffed or injected under the skin or into a vein. Street slang for heroin includes "scag," "smack," "H," and "junk."

"ON THE NOD" or nodding—the state produced by opiates: like being suspended on the edge of sleep.

MAINLINE or "to shoot up"—injecting a drug into a vein.

SKIN POPPING to inject a drug under the skin.

"A HIT" an injection of drugs.

WORKS the apparatus for injecting a drug. May include a needle and a bottle cap or spoon for dissolving the powdered drug.

A FIX one injection of an opiate, usually heroin.

JUNK heroin, so named because as sold on the street it is never pure.

JUNKIE an opiate addict.

A BAG packet of drugs, or a single dose of an opiate. Amount of the drug in the bag is denoted by price: a nickel bag ($5), a dime bag ($10).

"COLD TURKEY" the withdrawal that occurs after repeated opiate use. The addict can become irritable, fidgety; perspiration increases; there is a lack of appetite. The main problem in discontinuing opiate use is not *getting* off the drug, it's *staying* off.

TRACK scars on the skin left from the repeated injection of opiates.

ADDICTION physical dependence on a drug, so that when the drug is taken repeatedly, and stopped suddenly, physical withdrawal occurs.

OVERDOSE cause of over two hundred teen-age deaths in New York City last year. Death results because the part of the brain that controls breathing becomes paralyzed.

☛ STIMULANTS

These drugs stimulate the system, or make a person more lively. While they are not physically addictive like the opiates, they produce a psychological dependence or craving.

AMPHETAMINES stimulants taken in tablet or capsule form, or injected into the bloodstream. Among the widely used amphetamines are:

    Dexedrine or "dex" or "dexies"
    Benzedrine or "bennies"
    Methedrine or "speed" or "crystal meth"
    Biphetamine or "footballs"

COCAINE another kind of stimulant, derived from coca leaves. It is sniffed as a white powder, or liquefied and injected into a vein. It produces a fast and powerful feeling of elation. Cocaine does not produce physical dependence (addiction), but does produce a strong psychological craving.

COKE cocaine.

SPEED FREAK a person who repeatedly takes amphetamines or "speed," usually intravenously.

MENTAL EFFECTS OF "SPEED" decreased sense of fatigue, increased confidence, talkativeness, restlessness, and an increased feeling of alertness. As dosage increases amphetamines can produce irritability, distrust of people, hallucinations, and amphetamine psychosis.

AMPHETAMINE PSYCHOSIS a serious mental illness caused by overdose or continued use of amphetamines. The person loses contact with reality, is convinced that others are out to harm him. The most frightening part is that this psychosis sometimes continues long after a person has stopped taking the drug.

RUSH the brief heightened state of exhilaration at the beginning of a high.

CRASHING withdrawal from amphetamines: the swift descent from an amphetamine high to severe depression.

☞ PSYCHEDELICS

This is the medical classification of all mind-altering substances. "Psychedelics" change a person's perception of his surroundings.

HALLUCINOGENS those psychedelics which cause hallucinations.

LSD probably the most powerful psychedelic. Reactions to LSD are extremely unpredictable: distortions in time and space; brighter colors; vivid sounds; feelings of strangeness; a sense of beauty in common objects; sometimes fear and panic; sometimes even psychosis.

FLASHBACK a user thrown back into the LSD experience months after the original use of the drug. Other possible risks of LSD, which are being thoroughly researched, include brain damage and chromosome breakage.

ACID LSD. A frequent LSD user is an "acid head."

DROP to take any drug orally. LSD is usually dissolved in water, and may be placed on a sugar cube. The term is to "drop acid."

DMT a powerful psychedelic prepared in the laboratory as a powder or liquid. It is usually injected into the vein or smoked along with marijuana or in cigarettes.

PSILOCYBIN a psychedelic taken from a mushroom. It is less potent than LSD and takes a larger dose to get the effect.

PEYOTE from the peyote cactus. It causes pronounced visual effects. It is used in a religious ritual by some Southwestern United States and Mexican Indians, and its use in these rituals is legal.

MESCALINE or "mesc"—a drug which also comes from the peyote cactus. Stronger than peyote itself, mescaline also causes vivid visual impressions.

DOM   called STP by users. The effects of STP can last for two or three days.

MARIJUANA   the crushed and chopped leaves and flowers from the hemp plant. Sometimes smoked in cigarette form, sometimes smoked in pipes. Reactions can be: a giddy feeling like drunkenness; changes in perception and mood; feelings of well-being or fear; and possibly hallucinations. Slang terms for marijuana are "grass" or "pot."

JOINT   a marijuana cigarette.

ROACH   the butt end of a joint.

STONED   describes the intoxicating effect of marijuana, or really any drug including alcohol.

HASHISH   called "hash." Also prepared from the flowering tops of the hemp plant. Hashish is smoked in a pipe or taken orally, and is more powerful than marijuana.

THC   or tetrahydro cannabinol—purified extract of the resin of the hemp plant. Also made in the laboratory. It's thought to be the substance in marijuana and hashish that causes the mind-altering effects.

TRIP   a name for the reaction that is caused by a psychedelic drug. A "bummer" is an unpleasant or frightening trip.

HEAD   someone who uses drugs frequently.

☛ DEPRESSANTS

The category of drugs that depress the functions of the brain.

"DOWNS"   street slang for depressants.

ALCOHOL   ethyl alcohol, a depressant because it slows the functions of the brain that control thinking and coordination. In high doses it produces drowsiness and sleep. Alcohol is an addictive drug, since after prolonged or continued use, it can cause physical dependence (alcoholism) and, when discontinued, causes with-drawal symptoms at least as serious as the other addictive drugs.

BARBITURATES   in the group called sedatives—medicines to make you sleepy. Barbiturates are taken in capsule or tablet form. They cause physical dependence (addiction) and, after repeated use, physical withdrawal does occur when these drugs are discontinued. Among the common commercial names for barbiturates are:

Seconal or "red devils"
Nembutal or "yellow jackets"
Amytal or "blue heaven" or "blue devils"
Luminal or "purple hearts"
Tuinal or "rainbows" or "double trouble"

TRANQUILIZERS   drugs that calm tension and anxiety. These drugs do not cause sleep except in high doses. Tranquilizers are taken in capsule or tablet form. Some common commercial names for tranquilizers are Equanil, Miltown, Librium and Valium.

INTOXICATION   sedative or tranquilizer intoxication is similar in its symptoms to alcohol intoxication. Driving while intoxicated can be extremely dangerous, and is thought to cause at least 25,000 traffic fatalities a year.

BARBITURATE OVERDOSE   more people in the United States die as a result of an overdose of barbiturates (usually suicide) than of any other single substance.

Interview
by Bud Scoppa

THE BYRDS

BUD: I don't think it is a dumb idea, it's just that . . .

ROGER: It's a fine idea; it's just done because we made a production out of it. Really, I made a production out of it, but you asked me to put it on my machines and I . . .

BUD: I thought I'd never see a ——— against the Rotary Club—in Kankakee, Illinois, or something.

ROGER: As Chairman of the Rotary Club here in Kankakee, I'm sure all the members out there, all you guys, are very proud of the great success we have had with putting up the ornaments for the upcoming celebration of the Rotary Club for 1936. As you know, this year 1936 has been our best year for rotating everything, including soil and crops and wheels and indeed our own planet. And now, in my official function as Chairman of the Rotary Club of Kankakee, Illinois, I would like to bring up to the podium our beloved brother and fellow rotar, Gene Parsons. Gene, come up to the mike. Let's hear it for Gene.

GENE: I ain't talking while the flavor lasts. I hereby pass it on to fellow brother, Michael. Come up to the microphone, Michael.

MICHAEL: ———

BUD: Well, I guess historically there are some things I'm not sure about. Am I not pushing onward?

ROGER: Are you engrossed in the TV set? No? Well, push the button on top—the white one . . . Here we are at the Tip Top

Lounge of the Newbury Cafe located in downtown Omaha, bringing you the All-Night Show brought to you by the Corn Huskers Revenge. Corn Huskers Revenge, remember, comes in convenient packages of family-economy size, regular size and baby size. So don't forget to get a package . . .

SPLICE: Splice!

ROGER: . . . *Rebel Without a Cause*—I've seen that twelve to fifteen times. Last time I couldn't keep my eyes off of him. I knew which shots they cut. I was watching every little lick in there. I was watching Dennis Hopper's face and getting into—I mean, I'm past watching Dean doing his soliloquies, and Hopper is in the background making facial expressions, y'know.

BUD: Oh, really?

ROGER: He was trying to steal the scene with his face. If you weren't watching Dean, he would be, y'know.

BUD: Things don't really have to be universal to be valid at a particular time. *Hard Day's Night* really was saying something.

ROGER: So was Spock, man.

BUD: Yeah.

ROGER: Nobody dug it at the time, though. It boils down to if you are appreciated in your time, your value is limited. It's true, you have to die and be a martyr before they will love you in a couple of hundred years, forever. Not necessarily, with the current media . . . it might readjust the situation. So I take that back. You can be good and still be appreciated, but not as much as you will be when you kick off, because everyone loves you when you kick off, because you can't hurt them any more.

BUD: I'm really having trouble following you.

ROGER: There's nowhere to go. We are stuck here on the earth, together. With all kinds of bad scenes going on. Making the best of it.

MIKE: Yeah, right. All the ways they are trying to kill us. You have to do something.

GENE: Wake up, Clarence.

MIKE: Really, they're trying to kill us.

ROGER: Let's hear it for ecology.

GENE: Yea.

MIKE: [Slurs] What college?

ROGER: What do you think about the euthanasia situation?

MIKE: Too expensive and what do you get?

ROGER: Yeah. You get killed.

GENE: Shot.

BUD: Let me try again.

ROGER: Take two, roll on. Speed.

MIKE: You're writing on the Byrds, right?

BUD: Yeah.

MIKE: A book on—all the way from the beginning—all the way through—you want the whole smear in a nutshell?

ROGER: That's what he wants—in a nutshell, man. All on a sixty-minute tape.

MIKE: Well, it's going to be difficult.

BUD: Well, I've got about thirty minutes more.

ROGER: What do you want to know?

BUD: What do I want to know?

ROGER: Yeah—specifically. We'll tell you in a nutshell and then we'll tell you . . .

BUD: That's really not an easy question. I want to know the things . . .

ROGER: You mean you don't know?

MIKE: It was so far-out, man. It's always been far-out.

ROGER: We don't even know.

MIKE: There is just so much . . . Yeah, we don't even know.

ROGER: I don't know anything, actually, about what happened. It's just a big blur to me.

BUD: Well, let me try it from my point of view, you know, like . . .

MIKE: You guys threw it at us, man, that's what happened, man.

ROGER: You're making an academic situation out of something that is a life experience, right?

BUD: Yeah.

ROGER: In other words, you are reducing it to type, which is limiting and also leaves you—which is nice because it lets you— it's got a flower quality to it that blossoms and everybody says it differently, when you write something.

BUD: It's not like music, though.

ROGER: Well, it's an art form. I would certainly say it was an art form equal to music. I wouldn't put it down. I think I'm really more of a fan of audio-visuals than I am of black-and-white print on paper because it takes much more work and you don't absorb as much per minute. I'm sort of a futurist . . . and some people are, like, intellectually reactionary, but not necessarily politically so. Like people who live in a baroque period and are militant liberals at the same time.

BUD: Yeah. The thing is, with audio-visuals there is a different kind of language and people really don't know what that language is. Perceptions, when they are flashing at you, are a lot different in form from words on a page, which you can go back to.

ROGER: Yes, that's right. One is totally linear and the other is almost horizontal and vertical at the same time. You can return to it.

BUD: I don't know what to call that.

ROGER: Well, you can return to it; it has a—you can return to the tape or recording. It's a recording, you see. You can also return on film but you have to have access to the control of the film. You can return to it, go back to it like you can a book. It's the same thing. It is merely a matter of giving everyone the facilities required to do that. You know, a book is less expensive and therefore more popular. If they could get cassette video-players down to the same price as a book, like the six ninety-five or seven ninety-five that you pay for a hardbound copy, then you get a cassette and you already have the equipment to play it with. They could get a whole book down on one of those, right? Video, video-color, perhaps three-dimensional, with stereophonic sound. Whatever they want.

BUD: How would you illustrate a book like that?

ROGER: Well, you would have to think a lot more visually than you do when you write. Provided you have an imagination which gives you—when you are writing a book, you're putting your imaginary trip into words. Right?

BUD: Yeah.

ROGER: Where it immediately takes on an ambiguous overtone. It's ambiguous unless you put it into words, unless you are extremely specific, which is scientific—not entertaining to listen to or to read. Do you know what I mean? Beauty is inherent in literature. Like people can misinterpret the Bible, right? There is not one interpretation literally. There are a number of ways of looking at it literally. I don't know. I'm sort of a word fascist, actually.

BUD: Maybe that comes from being . . .

ROGER: Well, I'm from a word environment. My parents are both writers.

BUD: Yeah. I saw something about that on a xerox copy of a page with your parents' names on it. I also found a picture of you in the files, and it said, "Jim McGuinn, fifteen years old." You've got a flat-top and you are holding a banjo. You have this plaid shirt on.

[Laughter]

GENE: A flat-top?

BUD: Yeah.

GENE: I thought you said you never had a flat-top.

ROGER: It wasn't a flat-top—well, it wasn't with fenders, anyway. That's what I thought you were talking about.

BUD: It was an official football practice.

ROGER: Yeah. I had an avant-garde, Aspen, Colorado, ski haircut. That's what it was at the time.

BUD: I think it was 1957.

ROGER: Yeah, it was very hip in 1957 if you were in Aspen, Colorado, skiing, which I wasn't. I was into people who were. It was a vogue thing just like long hair is now. You can laugh at long hair in ten years. You can say, "Ha, ha, you had your hair down to your fuckin' ankles."

BUD: That's the problem. I've tended to be scared away from vernacular language, faddish language, because I was just thinking, what if I write that down and read it in five years. It will look really ridiculous.

ROGER: Well, then anything you do, unless it is tuned to infinity, will look ridiculous.

BUD: I guess everything's relatively ephemeral. Even a rock.

ROGER: Well, you can attempt to tune to infinity. There are a number of available methods; they are all—look in the yellow pages under "Infinity" or "Tuning." Go look in the index in the front—"We're Tuned to Infinity." See if anyone has picked up on that phrase yet. It would be a good one . . .

BUD: It would.

ROGER: Metaphysical trips aren't in the yellow pages yet. They are not accepted and approved by the Good Housekeeping Seal.

BUD: The stuff that you are interested in—like, you can just buzz away on a lot of different kinds of topics. It seems to be in a lot of the music you've made. It's really nice to be able to think about things and enjoy certain things and then make your living by talking about them. I don't know . . .

ROGER: I've always felt fortunate to be making a living doing what I like to be doing.

BUD: I mean, is this what you like to be doing? I'm not just asking you, but everybody.

ROGER: Yeah. Oh, man, otherwise I wouldn't do it.

GENE: The only thing I like almost as well is pumping gas. I like to pump gas.

ROGER: I do, too. When I go to the gas station I jump out and pump and the guy gets—I love to pump gas, but I wouldn't want to do it for a living. I pump gas for myself, for my own pleasure. You start to sniff it, you know, while you're pumping it. You can't help it . . . standing there sniffing it. You get stoned on gas, man.

BUD: I always thought it would probably taste good.

ROGER: It doesn't taste good to drink, man, unless you really cut it down with water.

BUD: It has a nice smell to it.

ROGER: Oh, it smells good.

GENE: I've siphoned a lot of gas, and I know what it tastes like.

ROGER: It tastes lousy.

GENE: Yeah. It doesn't taste very good.

ROGER: Skip it.

BUD: If you had it to do all over, would you go the same route?

ROGER: Definitely. It's like I had no choice. I'd try to.

BUD: You had no choice? You mean destiny?

ROGER: I had a bunch of choices, but they all would have wound up as the same thing, more or less.

BUD: Do you think that is true of everybody, or just you?

ROGER: I don't know. Do you think I'm special in that respect?

GENE: I had a lot of choices.

ROGER: I had choices, but somehow, regardless of what choice you make, you come out the same place in the long run. It always sort of turns to something—like what Alfred Hitchcock is into, Rod Serling, the same thing.

BUD: No matter what happens?

ROGER: You can take the wrong track—not in train talk—you can't take the wrong track and avoid an oncoming train. But—yes, in train talk, you can take the wrong track and switch onto the right track before the oncoming train gets there. You dig? I mean, there are ways to do it. There definitely are tracks—there are tracks. Like, the spaceship Earth that we are living on right now is on tracks, huh? With environmental control on auto-planet, the spaceship Earth on auto-planet, just flying through the air at countless thousands of miles per hour down-range every day, rotating around the sun. But the entire galaxy is moving at a different speed, and the rotation is 18,500 miles per hour. The spaceship Earth that we are sitting on, here talking normally about trivia, is on tracks, man. You can't change the course of it. Right? I state like a hypothesis or postulate, you know, that everything is on tracks within the structure of the universe.

BUD: But the game is, it's not apparent where the tracks lead, you know, which leads you to a Hindu type of conclusion. There is a game involved. Maybe you don't necessarily have to think that.

ROGER: Well, you can interpret it to be a game. A game is merely—a game is a reproduction of reality. It's like Monopoly is a reproduction of real-estate sales—you know, capitalism. The game Risk is a reproduction of international warfare extending over the entire globe. Games are just reality, so you can interpret everything in actuality to be a game, which in a way it is. But it's a real game, played for life-or-death stakes instead of money or points, whatever you call them. Too bad Jim Dickson isn't around here to answer that.

BUD: Jim would just take it away.

ROGER: He will for about thirty minutes.

BUD: I already got forty-five minutes of that. It's really interesting.

ROGER: He's fascinating.

BUD: Yeah.

ROGER: He tends to harp.

BUD: He's obviously older. He's . . .

ROGER: Older, yeah.

BUD: He's like a professor . . .

ROGER: He's definitely a teacher. He's a schoolteacher. He's got a schoolteacher quality about him. I wouldn't give him a professor—like Ph.D. professor—rating. I'd rate him more like—he's an M.A. kind of teacher.

BUD: Did he build anything into the Byrds at the beginning? Was he a . . .

ROGER: Yeah, he built Dylan into the Byrds.

BUD: Yeah.

ROGER: Yeah, which was our central ingredient. He did it against my will and everyone else's, initially, but then I started to dig it.

BUD: You knew Dylan in the Village?

ROGER: Yeah, but he was my enemy.

BUD: You didn't like him?

ROGER: No, man. He used to—it was competitive. Everybody—
he had like twenty little girl fans and I didn't, so I was pissed at
him. I didn't particularly dig his imitation of Jack Elliot or
Woody Guthrie. I thought, O.K., anybody could get up and do
that. He was sincere about it, so he carried it off. That's why he
made it, because he was sincere about whatever he tried. You
haven't heard his latest album yet, have you?

BUD: No. Do you have the tapes?

ROGER: No. I was allowed to listen to it. But I haven't been given
a copy.

BUD: I think I heard one track on the radio yesterday. It was very
mellow.

ROGER: It wasn't "Blue Moon," was it?

BUD: No. This was mellower than *Nashville Skyline*.

ROGER: He's got some leftover stuff from Nashville—six cuts,
leftovers from the Nashville session that would have been in
Nashville Skyline. He's got about eight cuts that were made in
New York that are real crappy—you know, just reach in, scrape
the bottom. It's just god-awful stuff, and Bob Johnston put god-
awful voices over it.

GENE: Oh, did Bob put voices on it? He did his thing, huh?

BUD: It's like "Lay, Lady, Lay."

ROGER: Yes, he did a "Lay, Lady, Lay" on Dylan.

BUD: I think he said that Dylan was there on the mixers with
Johnston.

ROGER: I hate to lay a dupe, man, but Johnston is an insidious
dupe artist. He can get you because he comes on so strong.
Country-like, he tells little funny stories and then he cons you
into his game and you don't know it, because if you know it,
then you—

BUD: Is it a bad album?

ROGER: Clive realizes that there are bad aspects to it, but he loves it just the same. I told Clive what I'm telling you. Dylan doesn't particularly like it. He's working on another one right now, to prove the point, yeah. He's going to cover himself before it's too late, like the sessions with Harrison and all.

BUD: Did you guys—I've been wondering about this for a long time. The first time I heard "Sounds of Silence," the single, I was wondering if any of you, and particularly you, had played on either Highway 61 or Blonde on Blonde. There are a couple of tracks that are direct cops.

ROGER: Nobody invited me to.

BUD: No?

ROGER: It was probably Robertson.

BUD: In the "Sounds of Silence" it really sounds like a twelve-string Rickenbacker.

ROGER: Well, Simon and Garfunkel—

CHRIS: I remember Roger even saying something about it when we heard it on the radio, while we were on the road, that it was a cop.

BUD: The strange thing is, I just realized it about a month ago, you know, after hearing the song about a thousand times. Then I thought of a Beatle song. Was it "Nowhere Man"?

CHRIS: "If I Needed Someone."

ROGER: Yeah. That was Harrison. He admitted to me that he was doing a "Bells of Rhymney" imitation just for fun.

BUD: "If I Needed Someone"?

ROGER: Yeah. He based his tune on the guitar on that, which is something I took from Joan Baez or someone a long time ago. It was a folk riff that everyone was doing, dropping down a note.

BUD: Seeger.

ROGER: Yeah, Seeger. All the folk singers were. They would hammer on, you know, a half tone up and then they would drop down and back to zero again.

BUD: Is there a formula for a Byrd song?

ROGER: No, not—well . . .

GENE: Ask Dickson.

ROGER: Yeah, ask Dickson. He'll make one up for you on the spot. He had a formula for "Tambourine Man." He developed that. We really weren't in control on that at all. We were sort of puppets at that point. It's strange that it was one of our best records till now. A lot of people like *Notorious Byrd Brothers* and comment about it.

BUD: Yeah, that seems to be the critical choice.

ROGER: There's a lot of extra gimmickry on that, but there is also some good material, like—

CLARENCE: It's a good album. When it first came out—

GENE: I really like the album. I think it's great.

ROGER: Chris filled it out, really. He had some good stuff on it. Really good. I mean lyrics. How many cuts did you have on *Notorious*? You had about four, five?

CHRIS: I don't remember what's on it.

BUD: His high was *Younger Than Yesterday*.

MIKE: Right, *Younger Than Yesterday*.

BUD: I think that's my favorite. I really like *Younger Than Yesterday*.

MIKE: I like both of them, *Younger Than Yesterday* and . . .

BUD: Of course, the first one has its special kind of place, too.

ROGER: Yeah. That's more intense. We were trying much harder.

BUD: What happened on that second album? I can remember being very disappointed when I heard that.

ROGER: Which one was that?

BUD: *Turn! Turn! Turn!* It's never been one of my favorite albums.

ROGER: It's one of my lousiest—it's painful. It's okay up until the last four cuts.

MIKE: Everybody likes the cover.

ROGER: We were all stars and we were punching each other out to prove it.

BUD: Punching each other out?

ROGER: There were fights, man. Dickson and us would fight. We would fight about the material and all. I can't remember. I wish I had a film of it.

MIKE: They'd have to speed it up and make it look like Charlie Chaplin. Otherwise, it'd look real and very violent.

BUD: Do you think that the ego thing kept you from becoming as big as you were probably entitled to be?

ROGER: It's on tracks, man. We got as big as we got.

BUD: If you talk to people, "Eight Miles High" is like their favorite Byrd song and . . .

ROGER: Let me say something in that respect. Financially and by world acclaim, the Byrds never reached the pinnacle that the Beatles got to, but take a look at George Harrison now. Pathetic questions like, "What group would you like to tour with?" "The Beatles." Well, there isn't one, really. I mean, the price to pay for coming off a high like they had is much heavier than the price we all had to pay. So you get what you pay for, and you pay for what you get. You pay the piper. But I don't begrudge the fact that the Byrds didn't reach the Beatle point. I also think optimistically about the future. [dialect] I'm very optimistic about the future.

BUD: I was just wondering if there was a large, even Santana-size, audience for either the Byrds or the Burritos.

ROGER: What is the Santana-size audience in thousands of people —twelve, fifteen, twenty, thirty, forty, a hundred?

BUD: Well, the album sold . . .

ROGER: Oh, record audience. I thought you meant personal-appearance audience.

BUD: I guess it is tied in together. I don't know—

ROGER: Well, Steppenwolf runs fifteen to twenty thousand. Right? At least they did six to eight months ago. I'm not sure if they still do.

CHRIS: They don't any more. They broke up.

ROGER: They broke up, I'm sorry. They did. The Airplane can draw similar numbers.

CHRIS: The Airplane can draw about twenty thousand.

ROGER: About twenty thousand and make twenty grand off of it.

MIKE: The Dead can draw a few, too—

ROGER: The trouble is, money being as tight as it is now, people don't want to pay seven fifty to get in, or whatever. They would rather go for a group that makes more like five thousand dollars than a group that makes twenty thousand because they are going to have to pay more to see the twenty-thousand-dollar group. So groups that require—like, Crosby, Stills and Nash were in that position, where people were boycotting the concerts because the prices were too high, fifteen-dollar seats or something.

BUD: I just wondered if you thought the climate had finally changed to permit music of that—I hate to say type, it isn't a type—music on that level . . . you know, success?

ROGER: What level?

BUD: I mean music on a higher level than . . .

ROGER: I don't follow your last question, what music is that? Music reached that pinnacle, and I was wondering what pinnacle. Do you mean the Beatle level? Do you mean if music can be appreciated on that level? That was mass hysteria like Frank Sinatra or . . .

BUD: No, no, I don't mean that at all.

ROGER: Like Elvis Presley or that kind of thing?

BUD: I'm talking about the quality of the music rather than the charisma attached.

ROGER: I think the quality of the music will be unrecognized but nevertheless will reach that level in the future.

BUD: What I'm saying is, Will it achieve a popularity?

ROGER: That's the charisma that you were speaking of. The quality will be—

BUD: In other words, it doesn't have anything to do with the music.

ROGER: Yeah. I've decided that the success of a record has—no, I won't say *nothing*, it has *something* to do with it, but it's not totally dependent on the quality of the music. The success of a record, for instance, like Bob Dylan's latest release—it will be out the day after tomorrow, or something, selling at six ninety-eight in special thrift-shop record stores. It's a lousy album, but it will sell over a million copies.

BUD: It probably had advance orders.

ROGER: Right. I'm saying Dylan can get away with that for a short time if he bails himself out on the next one—similar, in fact, to the Beatles white-covered album called *The Beatles*. It's sort of half good, half bad.

BUD: I never thought that was a bad album, though.

ROGER: No, it wasn't a bad album. It wasn't like—I'm not equating this with Dylan, with the white-covered Beatle album. It's much better.

BUD: Could there have been the Byrds if there hadn't been the Beatles beforehand? That's a lousy question; I take it back.

ROGER: No, I don't think so, man. There would have been no Byrds. There would have been no—

CHRIS: That's what music involves though, man.

BUD: Yeah, I'm not—

MIKE: That's how they saw the Everly Brothers.

ROGER: There wouldn't have been the Beatles if there hadn't been the Everly Brothers—and like all the other influences, like Chuck Berry, all the rock 'n' roll people, Elvis. They were largely based on Elvis and Chuck Berry and the Everly Brothers.

BUD: If you talk about those routes, the Byrds weren't really a rock group.

ROGER: No. We were a folk group. We were going to use rock instruments . . .

CHRIS: We were the epitome of a folk-rock group—folksy-rocksy.

ROGER: In it were folk musicians, prior to their joining what we did. Like four out of five . . .

BUD: All five of you?

ROGER: Michael, what kind of musician were you before you joined the group, man?

BUD: You weren't a drummer before, were you?

MIKE: Truthfully, I wasn't any kind of musician.

ROGER: He was. I first met you in San Francisco at the—

MIKE: I was digging on him in—he was playing Beatle songs.

ROGER: Right.

MIKE: No one else was playing anything.

ROGER: I might credit myself with being the first American folk-singer to pick up on the Beatle music.

BUD: Yeah.

ROGER: The day after I heard it, y'know.

MIKE: It's true.

ROGER: I don't know anyone else.

BUD: Did you dig it right away?

ROGER: Right the second I heard it—the second I heard it. I could play it on the guitar and sing it, too, at the same time, because I'd been writing songs for Bobby Vinton and Bobby Dee and stuff, and Bobby Darin, y'know.

BUD: Most folkies really resented the Beatles.

ROGER: Well, I wasn't on the inside snob trip they were on, with electric instruments and stuff.

BUD: I guess really the whole thing has been folk all the way up. I don't know what the definition of folk music is, but I think the new album we listened to tonight is kind of a folk album in the same way. Rock 'n' roll is kind of a folk music. This is the first time I ever heard the Byrds do that particular area of folk music, if you want to call rock 'n' roll folk music.

MIKE: What area?

BUD: This is the first funky Byrds album, I think—the next one.

MIKE: Yeah, it's kind of funky.

BUD: I wonder if long-time Byrd fans will accept that.

CLARENCE: Fuck them.

Sandy Pearlman

EXCERPTS FROM THE HISTORY
OF LOS ANGELES: 1965–1969

🖙 PART I: LIFE ON THE STRIP

Saturday night on the Sunset Strip exhibits a certain density. As if—but I can say no more. Then one Saturday night this guy appears. He's of the species sleaze. With a Lord Sutch cockade in his green beret and all he says; "Slip me an anodyne, mate. For I am ill." With an illness of the body? of the mind? of the soul? Well, I don't rightly know. And out there on the Strip no one seems to care. Including the sleaze himself, who, totally ignored, pads on down the street, bent upon his business, oblivious to the fact: Where he is sympathy does not exist.

That human imagination is manifest through forms. That these forms are known to the imagination and taken by it. That sympathy itself is a form of imagination . . . None of that should surprise the serious analyst. But still and all, out there on the Strip one oddity obtains: An actual near Manifold of Imagination, an extraordinary condition, whereby the Strip and its denizens manifest all the forms of imagination save that one which is sympathy. As if out there on the Strip, the human imagination came somehow to prefer all its forms to sympathy.

1969! Quite a year! Quite a number! I mean 69—what with infinite visual (rather than mere numerical) symmetry achieved through the reversal route, 69 will always symbolize (to me, at least) perfection in form. And how the Strip was humming back in December '69. Not too late, but not too early. Before Christ-

mas, but after Altamont. You know when. When more than one
dozen Hare Krishna packs ranged the sidewalks as if at will. These
guys meant to beg and they did. Especially impressive were the
ones with flyers' helmets. What a coup! They shaved their skulls!
They had no hair! It was December! Their eyes were cold! They
were cold! Perhaps. And what the hell if the mercury was more
than seventy, but less than eighty. Other religious fanatics proved
no less imaginative. From the Assembly of God hailed one rough
bunch whose sheer delight was posing for pictures late at night,
pissing on the side of a VW bus marked "Assembly of God."
Strangely, these bravos received little police harassment. But the
biggest bravos of them all had to be of Transmaniacon origin:
Transmaniacon M.C. Once considered just a story, Transmaniacon was just that, indeed, until the world figured out no
more stories would be told. ("They came late to a story that had
been, but early to a riddle not yet begun.") Then and there,
Transmaniacon became all too real. Tragic consequences, I know,
and quite an old story. Gaudy, sensational rags might easily label
these bravos "outlaw bikers," but that would be more than a slight
inaccuracy. The Transmaniacon M.C. is not outside the law per
se, but rather beyond it. All its members are philosophers, as all
Angels are poets. And the true philosopher stands not within, but
astride culture. So these bikers claim "Dominion on the Strip
today and then for California." They'd love to unleash pox madness. Pox madness in the streets. Pox madness on my mind. Pox
madness is politics these days. "We proved it at Altamont" reads
the sign. And you know it. More colorfully, perhaps, they drink
the warm and humid stuff. Their colors feature a Babylonian
vampire image straight from the Louvre. They hang out under the
actually rotating Bullwinkle monument, which Jay Ward erected
in his own honor. They know, perhaps, more than man is meant
to know. The obscure, albeit frighteningly real, connection between
the Hog and the Star named Wormwood does not escape them—
and never has. After Altamont, though, they became well-nigh
insufferable. And why not? "Who took care of the nigger—by
hand?" (Offed him.) They ask appropriately. Yes, cruel things
don't escape such bravos. Cruel things like when evil itself decays.
More than a form/content dilemma, decay like that touches upon

the very assumption of an evil incarnate, of an evil that will stand, as a cruel dialectic unfolds. And forever between: an imagined ideal and debased execution, twin poles, no less, of some continuum, process, whereby life betrays our dreams and us. The process seems rightly called by some, "Evil," and by others, "Corruption." As if corruption was the Dance of Life danced by Valentino:

> Rudolph Valentino died at the age of twenty-nine
> And his eyes were never red
> And all the girls he knew
> Thought them blue.

And while we're on this death trip, called by some the "ultimate," let's not forget that which death calls to mind inevitably, by which I mean both sympathy and its very perverse, that form imagination takes, known simply to us all as terror. To have known terror is to be capable of terrorism. A certain effective identification . . . the cruel irony known, above all, to Transmaniacon, the cruel irony of the terrorist being terrorized. Yes, in that District of Forms willed by imagination, in that District of Forms which is the Strip, Transmaniacon plays an inevitable role: The Monster of Will. And make no mistake, they are a monster. Without the mercy that leavens. Out there where no sympathy exists. And they even had a song on the charts:

> With Satan's hog no pig at all
> And the weather gettin' dry
> We'll head south from Altamont
> By California 93
> So clear the road, m' bully boy,
> And let some thunder pass
> We're pain, we're steel
> A plot of knives
> We're Transmaniacon M.C.!

> Dominion on the Strip today . . .
> And then for California
> Dominion on the Strip today . . .

And then for California
Dominion on the Strip today . . .
And then for California

Behind the pantry, behind the tree
In cold blood traveled trance
The Ghoulies' chute adopts that form
Whose name exists forever
Whose name resounds in terror
And I'm no fool to call that Hog
'Cause, man, I remember.

And surely we did offer up behind that stage at dawn
Beers and Barracuda, Reds and Monocaine
Pure nectar of antipathy behind that stage at dawn
To those and all who would resign their souls to Transmaniacon

So won't you try an unknown form
Terror's here with no form
Cry the cables Ghoulies try
And won't you try this tasty snack
Behind the scenes or/but the back
Which was the stage at Altamont
My humble boys of listless power!

PART II: THE ALTAMONT PLOT

Echoes come and echoes go. Echoes send and receive. The same thing but the order's different. One winged rodent, and every sonar device, finds distance by length—the length of a send-and-receive cycle. The rodent is a bat. And bat guidance is not invulnerable. Make no mistake, an interference effect exists. Bats know it. Bats fear it.

A recent survey reveals the Echo Park district is bat-free. Big surprise! Though obscure, the district was not randomly named, featuring, as it does, an actual Echo Park. And a lake in the middle of the park. And an island in the middle of the lake. And an interference field might be an actual Echo Park. Anyway, where would bats live? Like ducks on the lake? Not likely. On the island? People hold meetings on the island. If you live there you know that. And who knows if you don't. But bats? Bats need caves.

It's as hot as L.A. And part of it, too. It's Echo Park. The Mexican neighborhood. There are no bats. Are there echoes? You'd expect them. I don't know. If so, they'd issue from the island—mathematical focus of echo, this island. Some say it is the heart of Echo Park, where words spoken (or whispered) circulate the district, the city, the air, insinuating themselves perhaps beyond where, off the Straits of Magellan's windy shores, a Fuegian gets word from Echo Park, where, well, wherever air is capable of motion. But, in truth, Burrito King, a Burrito joint, is the heart of Echo Park. And what's a *burrito?* Once a little donkey—now a tortilla wrapped around beans and something else, i.e., beans *and* cheese or beans *and* sausage *and* eggs or beans *and* you know. Burrito King's crest? A little donkey crowned. Burrito King's on Sunset, across from the pastrami and shake joint, next to a carwash. You can't miss it.

To T.J. and back—I've been there. To Red Robin for the Stalk-Forrest Group. Or was it the Club of Los Maniacos Busboy? My memory fails. On a Tuesday I skipped San Diego. Hungry for food, not tattoo. Hungry, but selective, I had eyes only for the King. People go there to eat. I did. But I stayed to talk with Macrobius Carl (his real name). How his face had changed! Road manager to the Santos Sisters, a Bidet, Louisiana, group, before—not since—Altamont. "Funny," says Macrobius, "I've drawn mud and water with the Sisters. I've licked brick. Floods convinced us to quit the bayou. Plagues of gnats, y'know. But Altamont was . . ." Well, then she appeared. She was just seventeen. Her face was . . . Not exactly his girlfriend, but a constant female presence. The lovely Bel Punice. Composure was her gesture. Maybe she was surly. A girl to be called Cataton. A face known by heart. He'd heed what she said: "Let's conspire on the island."

They danced like sinister kangaroos—awkward, yet graceful. A mechanical component to their dance. 2 on 2, 4 on 4, 8 on 8, then 12 on 4. 16 girls. All good-looking. Were they innocent? That's a lie. They were perfect! Two hundred feet from the stage. To the right, really. And the crowd gave them ground. Immediately. As if afraid. The first Angel to see them was incensed. From San Jose, wearing a wolfskin, he hung from the tower and dropped to the

ground like bum sub dives. Only then was there a commotion.
Angels followed. The crowd panicked. "Under My Thumb" was
ten seconds away.

Bel Punice told that tale on the island. About Altamont—how
far did it go? To Altamont itself? I mean, her words as sounds.
Another sound was heard. The only other. A mariache band!
Don't laugh! An Episcopal church faces the park. Made of thick-
sliced dark wood, maybe stained. (Should our climate shift, this
church will stand.) With a big porch. Maybe too big. Big enough
for a mariache band. Dressed in black formal boleros. Each
guitarrón is bigger than a picture. Disproportion is one surprise.
Especially when it's not. An extraordinary acoustic inversion,
which may be ordinary, made this band audible to the island. But
unsuitable for dancing. Anyway.

"That's when I got hit," says Macrobius. "Man, take a look at
my face. Hit from behind—with some pool cue, loaded, most likely.
Y'know what these Angels are? All the time. Back of my head.
And hair hides the scar. Right there, man. You can't see it. Take
my word. My face got twisted outa line. I've got permanent nerve
damage. I'm digging the sounds, man, near the stage, and I get
nerve damage. Far-out."

I said, "Just an innocent bystander?"

He says, "Yeah."

She says, "That's a lie."

Bel Punice contends: Evil Kneevil was no isolated incident. A
plot exists, code named Transmaniacon, M.C., a plot of long
standing, a plot against the moderate Angel leadership: Sonny
Barger, etc. That famous moderate Angel who got it recently. He's
called . . . ? They say reds got that Angel. Or something else. I
don't know. Did he buy a farm? Or was he sold one? Know what I
mean? Anyway, advised of the Angels' presence in advance, by pals
in high places (concert command), these plotters, including
Macrobius Carl, met on "this very" island on the fifth of December—one day before Altamont. They'd penetrate the stage area, it
was agreed, as fools, dopers and drunkards. "Why else was Mere-
dith Hunter armed?" But this being Echo Park, "they got wind up
north." San Jose Angels were assigned: "Crush the plot. Any way
you know how."

Macrobius says, "And I went to help the dancing girls. And got . . ." "A provocation," says Bel Punice. "Far-out," says Macrobius. "You don't know you plotted," says Bel. "Your nerve damage was brain damage."

Who is Bel Punice? An imaginary newscaster. Not imaginary herself (though she looks it). No, she's quite real. Like you. Like me. But she broadcasts imaginary events. Not unreal. Imaginary. They could've happened. Maybe they did. But their image is their lure.

Movies are more important than anything. Their budgets are high, their images plentiful; they encourage a rich fantasy life.

Hell's Angels was first a movie title, then a club, then a movie again and again.

A sticker seen on La Cienega recently, between Elektra and the Climax: "We proved it at Altamont."

Imagery is superior to ideology. Ideology justifies imagery, sure, but posthumously.

"That night at a fund-raising party in conservative Ontario, the governor was cheered when he denounced the demonstrators as cowardly little fascist bands."

Governor Reagan was "the Governor."

America's so rich that even the marginal spillage of wealth frees millions (of citizens) for a rich fantasy life. Subsistence income— if only assured—generates enough irresponsibility. American schools are strongholds of irresponsibility. Therefore action. So are wars and revolutions. Margin of events. Situational similarity.

Action conforms to preexistent imagery. Action has the precedent of image. Action is validated, not by biblical or rational accounting principles, not by ideology, but by the concrete lures of imagery.

The Coast press made too much of traffic jams at Altamont. They were imagery: the Woodstock precedent.

Action is inherently more comparative than compensatory. Romantic gestures preface themselves with this remark: What would the appropriate hero have done? Irresponsibility, therefore, toward even yourself. The distance from self can't be missed. "I don't feel like I did it."

The preeminence of entertainment means, above all, that images exist as mere images, rather than ideological symbols or seductions. Image as image.

The fantasy of Altamont, of leadership and conspiracy: the conspiracy is truly anarchic. The sum total of every lure cost to date by imagery in America. At Altamont—for an instant—image became action, then returned to image. But action will be used, on the most convenient people. And ideology will choose them.

Plato's conception was the idea and image synthesized as ideal. Now the image component comes alone to the fore. It has no, needs no justification. It is the most radical factor. Images are free these days and what can survive them?

☞ PART III: THE TREATISE ON IMAGINATION

The Prester John Army was forming on the Strip. A battalion appeared on my right. Then the recruiting booth closed at last: "Quota fulfilled," signed the sign. Yes, soon they would leave for Tokyo, Jerusalem or Osaka. I don't know exactly where, but please observe how power does shift toward the Orient. And so begins in high optimism the campaign of Prester John, the Great Treatise on Imagination. And in that campaign but one thing mattered—one's immortal soul. The survival of souls before death constitutes the Magna Wonder, the cause for optimism, the ground of optimism and its possibility.

And as for that army's leader, he had but one fatal flaw: though always implacable, relentless and quite ready to send the opposition to the wall, he could never quite do it. Oh, how this leader admired Macduff! But when the chips were down, he got to know the opposition and other people as well and his recognition was sympathetic. An oddity on the Strip? I'd say. But like all the others there, he could be moved by the power of music:

> Redeemed at last from the ice
> Redeemed from the cold
> Redeemed from the cell
> Into which I've been thrown
> Redeemed by virtue of a country song

> And I believe, Good Lord,
> It won't be too long

Yes, that was his favorite, "Redeemed," the story of Sir Rastus Bear.

Imagination redeems revolution.

Imagination permits optimism.

Perpetual invention degrades wonder.

Wonder is a secret.

One Heraclitean urge leads one to irony, cynicism, even motion sickness. But a mere advanced Heraclitean urge leads beyond all that. Abnegation of the Law of Contradiction follows as night the day. Post-cynical phenomenon seems curiously harmonious: savagery to numb the imagination, plus the long-awaited Lion/Lamb consort.

In retrospect, how obvious: the Law of Contradiction is a Law of Motion.

Meanwhile these days, Pool, that ever-descriptive metaphor for culture, reduces logic to a relative motion. Infinite variation, true, but within a closed set. That leaves no room for contradiction. All motion owns a relative. Ultimate, but immediate, location of affinities which merely await. Contradiction is therefore but a facet of harmony . . . or occasion for it.

And what is imagination? The human face reveals it. The human face is a composition of elements: eyes, nose, mouth, ears, tongue. And what composed them as a face? Why, imagination. Imagination is the will that binds. Imagination is the will to affinity. And make no mistake, if an affinity's been discovered, that's no different from imposed. And if an affinity seems retrospective, do remember please: imagination precedes everything. It is will—the will to form.

The truly random and ambiguous are untouched by form and therefore imagination. Innocent of imagination. What would that be like? Yet such things exist, and increasingly.

In American scenes, the dynamic has been vulgarity versus the cipher. Cipher system irony is no more, no less than the fixture of the form in itself. Not the Meltzerian flux irony. Not the interference effect. Fixture and flux are aspects of Transmaniacon. But fixture is more modern. It requires some technology: A Communications Network.

In truth, abstract forms don't result from purification, rather, its saturation in the saddle. Saturation of form, of meaning, exhaustive surface content, blatancy, in other words, that's the ticket. Form and content: let's see where the balance really is. Pure form, traditionally, that was abstract. But so seductive of meaning which seems always, via association, to inhabit pure form. But if pure form draws meaning to itself, does blatant content just chase it away? I'd say O.K. Here's why: Blatancy, or saturation with meaning, is a state of nearly too much content—"nearly," 'cause can there ever be too much?

Form is the logic of content. But logic is the content of form. In this scene of terms (form, logic, content), each term can assume the other's role, while, by contrast, once-upon-a-time the split-screen role of form/content seemed so apt. Is this confusion or an a-entropic circulation process? Yes, it's the latter. Form/content, the split-screen role, is rigid configuration, at any given moment. Like the relationship of image and mirror—which is rigid and split at that moment when the image is cast—it can be flopped. A logic mediates the form/content role. Form does become content and the other way around, too.

Mirror, image, mirror of images, mirror for images—the mirror itself, which is more profound an image than I'd ever imagined. The mirror image is the tributary image reversed. Reversed—this word origin recognizes an interchangeably logical poetry: verse. (Verse, i.e., dynamically inevitable word logic. Prose, i.e., meaningfully inevitable word logic.) For Sherlock Holmes, Professor Moriarty is the mirror image. Faithfully mirror-like, Moriarty's actions are Holmes's moral, or at least legal, reverse. The verse of reverse, the version of reversion . . . um, yes, so far reversal remains verbally obvious, but what about the form of content? The form of content! Yes, that form, form in general, traditional abstract form. Though incongruous word-wise, form relates to content as mirror to image—a relationship of reversal.

In the company of that girl of ancient lineage, of that beautiful Anglo-Egyptian girl, Boris Karloff as the Mummy said, apropos of his Pool, "I shall awaken memories of love and crime and death."

And like certain other Pools, the Culture Pool does encourage reflection. Then, it's a mirror. I've seen this mirror. It would be spherical but for an imperfect surface, broken by more facets than I can count. An infinity of reflections projects beyond, through a surface which passes images out of the sphere—never into it. Inside the sphere itself is a view of magical confusion; outside, a comprehensive projection. Apart, neither exhausts the imagery. But together, what would that be like . . . ?

Ciphers: invented by seductive game masters, who could alone afford to actually encourage such blatancy. Ciphers: the truest issue of a technological system grown proficient enough to sponsor unparalleled levels of information density. Ciphers: an almost physical anomaly—the only time, or place, for combination to exhaustion of the Culture Pool's internal and external imagery.

PART IV: THE GROUPS OF L.A.

Edd "Kookie" Byrnes

If you're a human being, a real human being, not a punkoid or a subhuman, the first place you'd head for upon hitting the Strip would be Dino's, better known as 77 Sunset Strip. Better known as Great. Your roots are there. My roots are there. Yes, it's still there. But the last time I went I noticed something missing—namely, most of the parking lot. Where week after week, Edd "Kookie" Byrnes would ply his trade(s): parking-lot attendant and part-time private dick. Where is that lot today? Well, no one seems to know. And as for Edd "Kookie" Byrnes, a star of 77 Sunset Strip, a cameo star of Marjorie Morningstar, a recording star in his own right . . . where is he today? Well, no one seems to know. But, y'know, there is one token to remember him by: the great hit record, "Kookie, Kookie, Lend Me Your Comb." It's an emotional tune on that old black magic theme—and I mean love.

The Byrds

Five years ago McGuinn and Crosby saw Hard Day's Night and said, "That's for us." The Byrds' birth was inspired by this hit

mythic image of perfectly triumphant Beatles. Clark, Clark and
Hillman joined and they stood—five bland Apollonians—as dedicated leaders, not followers, of fashion (McGuinn's glasses,
Crosby's hats and cloaks). Back then, Byrds' performances were
visually elegant. People danced while the boys looked on, so
detached and indifferent as to conjure images of both Descartes
and Apollo. Yep, the Byrds kept up appearances. Only the Stones
rival them in high gorgeous album percentage. Only John Mayall
(who often fires men) could compete for this title. God with a
thousand faces. As the Byrds appeared and moved on, they inevitably left a residue of visually perfect mythic imagery.

Bundles of nostalgic technologies: they supply the *real* themes
for Byrds tunes—and/or broadly defined technologies we yearn for
to organize and/or operate the world with *absolutely* perfect
consequences. Mere technology (transistors, airplanes, tires) and
legends and magic are all nostalgic technologies. But their in-
tended perfect consequence is so unnatural it's mythic, and they
live happily ever after there. Mythic operators execute in unnatural
perfection, whereas your natural operator is accident-prone. Byrds
tunes have worldly irrelevance.

There are important and poetic affinities between all nostalgic
technologies. All of 'em are formally equivalent, therefore mutually
modular. On a subterranean level they all intend *perfections* of
vision and action in structure—eventually consequences—which is
to say perfect consequences, and that's unnatural and that's mysterious. Well, then, the Byrds swim in mystery, but do perfect
circles, taking wing before your staring eyes. So worldly irrelevance
isn't all that special. Anyway, knowledge of subterranean affinities
opened up whole new ways to say the same thing. A regular poetic
license. Murray the K equals my dog, Blue . . .

Some nostalgic technologies: magic, science and religion, sci-fi,
Child ballads, hill ballads, "serious" C & W chestnuts, other folk
(i.e., the Joan Baez songbook), Dylan. (Oh, Dylan, he's big, but
closed, hence little—the universe of discourse forms everything
nostalgically, especially the last few LPs since his death.)

The first Byrds LP has but three mythic visions: "Mr. Tambourine Man," "The Bells of Rhymney" and "Chimes of Freedom." Gene Clark, who wrote most of the Byrds' words in those

days, didn't prefer the mythic visions. He'd do his ad hoc Bizarro
Beatles or his Everly Brothers. Today McGuinn says, "I'm glad he
left, actually. 'I Knew I'd Want You' had the exact Beatles 'Oh,
yeah.' It recalls Bobby Rydell's 'World Without Love,' which
perhaps you recall. Also Gene Clark intrigues me more and more."

   Turn! Turn! Turn! was nearly half myth: "Turn! Turn! Turn!"
itself, and "Lay Down Your Weary Tune," "He Was a Friend of
Mine," "The Times They Are A-Changin' " and "Satisfied Mind"
were meaty affinities. They were affinities between revealed religion ("Turn! Turn! Turn!") and political legend ("The Times
They Are A-Changin'," "He Was a Friend of Mine") and mere
nostalgia (i.e., what's left).

   Fifth Dimension was the last big thematic move: "5D" was new
(science, sci-fi and drugs—a real "rich" tune), "Eight Miles High"
was new, the "2-4-2 Foxtrot" was new (both these latter tunes
have the romance of mere technology, and lotsa traditional myth,
too). "John Riley" is, of course, Odysseus. I could go on . . . but
it was mostly mythic. And then the thematic repertoire was full
up; the boys could go whole hog.

   Cut to all-myth *Younger Than Yesterday;* an all-myth *Notorious Byrd Brothers;* to *Sweetheart of the Rodeo,* which was, despite
a promising title, mostly C & W ready-made chestnuts (but "You
Ain't Going Nowhere," "Pretty Boy Floyd," "Nothing Was De-
livered" do close a cycle—the Byrds play Guthrie and Seeger and
Dylan . . .); to *Dr. Byrds and Mr. Hyde,* which is their own ready-
made, from a hitherto unfilled period between, say, *Fifth Dimension* and *Younger Than Yesterday,* a great posthumous album that
includes "Baby, What You Want Me To Do?"; cut to *the music.*
Cut to *Easy Rider, Untitled,* etc.

   It's been said and assumed the Byrds are eclectic. (On the *Turn!
Turn! Turn!* notes, the guy said, "This album's eclectic.") Let's
look at the record. Really, they've made but one musically eclectic
LP—then first, with shades of the Everlys ("I'd Feel a Lot Better,"
etc.), mid to early Beatles, that Jackie De Shannon tune done to
Bo Diddley's beat/arrangement copped off "Mona" (*The Rolling
Stones Now*) and, of course, the cycle-form tunes ("Mr. Tam-
bourine Man," "The Bells of Rhymney," "Chimes of Freedom").
From then on the Byrds were only "credit" eclectic, i.e., as writers.

Cycle forms induced musical homogeneity, and cycle forms were all the rage until the advent and end of the Gram Parsons era, *Sweetheart of the Rodeo*, which killed time between *The Notorious Byrd Brothers* and *Dr. Byrds and Mr. Hyde*, and the latter is not all that disappointing by virtue of being an old friend returned.

The cycle forms deny entropy (don't run down . . . well, nor up), therefore "they'll" sound unnatural. Energy-wise, they seem symmetrical. And their relationship to normal, variable, accident-prone sound is otherness. They're an archaic (or prophetic), deeply musical order of sound. Mathematics and the Music of the Spheres, etc. In other words, a sonic perfection—the sonic affinity and analogue for mere technology, legend, magic and the nostalgic technologies. Naturally, cycle forms have automatic precognitive efficacy. The sound of the Byrds is so symmetrical, it's in automatic contrast with worldly sound—what you hear waking up, or in the car, the pool, or from Canned Heat.

With the Byrds, the cycle form executes via a dense, textured drone. The music has a fundamental ground, i.e., the drone out of which all variations seem to rise. The drone is executed via bass and drums (a constant), and guitars and harmony (sometimes). Vocals or guitar rise outa the drone as surface variation. As an American group with research curiosity, the Byrds' form must be inspired by sources: Famous Raga and American Hill/Country drone (Fundamental Background Drone), Everly Brothers, etc. . . . C & W harmony and technological regularity. "They're the mechanical sounds of the era," said McGuinn (foreground drone). Raga once more. Hill songs. Child ballads (real hard-core ethnic cycle forms). Muzak (silence denial, nook-and-cranny-packed total sonic space occupation). And synthesis of these into a strong cycle form made possible the subordination of most other plausible music styles: Beatles tunes, C & W, Dylan, the classics, i.e., "CTA-102" or "Old John Robertson," etc., etc. With this form, only the credits could betray the eclectic.

The cycle form homogenizes and leads to a context of music as energy. With it, the Byrds could've made LPs as Energy Flow Charts. Get working on chart structure and organization—the energy surge and Turkey Tongue, for example. Even proceed to

Molecular Sound Organization, a region wherein mere silence denial ("mere" as in V.D. Parks or Phil Spector) is surpassed by the self-conscious conversion of sonic energy into space: universal organization of all available space by energy.

The first two Byrds albums had pre-pubic instruments that were not very heavy, so the vocals predominated. Yet they did begin to stride on *Turn! Turn! Turn!* Conceptually, a "Turn! Turn! Turn!" title meant the Byrds knew their mission. On that album they introduce the Byrds' "surge." A surge is simply an alteration in energy level: energy-symmetry is preserved by cycle-form tunes. Each tune has its energy level. Energy variations (surge) would distort, therefore organize, any LP charted for flow. *Turn! Turn! Turn!* was organized by its flow and surge. For the first time, an LP combined a proper musical context and programming to cumulatively read out as symmetrical energy flow. (Cycle form expanded LP wide.) Energy-wise, *Turn! Turn! Turn!* was not progressive; it wasn't dramatic. To begin or end, you just insert your ear in any cut. Motion, surge, organization, all came on the heels of subtle energy variations, minor clues. Some move into the dynamics of statics. I'd say!

And then for necessary refinements: *Fifth Dimension* and *Younger Than Yesterday*. *Fifth Dimension* was a mixed move: random energy levels like a Beatles album, but musically post-public. On it the Byrds become the first technological band ever. And McGuinn the first technological guitarist since the prophet Lonnie Mack recorded his Fraternity label LP, *The Wham of That Memphis Man*, in Cincinnati in '63. On "Eight Miles High," the boys occupy all available sonic space (Molecular Sound Organization) and McGuinn sounds quite unnatural. I mean, his lines have geometric, not organic, shapes. (While blues are organic and natural.) But, of course, technological guitars have these ultra-modern mechanical models. So *Fifth Dimension* is one of the world's great guitar LPs, and its sci-fi and technological tunes finished up the Byrds' music style repertoire. Like nostalgic technologies, music styles had been subordinated into neutral modules to be placed by the cycle form. And the *Younger Than Yesterday* refinement was Ecstatic programming, especially Turkey Tongues, a type of Unknown Tongue wherein the next cut completes the *preceding* one in ecstatic union. Turkey Tonguing requires a matched pair, the preceding "Turkey" and the "next cut." So "My Back Pages" acted to resolve "Mind Garden," which was the "Turkey" for "My Back Pages." Obviously, Turkey Tongues occasion a mammoth surge.

The Notorious Byrd Brothers: (McGuinn) "You're saying, Am I happy with Gary Usher as a producer?" (Question) "He used to work with Brian Wilson . . ." (McGuinn) "I don't know. He worked with . . . somebody." Well, ever since the Peanut Butter Conspiracy boner and the mysterious Sagittarius affair (the letter allegedly causing Brian Wilson to sever his old pal, Gary Usher, forever leave the Columbia studios, and build a studio for himself in his basement), I've heard no good of Gary Usher. (Now V.P. at RCA.) And yet, this man collaborated with the Byrds on *Younger Than Yesterday, Sweetheart of the Rodeo* and oh, so 'specially, *The Notorious Byrd Brothers*. And *The Notorious Byrd Brothers* is, I'd say, one of the best rock 'n' roll LPs, and the best producing job. All previous Byrds LPs were its necessary preparation. It is, after all, a real, accurate, pale reflection of the Music of the Spheres and an unprecedented penetration into Molecular Sound Organization.

Previous crucial penetrations would be Phil Spector (the Bronx Genius; *Cheetah* called him "Grey Eminence")—a primal genius *with* the (early) Righteous Brothers, Ronettes, Crystals, Ike and Tina Turner, etc. (He disappeared and then just months ago reappeared with—the Beatles!) Another penetration was made by V.D. Parks' *Song Cycle* (*Cheetah* called him "a genius"). This guy's move was Silence Denial: sound treated as "molecules" to be organized into dense structures that deny a silence always implied by its own absence ("present through absence"). Spector is ground-oriented, essentially musical. His structural analogue is oceanic. Wave-like rise of variably familiar sounds from a fundamental ground. As for V.D., while he does mine a ground vein, he's more oriented toward *cognitive* syntheses of ready-mades. (That old cynic: he started with cynicism, then proceeded to postcynicism.) His song, "Cycle," is a cognitively directed American fantasy. Synthesized out of ready-made American modules, it's suitable for mass production.

Let's check the front side of *The Notorious Byrd Brothers* album. It's typical. The first tune is "Artificial Energy." Real appropriate, eh? Its arrangement is so structural, it's an energy chart, assigning energy roles and levels. Maybe the Byrds' greatness as working musicians is in arranging. That's not to belittle . . . they are absolutely adequate, meaning they know exactly what sorta energy instruments imply or pipeline. With Molecular Sound Organization their arrangements occupy all sonic interstices. (No more holes.) *Younger Than Yesterday*, the old density champ, seems by comparison thin as dogs' ears. One channel has drums, brass, bass, traditional Byrds chorale and some electronic noisemaking. The other channel has John Philip Sousa's bass drum, brass, Byrds chorale, *acoustical* piano and chimes. Since sonic density is not mere accumulation, these sounds aren't stocked (which spells mere weight). Rather, they're subtly woven, interwoven, interfering, to finally coalesce, not disintegrate. Coalescence through opposition. Recall magnetism. Negative pole to negative, positive to positive. (They're held apart by what binds them and so forth.) Rhythms against counter-rhythms. Mechanical John Philip Sousa bass drum repetitions (oom-pah-pah, oom-pah-pah) against the bass, so great and flexible with its liquid tone patterns. Energy type against counter-energy. Linear brass (moving diagonally) against the flowing wave notion of a Byrds chorale specializing in ad hoc vocal phrases (not the word "ride" distended in the phrase, "my ticket to ri-i-de"). The mix is done with great delicacy—for example, the piano's barely audible resolution after the voices stop with "Do you think it's really the truth you see?" or the electronic noisemakers' fade to audibility *at the fade-out*. I could go on forever . . .

The primal-molecular-sound persons occupied and organized sonic space as if it were mere space, you know, a set of physical dimensions. Sure, the occupying, organizing sounds were energy. Energy is energy. Can't be denied. But energy's also flow. And there are contexts disrupting flow and contexts emphasing it. Dramatic moves, the build to climax, the stop/start scene, etc., are inherently disruptive: Phil Spector was a dramatist. As was V.D. Parks. *Song Cycle* is an American fantasy, with a cognitive foreground. V.D., it seems, told stories. His music served a purpose; it wasn't the absolute Music of the Spheres. V.D. was only being ironic.

By the time of the *Notorious Byrd Brothers*, the Byrds had recognized absolute affinities not between nostalgic technologies, but between nostalgic technologies, the cycle form and aggregates of cycle forms—across-the-board affinities. The Music of the Spheres. Oh, man, that LP was like energy's self-expression in words and music. Those Byrds respected flow. From molecular organization and occupation of sonic space they broke on through to energization of molecules. Sound that is space that is energy. Quite a compact collapse of former separate scenes.

If you're charmed by words or don't understand, the Byrds suggest entropic puzzles. (A) Cycle-form energy is symmetrical energy. Cycle forms possess motion, but it's static, not progressive. It goes somewhere, but nowhere. The collapse of static into dynamic, and the reverse. (B) Absolute Byrd sound, i.e., *Notorious Byrd Brothers* sound, denies silence so well, via space and energy, that silence (which you rarely hear these days) is fully recalled as a polar conceptual reality.

The Doors

When it comes to the pulp touch or modern, hard-core industrial and political spirits, it is, I think, safe to say no L.A. rockers can touch the Doors. The elegance of the Buffalo? Remains velveteen. The elegance of the Byrds? Is nothing less than timeless. Y'know, techniques well-known to the centuries which preceded this one: Romantic Buffalo and Mantric Byrds, Mystic Lyres at Marathon, the Banshee of O'Neill, etc., etc. . . . But the Doors? They're thoroughly up-to-date. Thoroughly determined by, say, the last three decades. And probably impossible before this one right now. In short, the Doors skirt dangerously close to such out-and-out lumpen moves as Steppenwolf (the group), with rescue coming only through execution, production, superlatives, superior personal appearance and elegant cultural warehouse plagiarism. Suffice it to say, the distance between "Hello, I Love You" and "Born To Be Wild" can be measured by such yardsticks as Kinks plagiarism. Just two years ago, a *Rolling Stone* reader kicked 'cause "Hello, I Love You" was blatantly copped off "All Day and All of the Night," that fabulous Kinks hit of just six years ago. And yet one performance index for today's warehouse culture is cop quality. Since no one's moved (or even able) to think up something new, to be, that is, radically creative, the question of sources becomes ever more crucial. Both the Stones and the Beatles made careers of Kinks plagiarism, and the Kinks themselves emanate from eminent sources, viz., a great American prototypical hit, "Louis, Louis." So, don't knock the Doors. And yet, such blatant cops do exemplify the Doors' peculiar inordinacy. In their prime (before their secret retirement—that tragedy of demise), the Doors hit upon inordinacy as a form: "I am," said Morrison, "the back-door man. The men don't know, but the little girls understand." Nothing less than the burly categorical statement of a tune which, after too, too many years of bluesy overuse, proves therefore not embarrassing at all. "I am." Absolute categorical assertion has here become systematically assertive. (If you say something strongly enough it assumes an inexplicable aura of strength.) The strength of this categorical assertion is so enormous that not only does it encompass the whole world (i.e., as a systematic construction), but it becomes, as it were, unnatural, surpassing all reason, arriving at Meltzer's categorical magical. Starting at household fornication, we've progressed to a magical collapse of the world. Absolute contextualization has fully directed our attention so that household phrases finally become inordinately expansive. Imagine "When the music's over, turn out the lights," winding up with the long-awaited resurrection. Imagine that! But we shouldn't be too shocked. Word expansion (via an explicit or implicit field) is an old trick of both Yeats and the Beatles, a famous pair, to be sure, and both of them well knew how words pumped with fire will expand until they shine with a spectral light—a pure light that's rarely seen. And how does the Doors' specter shine? With a plenitude of arrogance and assertive disorder, the pursuit of which proves more than ordinarily singleminded. As if, there in the background, a great world system can somehow be perceived. In which regard Morrison once said: "It is a search, an opening of doors. We're trying to break through to a clearer, purer realm." (And along these lines, don't you forget that the melody "For My Eyes Have Seen You" starts off like the Ajax ad, "Stronger Than Dirt.")

The Doors, in their success, did little more than *pretend* to provoke the imagination. They were wholly and obviously synthetic. Their originality was manipulative: a synthetic form which manipulates the overstatement inherent in every pulp artifact, a synthetic form which can therefore literally impose—as in brainwashing—certain select moods. The Doors are more authentically political than anyone, even Elvis, David Crosby, the Jefferson Airplane, because their politicalization is stylistic. They go in, *par excellence*, for the brute assertion—not the innuendo, not the imaginative provocation—repeated in a million different ways. The *Strange Days* album is typical. The first words are a simple assertion: "Strange days have found us." More akin to a command than a provocation. Nor is the music too provocative. There are many a priori mystery sounds, likely to conform to a listener's preconceived and typical ideas of what sounds mysterious. Movie music could have been a big influence. Check the surrealist organ on "Strange Days" and "Unhappy Girl," or that bass entrance on "You're Lost, Little Girl," which smacks of the pulp of mystery (crime-detective) movie music of the 1940 to 1960 era. I can see the Doors scoring the *Invasion of the Body Snatchers* or even the fabulous *Mysterians*.

Behind the Doors' success lay this discouraging fact: given an unqualified—and universally burgeoning—world-wide aura of familiarity, the bizarre itself had become impossible, had become, that is, replaceable by a synthetic bizarre, the bizarro. For, truthfully, nothing can be both familiar and bizarre. I mean, life these days is so consistently wonderful, and you see so much, especially at home on TV, that the formerly bizarre has become (at best) charming. Nowadays magnificent images seem played out at birth, and the very possibility of "going to the well," as it were, of provoking a response from within imagination, so to speak, does begin to seem mighty unlikely. So the Doors' feat was neither mean nor unworthy nor formless nor aimless, but certainly drilled, yes, drilled—a drilled repetition of too-familiar sentiments. That's the method, the academic/political/industrial method employed by the Doors for this sole purpose: entrée into the categorical magical in the guise of an absolute context. Therefore, and functionally speaking, the Doors' music is an absolute context. Certainly, inordinacy (or even simple overstatement) had much to do with this. That strikingly dense combination of more-than-mere-words, quintessential pulp sounds, Morrison's tone of voice, his garb, his grub, animal noises and athletics created a statement that no one could miss, or in other words, an explicit mystery field. They really stated this or that: "Strange days have tracked us down"; "You're lost, little girl"; "Unhappy girl, fly fast away, don't miss your chance to swim in mystery"; "People are strange when you're a stranger"; "The monk bought lunch"; etc., etc. And yet, as these mysteries precipitate like mad from the very midst of such unambiguous overstatement, doesn't a seeming anomaly likewise manifest itself and arise? Traditionally, mysteries constituted themselves through an epistemological lack. By dropping that quality, that state of lacking, by dropping that traditionally provocative appeal to the imagination-as-vacuum, the Doors stage-managed the divorce of mystery and imagination. In a major deal provocations were traded for instructions. Surprising? Ironic? Ingenious? Or more than inevitable!

Nowadays, it's Sergio Leone for great cowboy features, featurin' maybe Clint Eastwood, maybe Lee Van Cleef. However, in the TV '50s Gene Autry had this robotic cowboy serial—which, not unlike Judy Garland's big break (i.e., *The Wizard of Oz*), took place on or below Kansas . . . Today an owner of those (apparently) not unsuccessful California Angels, Gene once played singing cowboys and moved in horse and country-music circles. It's a singing image he had—guitar and horse together. Add that image to beautiful, albeit bickersome, nostalgic after-images outta *Lonesome Cowboy* and you've got exact sense of a tune, "Singing Cowboy," featured on Love's LP *Four Sail*:

> Singing cowboy
> Got a girl around your waist
> Wanta shoot a little taste
> At—
> Me and my boy . . .

Melodically, "Singing Cowboy" resembles "Hot Burrito #2" by bizarro Country and Western Burritos. For an infinite coda of "Comin' through to you . . . " "Singing Cowboy" supersedes even the "Hey, Jude" excess. If Jac Holzman found "Hey, Jude" worshipful, will "Singing Cowboy" run 'em over? It's an American tune, but likewise European . . .

Love: "Said to have been discovered by Jac Holzman, president of Elektra Records, at a Hollywood teenery known as the Bido Lido . . . " (Cash Box, May 1966) . . . R. Meltzer's top three American groups include Love, the Byrds, what else?

Touted as the "next Byrds" when they came up in L.A., Love has made Byrd-like moves. Until recently, no Love LP exactly duplicated its predecessor's personnel: Bryan, Arthur, Snoopy, John and Ken cut LP number one (Love), plus Tjay and Michael, LP number two (Da Capo, meaning a renewal—autobiography?), minus Tjay and Snoopy, LP number three (Forever Changes—autobiography?), minus Bryan, John, Ken, Michael, plus Tjay and George, LP number four (Four Sail), i.e., only Arthur Lee is still around, a leader, like the Byrd. And the Saturday Review said Love's the best in folk rock: "That is not to say that they are the best of the worst" (November 26, 1966). So much for perspective. Of course, it's a damn shame Love has now left Elektra, where they'd so much to do with corporate history and American history. Love was the first Elektra group and first in a long line of excessive Elektra groups: Love, Doors, Clear Light, MC5, (Psychedelic) Stooges, Wild Thing . . . yep. Four Sail is the last Love from Elektra. Love has signed with Blue Thumb. Upon leaving Elektra, Arthur Lee bought an $85,000 luxury home.

A group from Toronto, with a tune about donkeys, called itself Influence: why harp on influence? For Love it's always been crucial, later even necessary, to sound influenced. Influenced in the form of seeming ready-mades, riffs like modules, well-known before falling in Love, their obvious prior meanings could be counted on . . . to influence an audience.

Love: "If you like the Byrds and the Rolling Stones, you will love the Love," L.M., Memphis Commercial Appeal (June 19, 1966). Did L.M. know that Arthur and John hailed from Memphis? Love's LP, Love, well-praised on both sides of the Atlantic, was mostly and literally ready-made—Jagger and Southern California nationalism, mostly. "Hey, Joe" is there, not once, but twice, in earliest Byrds style, as "Hey, Joe" itself and another name ("My Flash on You"). About twelve whole tunes with "Chimes of Freedom"—"Bells of Rhymney" chords, etc. . . . Or do you recall Love's hit version of Manfred Mann's hit, "Little Red Book," a Bacharach-David tune from *What's New, Pussycat?* Behind Mann's by only one year and just as good, being just the same. More than we know, I'm sure, *What's New, Pussycat?* influenced Love.

Da Capo: "A record was cut off abruptly, the front curtain rose, a group of four whites and three Negroes was revealed, and the lead singer, dressed in a black stocking cap and brown vest, leaned slightly sidewise, yawned briefly, and began to sing." (*New Yorker.* Yep, Renata Adler!) Tom Jones' exclusive "What's New, Pussycat?" vocal, Johnny Mathis, jazz (impersonated in Tjay Cantrelli; he "blew" reeds), all influential on the *Da Capo* front side, true, but nothing next to "Revelation," the back side and extra excessive: "Revelation," often sneered at, it gets the airplay, a nearly twenty-minute fandango; John Echols and Arthur Lee, two gentlemen of color from Memphis, sang it in a style reminiscent of one you've heard—Mick Jagger!

Forever Changes: Bryan Maclean thought *Forever Changes* inferior to *Horizontal Bee Gees* . . . I'd guess in production terms, i.e., conventional beauty of the strings. Yet MGM thought Ultimate Spinach equaled the Bee Gees' "fusion of rock and the classics." *Forever Changes* finished what *Da Capo* began: Arthur Lee's insane mutation of Mick Jagger into—Johnny Mathis. Johnny Mathis, movie and show tunes, Muzak, particularly Xavier Cugat or Tiajuana Brass—they influenced *Forever Changes.* But the big ready-made must be what engineer Bruce Botnick did. He dubbed in literal Muzak, strings and brass, an afterthought, when the tracks were down, and Arthur Lee—his vision cloudy—wasn't happy.

Four Sail: Essentially Love's least excessive LP, *Four Sail* suffers from occasional inherently excessive wah-wah bursts and loss of elegance. *Da Capo* was elegant. But can even potent wah-wah explain *Four Sail*'s loss . . . ? Well, it's no coincidence *Four Sail* is less elegant and least excessive. Like libertines everywhere, Love discovered corrupt elegance in excess. Except for Johnny Cash's vocal ("Talkin' in My Sleep"), *Four Sail* got little raw influence beyond Love itself . . . Finally Love assimilated its own style.

Excess abounds in Love's story . . . The famous Houston airport incident, for example. In Frisco, the editor of the now-defunct *Mojo Navigator News* told me Love "was a bunch of hoods." A Big Brother member told R. Meltzer, "Their name is Love, but they're hate." My favorite is Arthur Lee, drummer. At Love's East Coast concert, Arthur sat in for his drummer, for a tune, and nothing special happened . . . Look, Cream was excessive, they play too much. The Fudge and Butterfly did it. I'm sure Blind Faith did . . . too much! So much for Atlantic. Those Atlantic groups are really heavy and excessive in one direction. But Love is excessive in contrary, therefore interfering, directions. Love looks good to people of Satanic imagination. Love's excess isn't wretched, it's plain corrupting. All corruption means is that meanings become questionable. Even a beautiful tune's got a meaning you could corrupt, i.e., its very beauty. Off of *Forever Changes* the tunes say "Live and let live," a chestnut, take it from me: "Oh, the snot has packed against my pants, it has turned into crystal, there's a bluebird sittin' on a branch, I guess I'll take my pistol. I've got it in my hand, because he's on my land . . . " But the music? Music? Beautiful music . . . Traditional tasties and something new, too . . . Beautiful enunciation: such juicy, precise sensuality, like Johnny Mathis. Also mincing, like Mick's "Lady Jane." Also English-style (British) harmony, likewise precise. The guitar's acoustic picked. Unforgettable music. But the spot for snot? Questionable . . . that's interference. Tough words like those hinted at interference, the Love LP was mostly ridiculous. After all, uncontrolled linear excess of its music ready-mades in no way accommodated the words . . . On *Da Capo* and *Forever Changes* ready-mades were synthesized, not literal. Seemingly, the words adjusted or determined the music. So the tunes became theatrical: at once dramatic, noncommittal, beautiful, chock-full of meaningful interference. It's no coincidence: *Forever Changes* sounds Broadway or Movie . . .

Yes, Jim Morrison sure knew his oats back in 1967 when he told that reporter from a pulp magazine: "Love and the Kinks, they're my favorites." A very significant statement simultaneously linking the Doors, Love and the Kinks. With Love as the actual and not merely verbal middle term, the synthetic operator, the archetypal ready-made manipulator of not merely Ray Davies but Mick Jagger, Jim McGuinn, even Johnny Mathis—all via the one, the only Arthur Lee! And Morrison should know. No doubt about it: Jac Holzman discovered the Doors playin' second fiddle to Love at the Whiskey. Later the Kinks would threaten suit over the origins of "Hello, I Love You." Love, the Kinks—most of all they share the interference effect. Yes, in retrospect it does seem true that no rocker from L.A. has ever done what Love has done in all its transit and motion: transmit imagery from an actual Manifold of Imagination. So please don't worry if discussions of Love's formal problems seem to lack terminology, like cycle form or geometry. Such a lack means only this: Love's form is hardly of this world, hardly physical, hardly quasi-physical. Rather, it's imbedded in the stuff of consciousness. And renewed there, too. Love has a strong and constant form, all right, one I've seen, one I know, one that's simply called—the grotesque angle.

Karlheinz Stockhausen
Introduction by J Marks

OPEN LETTER TO
THE YOUNG GENERATION

The music of this forty-year-old German *enfant terrible* (who directs the Experimental Electronic Studio in Cologne) is rebellious and youthful; it's music high on its own creative flashes. "Zyklus," for instance, is a mad percussive work, which beams out a drastic new musical message. It introduces the percussionist as a creative performer. "Gesang der Junglinge" (DGG 138811) is his most immediately moving monument of music; while "Refrain" is intimate and Asiatic in its simplicity of intent and its utter clarity. "Momente" and "Hymnen," contrastingly, are supracomplex electronic or orchestral looms of sheer invention—imagination on the brink of hysteria!

His experiments have nourished a whole generation of us with the bravery to be individual and with musical contexts which we could not have "heard" without him. Even if we've never heard his name, still his influence has been everywhere: from 2001 to "Strawberry Fields." In turn, the influence of our generation has fed back into his life as he has watched us swing a gigantic new political awareness and as he has heard us declare a gigantic new musical expression. In the following words, which I've tried to translate and correlate into the kind of language Stockhausen uses in our conversations, he describes the intricate interchange between his creative world and ours.

(Translation by J. Marks)

Again we are revolutionizing, but this time over the whole earth. Let us now set for ourselves the highest possible goal: becoming conscious that all mankind is at stake.

There was a time when consciousness became so strong in some animals that they finally became men. Now we are in a time in which supraconsciousness is becoming so strong in some human beings that they are close to becoming higher creatures. Here, on this earth. Only a few will manage it to begin with, but in every human being the longing is more or less strong to go beyond himself, to attain higher consciousness. Hence the crises which we are undergoing on the whole earth and whose nadirs still lie before us in this century. Everywhere in the world people sense the pressure, the panic, knowing that something lies before them which is comparable only with the emergence of the first animal from the plant kindom, with the emergence of the first man from the animal kingdom: a new stage in becoming conscious. So strong is the yearning in man for the next higher stage of being; so wild is his fear and his resistance to opening himself to this consciousness. Certain individuals, groups, parties and peoples believe that they have primacy and can oppress, literally devour, others. For we are unequal in respect to our mental power, and we know that only individuals will manage from inside out to become free, supraconscious, just as only individual animals managed to become men.

One can become a higher man only by overcoming his egocentrism and his fear of losing himself in that process.

Let us not endeavor in opposition to the systems which we wish to abolish—because they are too narrow and would exclude, oppress and reject too many others who think differently—in order to erect new systems. Our concept must be so broad that we see ourselves and the whole world from above, and let the old systems run out and not continue them and add no new ones with the claim to exclusiveness.

Systems are products of the brains which made our forebears the autocrat of the body so that the soul became its own prisoner because it gave all power to its whilom servant, the intellect. Let us make ourselves conscious that the human mentality, if it is not continuously fed by higher inspiration from the supramental, continuously makes different combinations of everything that is stored in it and that it can at any time assert anything arbitrary and its opposite. It can be used for anything, it represents any arbitrary opinion, it can justify, substantiate, refute anything, etc. And if we have not learned how to stop and start it, it races along without interruption. It is just a useful instrument, no more, no less: a model computer. But who needs it? And for what?

The supraego is supposed to give it thought, and the supraego receives its conception from the intuitive consciousness, and the latter from the higher and highest consciousness in which the consciousness of every individual unites with suprapersonal cosmic consciousness.

Why do I say something like this when, after all, I am a musician and not at all a philosopher or the like? Because we musicians must live entirely on intuition. Because I have found out that everything new begins when this consciousness is reached and ever higher ascents are striven for. One is a musician, a specialist, a man with a profession only secondarily. Primarily, one is an individual spirit, which must first take up union with the universal spirit before it intends to communicate anything essential to other spirits, anything that goes beyond that which is individual and has anything to do with every other spirit.

Music should not be merely a wave-bath for bodily massage, a sonorous psychogram, a thought program in tones, but a current of supraconscious cosmic electricity which has turned into sound. By far, most musicians who perform music today behave automatically, unconsciously, and they have lost the enthusiasm which perhaps once in early youth they had for a short while when they decided to choose the profession of musician. We must begin anew from the bottom up and reawaken this original enthusiasm in ourselves, or else give up the musician's profession.

Therefore, all orchestras and choruses should be dissolved for a rather long time and every musician be given the opportunity and allowed the time to go into himself, to meditate, to find out what he is really living for, why he is making music, whether he must make music at all. We would see that most musicians—who have already been in this profession for years and think that things will go on in the same way till death or pensioning and that nothing essential in their lives will change any more—would give up and do something else. Perhaps they would not do anything at all for quite a while (if their pay continued and their material arguments were thus removed), which could be wonderfully fruitful. The usual reasons for earning money—keeping oneself alive, satisfying demands which have grown up—are indeed only lazy excuses. In India, on a highway between Agra and Jaipur, I met a musician who played for me on a small handmade string instrument and sang in accompaniment. He was one of the very few wonderful musicians that I have met in my life. He literally had no possessions, and when I asked him if he could not sell me his instrument for twenty dollars—a sum which he cannot earn in many years (as the Indian driver translated for me, he receives at the most something like two and a half cents a day given him by passers-by or in the villages for his playing)—he looked at me, his composure lost, tears running down his cheeks, and he shook his head. I was ashamed to death.

Those who, following their higher voice, want to be musicians must begin with the simplest exercises of meditation, at first just for themselves: "Play a tone with the certainty that you have all the time and all the space you need," and so on. First, however, they must acquire a consciousness of what they are living for, of what we are all living for: to attain higher life and let the vibrations of the universe penetrate into our individual human existence. And musicians must prepare for the arrival of the higher man still hidden in us—so set the whole body vibrating down to its smallest components so that everything becomes loose and receptive to the vibrations of the highest consciousness.

I sense in advance your rejection of this "charter." It does not disturb me. It would be bad, however, if you do not have the least feeling that in your best instants you are inspired from intuition, and beyond that do not have the presentiment of a higher possibility of existence in you which keeps you alive. You should not want to keep living dully, but to achieve certainty, to become conscious of why, whither. And you should know that our incapacities and imperfections are only the indications that we are being drawn up, that the future in us—which is the supramental—is drawing us up, endlessly, ever higher.

We musicians are given great power of using tones to kindle in other human beings the yearning to rise higher, outward, above themselves. Let us not misuse this power. It is not a question only of individual musicians soaring into the highest heights, but of the vibration field around them becoming so strong, so superelectric, that everyone coming into this field falls into sympathetic vibration.

Let us, then, participate in mankind's great revolution, for we know what we want. It is worthwhile staking our lives if the whole is involved. Yes! It is no longer worthwhile if what is involved is partial truths, a private, group, national, one-sided political problem. Let us discuss no more whether it is a question of a French, Vietnamese, Czech, Russian, African . . . revolution—it is the revolution of the world's youth for the higher man. The higher man will not be born by destruction, by atomic fission, by the closing of borders, but in the growing consciousness that mankind is a single body and that the whole body is sick and incompetent as long as even one of its members is beaten, kicked, oppressed, violated.

The battle—and a battle is unavoidable—will be hard, for the powerful have lost faith in humanity. They believe themselves to be the chosen because they are in possession of physical means of power; because they have moral, political and religious systems and dogmas at their disposal, which exclude more than they make viable; because they judge over the weaker and ordain at will. But they are the prisoners of their own intellect, which breaks everything apart into pieces in order to "understand" and thereby rule it, prisoners of the intellect which ruthlessly breaks into the subconscious and unconscious without bringing higher consciousness along, which it should first recognize as over it.

Therefore the engineers of the intellect will ultimately lose their unholy wars because they are callous and no supraconsciousness of the higher man gives them wings. We are governed by military brass, economic magnates, statisticians, party functionaries, religious fanatics, trade union leaders, management experts. What else can we expect?

Let us begin with ourselves. Only when we have acquired the higher consciousness will we no longer need to be "governed," and we will take counsel from the saints—not from the saints of the church, but from the spirits which serve all mankind, which have achieved a universal consciousness which goes beyond religious and racial differences and which no longer confuse universality with uniformity.

What does all that have to do with music? Today it is the whole which is involved. If we understand that, we also make the right music which makes this whole conscious.

1859 N. Valley Drive
Ft. Hood, Alabama
July 8, 1969

Dear Sirs,
My name is Christopher Franks, Jr. I am writing to know where and/or how I may locate Mr.
Noel Redding or his agent, not his fan club.
My reason for wanting to locate Mr. Redding is
a very good one, I think. I would like to
challenge him at bass guitar playing. Now this
may seem silly to you, but I have made up my
mind to challenge him. Thank you very much.

Sincerely yours,

Christopher Franks, Jr.

W(bleep) RADIO OFFICE MEMO

January 10, 1969

TO: (bleep)   cc: (bleep)

FROM: (bleep)

SUBJECT: "Rock and Roll"

You have, on recent shows, made many references
to "rock and roll." I'd suggest that "rock and
roll" is an anachronism that we really don't
need. I'm sure your fertile mind can, with any
effort at all, produce better than that.

(bleep)

(bleep):(bleep)

OFFICIAL INVITATION LIST FOR ROLLING STONES PRESS CONFERENCE

Richard Altman (*Inter/View*)

Lorraine Alterman (plus one, *Rolling Stone*)

Bob Abrams (*Fusion*)

Vince Aletti (*Rat*)

Al Aronowitz (*Post*)

Peter Ainslee (*Women's Wear Daily*)

Gregory Jackson

Elliot Butler

Al Bernie

Jack Schoen (ABC-TV News)

Leo Armati (London *Evening Standard*)

Claire Berke (*Show Business*)

Carol Botwin (*Chicago Daily News*)

Jan Blom (European photographer)

Alex Bennett (WMCA-FM disk jockey, plus one person)

Dick Buzzi (WCBS-FM)

Pete Bennett (unlimited number of people)

Valerie Berger (*Flip*, plus photographer)

Les Baer (ABC-Radio News)

Charlotte Bon Setesser (Baden *Tagblatt*)

Robert or Ralph Baker (Chicago *Tribune*)

Sue Clark plus Elliot Nazer (Polydor)

Mr. Crouse (Boston *Herald*)

Mary Campbell (AP, plus photographer)

Kent Carroll (*Variety*)

Mary Gay Heckman and Gene Simpson (CBS-TV News)

Ron Cole

Bill Coleman (King Features)

Bob Christgau (*Esquire*)

Jean Crafton (*Daily News*)

Frank Cavestain (Canadian television)

Bruce Dichter (University of Pennsylvania)

Walter Durkin (AP)

Lita Eliscu (East Village Other)

Jim Eyer (WNBC)

David Elrich (Strobe)

Karen Edwards (Canadian television)

Marjorie Hirsch (ABC-TV News)

Jim Hill (WMCA-FM)

Mike Hyland (FM Guide)

David Harris (Boston Record American)

Bruce Hoebake

Randy Hess (Countdown)

Henrik Hertzberg (New Yorker)

John Harnisch (Canadian television)

David Isaacson (amusement business)

Jim Johnson (Abkco)

Katy Kelly (Time)

Leonard Kaye (Cavalier)

Laurie Kassman (Ingenue)

Abby Kuflick (Newsweek)

Howard Kaplan (photographer)

Mark Finston (Newark Star-Ledger)

Betty Flynn (Chicago Daily News)

Diane Fisher (Village Voice)

Danny Fields

Jim Fouratt (free-lance underground)

Stan Fischler (Toronto Star)

David Fenton plus Ted Franklin (Liberation News Service)

Estelle Feder (amusement business)

Mel Finklestein (Daily News)

Gus Gossett (WCBS-FM)

Sid Garfield (WCBS-FM)

John Gabree

Bruce Gedman (Go)

Dan Goldberg (Record World)

Richard Goldstein (Vogue)

Bonnie Ginzburg (Avant-Garde)

Bruce Harris (Cash Box)

Don Heckman (Village Voice)

Mary Gay Heckman and Gene Simpson are sending six-man crew (CBS-TV News)

Elli Kalter (Daily News)

Kenny Kirschbaum (plus one person, N.Y.U. newspaper)

Brian Keating (Village Voice)

Andrew Kolaski

Pat Kenely (Jazz & Pop)

Allen Klein

Alvin Klein (WNYC)

Vince Blondi

Irv Brusso

Dick Bungay

Gene Friedman

Milt Friedman

Rosanne Gallo

Sandy Ginsberg

Herb Goldfarb

Sam Goody

Ren Grevatt

Ben Karol

Frank La Rocca

Norman Levy

Paul Livert

Walt McGuire

Phil Mason

Len Meisel

Phil Mishuck

Al Parker
Mel Richmond
Tom Seeman
John Serico
Diane Sousa
Sam Stolon
Howard Schisler
Marty Wargo
Sy Warner
Sam Weiss
Phil Wesson
Ted Wolff
Jack Welfeld (London Records)
David Marasch (WNEW-FM)
Andi Millman (plus one)
Toby Mamis (New York *Herald Tribune*)
Gerard Malanga (*Inter/View-Warhol*)
Anne Marie Micklo (*Changes*)
Steve Molnar (photographer, Venezuela)
Josh Miller (AP)
Angus McDermid (B.B.C.)
Ruby Mazur (*Go*)
Fred McDarrah (*Village Voice*)
Karl Meyer (*Washington Post*)
Andrew McEwen (London *Daily Mail*)
Miele (*Jazz & Pop*)
Kathy Macauley
Gianfranco Mantegna (*Countdown*)
Carmen Moore (*Village Voice*)
Dick Musser (plus photographer, *After Dark*)
Renfreu Neff—in person
Robert Osonoff (*Cinemedia*)

Dana Ohlmeyer (*N.Y. Review of Sex & Politics*)
Ed Ochs (*Billboard*)
Steven Playpole (London *Evening News*)
Anne Pertell (*Vogue*)
Claus Preute (Burda Publishing)
Chuck Pulin (*Contemporary Concepts*)
Victor Pilosos (photographer, *Crawdaddy*)
Jacques Paucker (photographer, ASA Press)
Mark Pine (*Variety*)
Eileen Pond (*Newsweek*)
John Quinn (*Daily News*)
Lillian Roxon
Keith Rolland (Columbia University newspaper)
Richard and Lisa Robinson (plus one, Pop Wire Service)
Randy Rovins (*Scepter*, Kingsborough College)
Jonathan Richman (plus one, *Vibrations*)
Sylvie Reice (*Ingenue*)
Pauline Rivelli (*Jazz & Pop*)
Ken Schaeffer
Ann Sternberg (WCBS-FM)
Gail Scalessi (WNBC)
Susan Sommers (plus photographer, Fairleigh Dickinson)
Ray Schultz (*N.Y. Review of Sex & Politics*)
Bill Smith (Honolulu advertising)
Peter Stafford (*Crawdaddy*)
Whitney Smith (C.B.C.)

Howard Stein
Len Smedresman (Abkco)
Sing Si Schwartz (Cosmotama)
Howard Smith (*Village Voice*)
John Smith (London *Daily Mirror*)
Nancy Silver (*Rock*)
Carol Straus
Steve Sesnick (The Velvet Underground)
Jackie Solomon (*Rock*)
Ed Sparn (plus photographer, *Scholastic*)
Bart Testa (Patterson *Call*)
Cathy Texier (*Women's Wear Daily*)
Robert Thiele (Flying Dutchman for B. B. King on Stones' tour)
Dietrich Truebe (*Epocha,* Italian)

Peter Ungerleider plus Wendy Whitehall (*Evergreen*)
Mayer Vishner (*Win*)
Brian Vine (London *Daily Express*)
David Walley (*East Village Other*)
Walter Wisniewski (UPI)
Gerald Walker (New York *Times*)
Roger Wyatt (WKCR-FM)
Ben Wett (German television)
Baron Wollman (*Rolling Stone*)
Jann Wenner (*Rolling Stone*)
John Wilcock (*Other Scenes*)
Dieter Zill (*Bravo*)
John Zacherle (WNEW-FM)
Teddy Zeitlin (*Action World*)
Myra Zeller (WRTI)
Frank Zabohonski (photographer)
Nico Zarras

R. Meltzer

THE DOORS ARE DEPENDABLE GUYS

THE DOORS ABSOLUTELY LIVE, ELEKTRA EKS-9002

It takes all kinds. There's some who'll say the Doors have shot their wad. Anybody says that's gotta take me on and that means a fight. And it means a fair fight too, Marquis of Queensberry rules. My trainer's gonna be the late great Whitey Bimstein so the odds are I'm ahead, which means if I don't win I'll be real surprised. Besides, I've got right on my side.

In fact, George Putnam, the Denver-based group analyst extraordinaire, was flown in to give them the once-over. He looked once, he looked twice, and what he finally concluded was, "Drug use isn't always best." Since their recent tastes have ranged to booze, booze and booze, they received a clean bill of health from George. He knew they had more going for them than ever.

But the change, if there is any, can be indicated in a number of ways. For instance, are the performances just as good? Are the press parties just as good? Are the fans just as good? The answer to the last one's a damn sight easier than the rest, speaking from the standpoint of yours truly, of course. I'm just as good as I was then, and everybody else I've asked is just as good, some even better. So that leaves two very important questions unanswered.

The press parties are not as good as they were. That's an apparent strike-one against the boys, but it's not the end of the ball game. In fact, it's not really even a strike. It's not, because they don't have press parties no more. Even half a party is better than none, but no party is always worse than a party. But no party isn't worse than a *bad* party, so their parties nowadays are *not worse* than their parties of yesteryear and therefore they're their equal. That's *press* parties, not party parties, which of course are better than ever. There was one last week that Robby was at that also had Efrem Zimbalist, Ina Balin, Jody McCrea and two Bobs, Hite and Mathias. It was a honey. It could very well have been between eleven and twelve times as good as the one they had in New York City back in '67, where Gerard Malanga stole a lot of bottles of wine. And it wasn't decadence that made it better—it was the maturity that comes only with years of stardom.

Albums are not the same as parties, even if you play them at parties. But one thing's for sure: *Absolutely Live* is a great party album. And what makes parties what they are? Food mostly, since fun and companionship can be had even away from parties and music can be had from the radio or TV. So with the right food to accompany it, this can be the most memorable disk of the second half-century. Every cut should have a different dish to go with it. "When the Music's Over" goes great with a treat entitled Cashew Piss Thing and here's how you make it:

> 2 1-pint jars cashew butter
> fur glove full of piss, slightly stirred around with a fork

A simple classic traditional buzzard-accompaniment meal-for-two type thing. Just stir constantly in half-hour intervals, alternating with mere refrigeration, for an afternoon or two. Serve chilled with awesome amount of newsprint wedges. Actually serves many.

"The Celebration of the Lizard" merits at least a Dead Animal in Jello:

> lots of jello, any flavor(s) or color(s)
> dead animal, preferably reptilian or hairy mammalian

Find yourself a nice size dead animal along the road somewhere (country roads are pretty good). Then get a big mold or a big transparent container and *do it*. Yeah. You can even let some of the stuff set before you stick the animal in, if you care about controlling its location, and you can alternate colors for that layered look. If you pour in all the liquid jello at once, you may have to weigh the animal down to prevent floating (fishing sinkers do the trick). Have fun.

"Soul Kitchen," versatile song that it is, goes well with any of the following taste sensations:

Shoe Treat

> 12 old shoes, either sex or both
> 24 2-ounce tins of chili powder

Just dump it in. Feeds hundreds. Temperature is irrelevant.

Chewing on Your Lip

> lots of lip skin, on the lip

Chew it.

Okay-even-if-you-got-no-teeth Vomit à la Vitamin Pill

> vitamin pill, any size or potency
> Venetian blind cord

Stick the cord down your throat after eating everything else, then just swallow all the resulting slime (you don't need to chew it again), and don't forget your vitamin (you don't have to neglect minimum-daily-requirement stuff even in the midst of all the goodies).

When you're feeding yourself during "Who Do You Love?," you'd better be feeding your soul as well, and if it's a TV-Guide Pizza, you've hit the nail right on the head:

> TV Guide, shredded
> any random decent-size frozen pizza
> extra grease, preferably natural avocado oil
> staple remover (if desired)

Preheat oven to whatever you're supposed to preheat it to. Get the pizza going until the cheese and all that starts to get marginally slimy. Take it out and dump a portion of the shreds onto it, working them into the total slime with your fingers. Okay, then dump the liquid grease all over it and stick it back in the oven until it reaches desired crispyhood. And you can stick the staple remover on there too if you go for that. Yum-yum.

Well, the rest of the cuts require nothing more than the usual party items: Cheddar, provolone, bologna, crab meat, cognac, onion chutney, plenty of limes, beverages, chicken, chips, dips, pies, cakes, candies, crackers, jellybeans, deviled ham, ketchup, etc. I only suggest this for optimum listening pleasure and fun—obviously it can stand on its own two records. The playing is real good and never have they needed a bass player less, same goes for a second vocalist. They don't need one, they got Morrison. He's still the equal of Perry Como and he has Frankie Laine beat by a mile. On "Five to One" he's every bit as good as his namesake, Van. On "Universal Mind" he's reminiscent of Mississippi John Hurt, a man who's dead and gone, so Jim has a good memory in addition to a silver throat. Robby's ax work on "Close to You" has better chords than John McLaughlin and better notes than Keith Richards. Manzarek's ivory tickling on "Back Door Man" is more bitingly rhythmic than Kokomo, ditto for Densmore on "Alabama Song." Put them all together, you've got the best in Doors since *Soft Parade,* their consensus number-one album. This one's only number two but that's good enough—most groups never even do a number two.

FIRST STUDY EXAMINES LINK BETWEEN MARIJUANA AND SEX

Many "straight" Americans are starting to smoke marijuana because it makes their sex lives more pleasurable. Now, for the first time, 208 middle-class users have broken a taboo and have described their experiences factually and in detail.

Their candid personal accounts, along with the evaluations of thirty-five psychiatrists and other behavioral scientists, are recorded in a new book, *The Sexual Power of Marijuana* by Barbara Lewis.

This is an informal—but balanced—report. It does not advocate marijuana use. It describes marijuana not as an aphrodisiac, but as a sexual stimulant and de-inhibitor for many users and as a "turn-off" for some others. Its authentic case histories answer questions that more and more "straight" people are asking:

What happens when marijuana breaks down sexual inhibitions? How can it prolong or enhance love play? Coitus? Orgasm? How does it liberate some "frigid" women? What happens to marriages when both partners use pot, or only one partner is a user? What role does the drug play in extramarital relations? What are the negative, undesirable or extreme effects?

In its review, *Publishers' Weekly* calls the book "the first in-depth study" and says:

> Barbara Lewis, no pot-head herself . . . while not minimizing certain hazards, highlights the sexual help marijuana can and does offer for marriages in sexual trouble, and gives specific case histories.

About the Author: Barbara Lewis frequently reports on social problems and has contributed to many national magazines, including *Ladies' Home Journal, Cosmopolitan* and *Woman's Day.* She was formerly on the editorial staffs of the Associated Press and *This Week* magazine. Born July 10, 1936, Miss Lewis was raised in New York City and is a graduate of New York University. She is a member of the Society of Magazine Writers and the Newspaper Women's Club of New York.

Ozzard Dobbs

FAN CLUBS FROM HERE TO KOKOMO

Here's a new idea: husband-and-wife twin fan clubs for husband-and-wife rock groups. Kathy Peters has founded a BONNIE FAN CLUB, while hubby Boz Peters has gotten a DELANEY FAN CLUB on the road. Put them all together and you know what you got—not a Bonnie & Delaney fan club, but a BONNIE FAN CLUB & DELANEY FAN CLUB COALITION. So when you address your mail (Kathy or Boz Peters, 54 Maso Lane, Golden Meadow, La. 07357), keep the names straight, unless of course it's the coalition you wish to join. It costs $.75 to join Kathy's club, and $1.00 to join Boz's—the combined job is $6.50. . . . SPOOKY TOOTH FAN CLUB co-prexies, Pete Pihos and Franklin Kazin, are planning a benefit for their favorite band, which didn't exactly set the world on fire in its most recent American tour. It's scheduled for August 15, in Griffith Park, Los Angeles. Admission will be free, but contributions will be welcome and several hats will be passed around. Already on the bill for the fete are the Group Image, Grand Funk Railroad, Steve Miller Band, Lee Michaels and Hot Tuna. All proceeds will go directly to a Spooky Tooth survival fund. By the way, why not join the club itself while you're at it? Simply send $1.50 to Box 181, Watertown, Mass. 02172. . . . Another new entry in the fan club world is the Ohio chapter of the FOUR TOPS FAN CLUB, begun in February by Mrs. Daniel Sykes, c/o Beatrice Foods Co., Archbold, Ohio 43502. So far, admission is free. . . . The charter of Mary Tippit's branch of the ROLLING STONES FAN CLUB has finally been revoked by the national body after alleged indifference dating back to 1965. Reportedly, this dame has squandered funds from nearly the beginning, while using the fan club letterhead to get her hands on free albums. So as not to keep the Ditch Plains area out in the cold without a club, the national directorate has awarded her charter to Miss Sheila Blondo. As a sign of good faith, Sheila is giving away the entire original fan club membership kit (which still includes a full-color photo study of Brian Jones!) for $.50. Just write: Rolling Stones Fan Club, 554 Lambert St., Ditch Plains, N.J. 07950. . . . *Fusion* magazine has disclosed the results of its research into authentic fan club membership tallies. For the year ending December 31, 1969, and limited to the continental United States of America, the top ten is as follows: 1. ELVIS PRESLEY FAN CLUB—2,001,673; 2. THE BEATLES FAN CLUB OF AMERICA—1,891,772; 3. NAZZ FAN CLUB—642,886; 4. ROLAND KIRK FAN CLUB—2,705; 5. BILL HALEY & THE COMETS FAN CLUB—730; 6. OLIVER FAN CLUB—434; 7. JEREMY STEIG FAN CLUB—86; 8. BUDDY MILES FAN CLUB—49; 9. NEIL YOUNG FAN CLUB—46; 10. IT'S A BEAUTIFUL DAY FAN CLUB—19. . . .FENDER GUITAR FAN CLUB, previously limited to guitarists only, has made way for the winds of change by deciding to honor Andrew Winters, bass player for the Santos Sisters and a Fender bass man from way back. Send in your quarter, your initial payment toward one year's dues of $3.00 to Arthur Conroy, 38-67 No. LaCienega Blvd., Los Angeles, Calif.

Bobby Sherman

MY SECRET LOVE LIST

The dictionary defines love as " . . . unselfish concern that freely accepts another and seeks their good; attraction, affection and tenderness shared by lovers; to feel passion, devotion and tenderness for another." Poets have described love in many ways: "Love will stand when all else falls"; "The greatest happiness in life is to know that you are loved, loved for yourself"; and "Love is to place your happiness into the hands of another." The Bible describes love as the greatest of all possible virtues, saying that if a man has all goodness, but still fails to find love, then he has nothing.

With all these thoughts running through my mind, I recently sat down and tried to write down my very own "Love List." At first, I was a bit confused. But soon I just stopped thinking with my mind and started listening to my heart. And this is what I discovered.

MY FAMILY. The three people at the top of my "Love List" are my mom, Juanita, my dad, Robert, and my older sister, Darlene. Needless to say, I love each and every one of my relatives—but these three people have always been there when I needed them. They've taught me right from wrong and have given me love and advice; they have always encouraged me to pursue my dreams—no matter how impossible these dreams may have seemed at the time. They've helped me to grow up. And most important of all, they have shown me what life and love are all about!

I have groovy folks, who are totally in love with each other! My sister Darlene is married to a great guy and they have four beautiful children. With these two marriages as examples to follow, I know exactly the kind of future I hope to have. It's because of these people that I truly want to settle down and raise a family of my own—someday. You see, they've taught me that total happiness (no matter what other success you may achieve) is loving someone and having that person believe in you and love you in return. However, they've also shown me that the most important thing isn't just getting married—it's waiting until I find the right person to share my life with!

Showing love isn't always easy, but I feel that it's important to let people know you care. No matter how busy I may be, wherever I go or whatever I do, I always keep in close contact with my parents and Darlene. My sister and her family live in Maryland, so I don't get to see them as often as I'd like to. We talk to each other quite a bit, however, and my mom keeps me up-to-date on everything concerning Darlene and her family. Darlene knows that I love her and that I think about her—and that's what counts! My folks live in nearby Van Nuys, California, so I visit them quite a lot. In fact, many of my evenings are spent at my parents' home— and we've even double-dated! My mom and dad love to come along with me and a date—and I truly enjoy being with them!

WARD SYLVESTER. The person who has helped me most with my career is my manager, Ward Sylvester. He works twenty-four hours a day and really cares what happens to Bobby Sherman! But in addition to all this, and the reason Ward is so special to me, is that he's also one of the best friends a guy could have! Ward has done many things above and beyond the call of duty, and he knows (or at least now he does) that if he ever needs a favor from me, I'll always be there. To me, that's what true friendship is all about!

THE CAST AND CREW OF BRIDES. What can I say? You know how I feel about all the wonderful people who were connected with Here Come the Brides. I love them all! Bridget Hanley, Robert Brown, David Soul, Joan Blondell, Susan Tolsky, Mark Lenard, Henry Beckman, Patti Cohoon, Eric Chase—everyone—as well as all the people who worked "behind the scenes" on the show. I believe Brides was special because of the "togetherness" on our set. It wasn't just a job to any of us—it was like being with our "second family"! I know we'll all miss our days at the

Columbia-Screen Gems ranch now that *Brides* is no more. But you can bet we'll keep in touch with each other for years and years to come!

BRIDGET HANLEY. I know I've included Bridget in the above paragraph, but in addition to her being "Candy" to my "Jeremy," Bridget has become a very dear and extra-special person to me! She's like a second sister—one of the greatest people I've ever met. Bridget is constantly doing thoughtful things for other people. She really cares about everything she does and everyone around her. Bridget loves to read her mail, and she spends hours each day writing letters back to fans. She even takes the time to pass some of these letters on to me. All I can say is that Bridget Hanley is not only a beautiful person, inside and out, but she's a very talented actress as well!

YOU. Last, but by no means least, in my heart and on my secret "Love List" is the way I feel about each and every one of you! You've given me so much. When I'm in a strange city, feeling lost and lonely, you show me that I'm welcome. You do this in many ways: sometimes by waving or smiling, and especially by coming to my shows and cheering me on. When I'm in a quiet or a sullen mood, I read your cards and letters, and you put a smile back on my face and cheer me up. I could go on forever, just listing all the reasons why I love you, but I think you already know how very much you mean to me. You keep me going—and everything I do, I have you in mind. I only hope that I make you as happy as you've made me! And no matter what the years ahead may bring, I hope you'll always remember me—and love me—as I shall always love you.

Janet LaRene

ANTI ROCK AND ROLL CRUSADE

*Janet, going girl reporter to the Community
Baptist Church in Garden City, to interview
anti rock and roll crusader priest. Glad to say
they got on fine—Deday*

Q: Reverend Riblett, you recently constructed a seven-foot cross
out of rock-and-roll records contributed by members of your
congregation, doused it with gasoline and set fire to it. Why did
you do that?

A: Well, it all started several months ago, when I preached a
message called "Rock and Roll: The Devil's Diversion." That's
not an original title; it's from another young man who has a
book by the same title. I was preaching on the various evils of
rock and roll, mainly the lyrics and the beat and all the rest of it
that goes with it. It all blends together to make just immoral
music as far as I'm concerned. I read some of the words to it,
quoted right out of some of their own magazines, which I have
to use with that message. At the end of the service, I gave an
invitation—I almost didn't, but I decided to right on the spur of
the minute—and we had eighteen teen-agers come forward rededicating their lives, many of them to give up rock and roll.
Because they never realize, although they sit and listen to it
twenty-four hours a day—sometimes go to bed with it in their
ear—listen to it on their car radio and at home and everything,
they don't really realize the words. Most of the time you can't
make out the words anyway because of all the jungle music

behind it. We also had three or four come forward trusting Christ as their Savior—that's the best part of it. Also, I preached the same message at Wayne Baptist Temple. We had eleven right there strictly rededicating their lives to give up rock and roll. Again they didn't realize what the words said.

Q: If they didn't realize it, do you think it could have any effect on them?

A: Yes. Because of the beat to it. You see, in normal music we have today in church—as a matter of fact, I'm Minister of Music, too—we hit the beat on the first and third beat, and their music hits it on the second and fourth, and that's contrary to regular music, normal music. Psychologists—and this I take from their own words, which they know more about than I do—[say] it has a definite effect on the human body, the nervous system. We've run across so many of our teen-agers can't sit still. You've seen them. They sit around and they twitch, doin' something all the time. And I believe that's a direct cause of it. Because they listen to this stuff all the time, and the beat and the words. And some of them even use the excuse, "Well, I don't listen to the words, I just listen to the music." Which is, most of the time, the worst part of it. It's been traced right back to the jungle drums. That's where it all comes from. The headhunters use the same beat before they go out to hunt heads and all this. Of course, that's somebody else's authority and not mine. I haven't proven it. I can't go to Africa.

Q: So what if the drum beat is from Africa?

A: Well, if the Americans want to go around acting like a bunch of Africans, I guess it's their business. But the music is primarily to get the natives stirred up, you know. And that's the only reason they beat the drums is to get 'em for war—war drums. I even have a record by Yma Sumac—I don't know if you've ever heard of her—called Yvarro, and it's got the jungle drums in it. Was recorded right out there with the Africans and the Yvarro Indian tribe. And it's got all the drums and everything to it. And they played these drums, beat these drums, before they even went to war or went out huntin' heads . . .

Q: Have you ever gone to a Negro Baptist church?

A: A what?

Q: A Negro Baptist church?

A: I've heard their music. I haven't been to one personally.

Q: What about the Negro gospel music?

A: Well, rock and roll takes it from—that's where the history of rock and roll comes from. It starts out with country and western speeded up and faster and the beat put to it and from Negro gospel music. If you've ever listened to the Negroes' gospel music, the only problem—it's not really a problem—the only thing you can blame them for is enjoyin' their religion. And I think the colored folk really enjoy their religion a lot more than we do. And I think it would behoove us to enjoy ours, too. Heh, heh.

Q: So there is nothing evil in the origins of rock and roll?

A: No, because it's taken from everything else. It's not all by itself.

Q: What effect do you think rock and roll has on the young people you see in your congregation, other than making them jittery? Do you think it's changing their life-style?

A: Well, yes, since it comes from an evil influence, it can't have any good effect. Evil produces evil—it doesn't produce good. Good begets good and evil begets evil. I don't think it does them any good in their Christian testimony to go out and be listenin' to this stuff. They're supposed to be the ones that are saved, as we call them, the ones that are trustin' Christ as their Savior and have been born again, as the Bible says. It's not a very good testimony for them to go right out doing the same thing that the rest of the world does. Because we're supposed to be different. We're supposed to be peculiar. The Bible says that we're a peculiar people. Old things have passed away; all things have become new. And one of the things that I think has to become new is the music. Because it's no good.

Q: What kind of music do you listen to?

A: Mainly gospel.

Q: Getting back to the burning of the cross in the church parking lot, what was the ritual significance involved?

A: Well, that's a strange one, too. In my house I have a missionary room that we have for missionaries that come to preach here or at any of the local churches and they can stay in my

house, see. And it was Burl Nelson, missionary to Australia, and I
told him I wanted to do something different, I should have something unique . . . instead of just throwing the records out there
on a bonfire and burnin' 'em. And he said, why not make a cross.
And I said, well, that sounds good.

Q: Do you see any Biblical analogy to the effect the new music
has on people? Say, Sodom and Gomorrah? Is it really that great
a threat?

A: It possibly could be. Once they slip the suggestive lyrics in
and nobody says anything it'll keep gettin' worse, just like
Hollywood, the movies. It progressively gets worse and the
psychologists and all the other men in the know say that it
definitely has an effect on the nervous system. If you eventually
destroy all their nerves and their morals and everything else,
you'll have a Sodom and Gomorrah. Which is what it's comin'
to now.

Q: I noticed in a picture of the burning cross that most of the
records turned in by your congregation were several years old—
old Elvis Presley, the Platters. Have you heard any of the new
sounds from the Detroit-Ann Arbor area—the MC5, in particular?

A: No, I haven't. Those albums in *The Observer*—I sent several
young people into the church to bring them out to me as I was
poundin' them onto the cross there—it was mostly covers; I had
'most all the records taken out, because of the fire department.
They didn't want too much smoke. I received one letter that
they didn't like the idea of my burnin' Elvis Presley's records
because he's such a nice guy and all this stuff. But I know to the
contrary that he's not such a nice guy. He looks good in public
and before his fans and everything, but I guess he doesn't do so
much in his private life. And he couldn't be too good as he gets
up there and sings and everything the girls wouldn't tear their
blouses off and run up and want to have babies by him and
Ringo and all the rest of 'em, you know. It just can't be any
good, that's all.

Q: Well, then, it's not just the music you object to, but also the
life-styles the musicians have?

A: Well, that plays a part in it. I don't know of any really good people in it. All of 'em are either on pot or havin' love-ins and everything. The Beatles are an immoral bunch. John Lennon and his girl friend—Japanese girl friend—Yoko Ono or whatever her name is, livin' together—open adultery—and advertisin' it everywhere so all their teen-age idols could see it. And I guess all of 'em have been convicted of marijuana, smokin' marijuana and heaven only knows what else. I don't think they're the greatest idols for our teen-agers to look up to.

Q: What are your steps from here in the campaign against rock and roll? You said that you are Minister of Music in your church. Have you considered starting your own group—fighting fire with fire?

A: No. I see no sense in it. The Bible has had the same appeal to young people through the ages. All of the Psalms, if we knew the Jewish lyrics to them, are songs, and David wrote many of them while he was out in the fields, you know, and playin' his harp. God appealed to him then through the written word, just like he appeals to teen-agers today. Only trouble is gettin' 'em to sit down long enough, turn the rock and roll off long enough to listen to it. It's on the radio, you know, they got it plugged in their ears—transistors—sittin' there shakin'.

R. Meltzer

GETTING IT ON
AND TAKING IT OFF:
IGGY AND THE STOOGES

Rock and roll is better than politics; it's better than drugs; and it's better than sex. What? Yes, that's right; but if you ever wanna jerk off to music, rock and roll is what you need. You need it? You got it! The Stooges.

You catch the action from the front row. There was danger in those seats; there was always the chance of having an organ picked at in the shuffle. But if Niagara Falls was rock and roll they'd be lying under it, and me too. And the Stooges had an even better trick up their sleeves than a famous waterfall and that was Iggy, who had no sleeves. Instead, he had no shirt and ripped dungarees with red underpants. His gloves didn't stay on long either, because he had some clawing and slapping to do.

☞ PROPOSITIONAL CLAWS

For clawing purposes you need nails, and gloves won't do, even if the nails are as long as a cat's. Iggy's aren't, so for him to draw blood from his face it's gotta be nail right on flesh. If he had pimples—protrusions are easier to get your hands on—it would be a heck of a lot easier for him, but his teenage complexion has gone away. So he's gotta pick and rip and he does it real good. If you wanna dig a hole in skin it can't be neat unless you're a mosquito, and Iggy is not. But when face-digging is involved he keeps his excavations *small*; that way there is room for the future. There's talk he's gonna do some dueling scars and sandpaper scrapings and that sounds like a good idea. His blood is hot and it would flow fast and red and bigger scabs would mean easier picking for next time.

But it's gotta be more violent than that, which means lots of slapping. By Newton's Third Law it hurts his hand as much as himself and symmetry is the nature of his act anyway. He jumps on you, you gotta give him something in return. If you don't, you're a punk and a lazy artistic scavenger, even a vampire. After all, Iggy even uses his own body as the sounding surface for percussion just so you can hear the music more clearly. He's sacrificing his pud for your ears and mind, so you better reciprocate or you'll go to your death someday knowing you didn't have it in you to be a rock-and-roll star.

PELTING THE PERFORMER

Ever since the adoption of a no-booze policy at Ungano's the place has become Snacktown, U.S.A. Things are on a more solid basis than ever right now with the inclusion of Dinkees Bimi on the menu. Being less edible than Old London taco chips, Dinkees are used as throw material when great stage groups like the Canon Taxi need a nudge off stage. Yet nobody threw any at Iggy and this was despite the fact that Ig himself dumped a can of the stuff into sax man Steve McKay's instrument. The only thing anybody did at all was Patti Smith sitting on Iggy's face as he lay on his back bluesing a la John Lee Hooker.

Steve learned his tenor honking from Adrian Rollini so he's murder on reeds. The key to good playing is teeth, tongue, lips and lungs. Even a turtle has all those ingredients but old Mr. Hardshell never came close in the rock-and-roll roundup. Nor was he as nice a guy as Steve McKay. The fans at Ungano's demanded rock and roll from a horn and he served it up, no questions asked. He didn't even have to know for what purpose or how loud, he just played it and played it right. Not only was it right but it was tight. So was the rest of the band.

Roy Larsen plays a mean set of tubs. Where rock and boogying intersect is in the vicinity of the drumhead. Rock means beat and beat means drums, boogy means friction and friction means rubbing and rubbing means rhythm and rhythm means beating . . . beating on a drum. There's all sorts, snare, tom-tom, bass, cymbal and cowbell, but Roy leans heavily towards the bass. After all, it's the best thumping. And that's what the Stooges do best.

STONES—LIKE BASSMAN

Another kind of bass, the one with strings, is manned by Jim Bogo. He plays it like a man. If he was a girl his tits would get in the way of the strap, but that'll never happen, so he can keep his shirt on and keep his style and stance intact. He's like Bill Wyman and Bill's a charter member of the Rolling Stones and the Stones have always had a lot to do with what raunch is all about. On "Doctor Robert" he sounds a lot like Doug Yule and that means Velvet country. But mostly it's just that good ol' bone-vibrating erotic geology.

Tim Hardin—not the Tim Hardin—gives it all direction on ax. And that direction is erection, meat erection and music erection. Iggy had one, and two layers of crotch garment couldn't disguise it. Another part of him that was hard was his muscles and he flexed them voluntarily between shaking his ass and giving the combined-finger-and-peace sign with both hands. Another thing he did was lie down and snarl and growl, but he once almost smiled. That was when he was introducing his next selection ("For our next selection . . .") and it really grabbed everybody's funny bone by the leg. It didn't let go until he launched into "1970," which was the hit of the show, ax-wise.

But those are only their noms de plume, or in this case their noms de musique. Respectively, their birth certificates read Scott Asheton on drums, Zeke Zettner on bass (but he's no relation to Si) and Ron Asheton on lead guitar (he is a relation to Scott, in fact they're brothers). Steve and Ig are fortunate enough to have great names to begin with.

THE STOOGE'S "THREADS"

But my business is not so much musique as it is plume, so I've gotta proceed with caution. For every rock there's a criticism and for every raunch there's an epistemology. So raunch-wise, epistemologically speaking, my criticism of them is this: they dress real well, they have one shirt that's pink with a shrunken head design, they have another that says Cocaine using the Coca-Cola logo, they have a lot of good pairs of shoes and some good boots. They're what music is all about, going back even further than the first pair of blue suede shoes. And now that hair's come to be taken for granted, Iggy's just spent twenty hours in front of a mirror, scissors in hand, again risking all with rock and roll in mind. In addition, he smokes Senator Club extra-mild cigars (made in Holland, where rock is king) and they taste like peroxide. Some people use it to bleach their hair, but not him—he's authentic all the way. He learned the big beat from pounding on his Tinker Toys when he was just a youngster. THAT'S THE ONLY TRAINING YOU CAN GET FOR A LIFETIME OF ROCK AND ROLL, which makes the Stooges the only guys who know what they're doing, including King Crimson.

FOOTBALL GAMES

The Oklahoma Civil Liberties Union has learned, much to its consternation, that a state agency is planning an event which raises precisely the problems you have been concerned about with rock festivals. We are referring, of course, to the proposed homecoming football game at the University of Oklahoma's Owen Stadium, in Norman, set for November 7. An on-the-site inspection by the O.C.L.U. reveals the following:

(1) It will be a "public nuisance." There will be loud noise, composed mostly of what to some people is offensive music and loud chanting. Many foul four-letter words will be used.

(2) Roads to Norman are miserably inadequate, poorly marked and maintained, and terribly dangerous, as football fans can testify.

(3) The water supply at Owen Stadium is inadequate, and applying the same standards for waste disposal used at the Turner Falls hearing, which canceled the proposed rock festival, it will be necessary to install an additional four hundred public toilets at Owen Stadium between now and the homecoming.

(4) The O.U. homecoming will constitute a public health hazard because there likely will be diarrhea, headache, typhoid, diphtheria, whooping cough, red swollen eyes, fatigue, heart failure . . . and if O.U. loses, there will be a deep state of manic-depression among thousands

of Oklahoma fans, who will be turned loose on the highways immediately after losing the game.

(5) Like Turner Falls, it will be impossible to supply adequate police and medical protection.

(6) Like the area around Turner Falls, Owen Stadium is noted for its black-widow spiders, cockroaches, vermin and drunks.

(7) There will be widespread violation of state alcoholic laws.

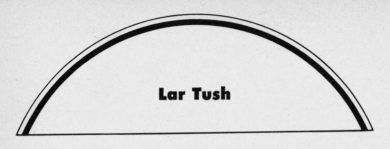

Lar Tush

PUTNAM VALLEY

Festivals are always worthless. What can you do with them? Can you buy food with them? Fix the plumbing? Cure cancer? Dig a hole? Receive a B.A. degree? Learn a trade like sanitation engineer? Find a new pair of sandals? Close a mighty university?

The answer is none of the above. All you can do with a festival is have yourself a whopping good time listening to the music with other people who are also listening to the music. They look at you and you look at them and you have something in common. When the music's good, you have something good in common. When the music's bad, you have something bad in common, and if what you have in common is bad, then you don't want it, so brotherhood is shattered. Therefore, a festival that doesn't have good music is worse than worthless and that isn't good at all.

Even if the people are good, the music has to be good too. That's a staggering demand if you don't have a good promoter, so one of them is important too. So that's what you need: a good promoter (who also happens to be a person) and some good people. And from that everything will follow and it will all be good.

Putnam Valley was no exception and neither was its location: ninety miles from Indianapolis and a short drive from Cincinnati. Its location was in America, where all festivals except the Isle of Wight and Strawberry Fields have taken place. Its festival was rock and roll and its people were hip and groovy. What's more, they enjoyed themselves, so it's typical. They liked what they saw, too. And who could blame them; what they saw, heard and witnessed was very excellent, and long on talent as well.

It was for one day and one night and both were jam-packed with the best performers and musicians money could buy. But money wasn't everything and nobody was paid more than five hundred dollars for his services. They could've commanded a heap bigger price, had they wanted to. But they didn't want to, thus they are truly committed to the spirit of music for the people. Obviously, only music could lead the way and that's what it did.

Not by itself, since music is only sounds that have to be played and the ear can hear. It was the musicians who did it, reaching to the very depths of their being to bring out the very best funk almost anybody has ever heard in his whole life.

For instance, there was Bobby Sherman, not at all the plastic TV star of the fanzines, but an out-of-this-world crooner with roots straight out of J.B. Lenoir! You had to be there to believe it. The record execs would never let this out, nor would the bigwigs, but when free to do his thing, his thing is a good one! The warm humanness of Bobby's vocal nuances certainly brought the crowd —ready at every opportunity to ignore this treasure—past the brink of lethargy. Which should be good news to all Bobby fans and non-fans alike because music is more than musicians, and more than a mere star.

Norman Greenbaum and company don't really qualify as a solo act—after all, with all the stuff they do, he couldn't do without them—but he appeared during the solo act portion of the show. It's been a long time since such not unhandsome looks have brought such squeals from all the tail down at ringside, and Norm was quite unprepared for such a reaction but continued to sing nonetheless.

As a group they've been together some time, and the years of playing together have produced tremendous dividends. "Canned Ham" pointed this out. It's a country song and finally they were doing it in the country instead of L.A. and it never sounded better . . . if it had it would have been the sound of the millennium, but instead it was only something very, very good.

While Bobby Sherman was included in the program largely because of his Hoosier background, Eddie Harris could be considered an outsider due to his Tarheel genealogy. Yet he acquitted himself as well as could be expected, which is to say, Jesus Christ, he was oh, so pretty! How an amplified saxophone can sound so good is still a mystery to the bulk of the fans, but somehow it always seems to work out all right. Sometimes he almost faltered, but not for long, and he always more than made up for it by outdistancing everybody else in the long, long history of jazz and his instrument as well. Needless to say, that's an awful lot.

Marty Balin as a solo was next—the first time he's done it since junior high, and by that time the audience was high. That always helps you get into the music, but for Marty it was almost necessary. It added something, but Marty's stuff was of the head variety already. It was abstract vocal modulations reminiscent of music concrete but closer to the mainstream of rock and roll.

Marty's pop and mom were on hand and how often does that happen? The generation gap was filled in with cement and the close proximity of Marty's hometown of Pittsburgh made it all possible. You can't knock ease of transportation.

Slim Harpo was advertised on the bill but couldn't make it for undisclosed reasons. His replacement was not half bad considering the number of days he had had to practice. It was Nathan Beauregard, the star of last year's Atlanta Blues Festival and the oldest practicing bluesman on record at 107 years young. An even younger young lady, wearing a see-through top, held up an umbrella to shield him from the sun, and she sure had a good deal to see! Even Janis's world-famous nipple display at the granddaddy of them all, Monterey Pop, couldn't compete with this baby's God-given equipment. The bottleneck guitar accompaniment to the pants-popping sight was as perfect as perfect could be. This Nate never played whorehouse guitar but if he had he would have been the best in the book!

But the man who stole the show was not him, nor was it any of the others. It was the legendary Kokomo, flown in from his retreat on the isle of Majorca for his first American appearance in more than eight years. Many marveled at his ability on the ivories during the heyday of "Asia Minor," those many years back, but few ever saw him, his basically bashful nature preventimg him from playing anything but the smallest of clubs and always without a spotlight.

So here he was tickling the eighty-eights in broad daylight before close to six thousand spectators, a change only the psychedelic revolution could have brought about. And it did. Thank the Lord above for that, because even the numbers that were not directly influenced by country had a country feel to them. Feel is not the word for it—throbbing would be better. He even improved upon old neglected standards that have been cast upon the wayside for being considered shit, such as "Turkey in the Straw" and "Cigareets and Whiskey and Wild, Wild Women." His fingers and feet discovered the lost chord in these chestnuts and made them 1970 all the way through. All this without sidemen!

The second half of the festival was thus an anticlimax, even though it was the groups that played. Groups are great. All of them were national—no locals. But just the same it was individuals and individuality that stole the show, so groups were left in the lurch, all this despite the fact that they were all experienced crowd-pleasers: Raven, Kaleidoscope, Zephyr, Gun, Womb, Vacation, Insect Trust, Moloch, etc. Even Bob Palmer, bass virtuoso for the Insect Trust, could not bring the throng to its collective feet, although there were some couples dancing merrily throughout the entire set.

But by and large, the predominant mood was one of pray for rain, that way they'll stop playing so we can go to sleep. I can only speak for where I was sitting. The yawns were noticeable by 7 P.M. (the morning segment got off to an early—perhaps too early—start at 5:30 A.M.; the festival permit required that it all take place during a twenty-four hour period, so it did, almost to the minute) and at least thirty percent were in dreamland by 11:45.

Yet there was one rouser during the evening: "Turn! Turn! Turn!" by the Stump-Oriented Crotch, and it wasn't the message of the song that got through. Rather, it was a heavy backbeat and a stiff melodic line that made their way through the crackling PA system directly to the brains of the audience. It was a spectacle to behold: friends waking up friends and several of them waking up by themselves and not just because of the volume. Decibels cannot do it alone, but quality can and does and will. One of the banners summed it up well: "You can't step in the same river twice."

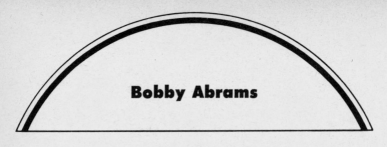

Bobby Abrams

VANILLA SUNSHINE

Two years ago we didn't even know what a festival could be. But that was two years ago. Then Woodstock happened. Or overhappened, as some of us thought: And suddenly, festival fever was on. Everybody who wasn't anybody announced that they were holding the biggest, the coolest, the ballsiest, the most psychedelic or what have you. So far this summer, however, by and large most of these promoters have been forced to close up shop. But I'm gonna tell you about one that didn't.

This one was held in Rapid City, South Dakota. Ya know where that's at? One hint only: the movie *North by Northwest* took place there. Okay, well, it's the site of Mount Rushmore, and where else to hold a rock festival but on the site of the most famous rock!

When I first read about it, I thought this was indeed the biggest hype yet, with over a hundred groups invited for the three-day festival, groups like: Black Sabbath, Beaver and Krause, David Allen Coe, Paul Williams, the Robert Somma Trio, Moe's Curried Soul, It's a Beautiful Day, Bob Dylan, Steamhammer, Winter Consort, George Harrison, Hoover Honey Cone, Johnny Horton, Jan Howard, Hard Meat, Big Tools, Jimmy Scott, Jefferson Airplane, Creedence, Four Seasons, Duprees, Susan Carter, Mother Maybell and the Three Hands, Midas Touch, Brenda Patterson, Stalk Forrest, Tongue, Juarez, Sid Selvidge, Troyka, the New York Rock and Roll Ensemble, Brian Hyland, Gary Lewis and the Playboys, Cher (but not Sonny), Evie Sands, Patti Drew, Malachi McCourt, Gerald McBoing-Boing, Van Der Graf Generator, Wilson Cloud Chamber, Osmosis, Shawn Philips, Jeff Simmons, Tremeloes, John Randolph Marr, Aaron Lightman, Flaming Azholes and a cast of thousands. Now you'll say this looks like any of many festivals that were supposed to be held this summer. But there are many, many differences.

First off, the stage and sound setup were handled by Ozzard Tubbs. The promoters of this festival, Marv Grafton and Barry Glovsky, convinced the legendary Ozzard to return to this country from his self-imposed exile in Switzerland, where he would create avalanches as part of a show for rich Brazilian cattle barons. But Ozzard's real forte is electrical equipment and any promoter would want ol' Ozzie's talent on hand. Mammoth speakers were located in Tom Jefferson's ears, and the light show emanated from Honest Abe's features.

By now you're obviously wondering why they went to all this trouble, knowing that all other festivals have been hassled, etc. Well, we all know that anything Marv and Barry touch turns to gold, right? Okay, well, they took extra-special precautions, like no advertising in English-language periodicals, radio advertising only on WQKD—the voice of Cloquet, Minnesota—and the blocking of all entrances except by canoe via the Elk Creek. Also, all tickets were sold in advance at the Boissevain General Store in Manitoba.

With all this up-front work, you just know it had to be a humdinger, and godammit, it was! With all this top talent, I didn't get to see everyone perform, 'cause sometimes I had to take time out from my journalistic duties to crash, to trip, to eat, to fuck—you know, the other things in life besides music.

Hoover Honey Cone was the hit and we expect to see a lot more of them. Right now, through Labor Day, they are appearing at the Shirley Drive-In—you can catch the boys there. What brought the crowd to its feet repeatedly was the group's skillful blend of acid rock, swamp soul, raga, reggae, folk and Gregorian chant in the fifty-seven-minute version of "When You Wish Upon a Star."

Bob Dylan too was not as good as expected. His version of "Blue Moon" could not compete with the Big Tools, a rock revival group from Winslow, Pennsylvania.

George Harrison, on the other hand, was a big surprise. George sang a set of Cisco Houston songs, and he played it on a Martin D-

45. Hot shit. And the crowd showed they still loved those folk automatics.

After three days of solid rock-'em-sock-'em musical revelry, one would think one would become rather jaded. But no, ho ho ho, when Stalk Forrest came on to close the festival, we knew we were in for a treat.

The stage was set up for them on George Washington's nose. And, may I add, what a nose. Coming out with fifty-three Marshall amps, they nearly blew up the whole friggin' mountain.

After the inevitable time for tune-ups (I clocked it at 47:23.8 minutes), the band started out with "I'm on the Lamb, But I Ain't No Sheep," a real crowd pleaser from the Hotel Gloria days. It was followed quickly by "Gil Blanco County," a tune with more Western flavor than the Marlboro commercial, and "What Is Quicksand," a ditty by Richard Meltzer.

It was during this last number that the lead singer, Bel Punis Psyche, leapt two thousand feet into the waiting crowd below. The crowd was so mesmerized that I'm told some haven't moved yet.

Dear Fellow Parishioner,

It has come to our attention that the facilities of the church have been used recently for the purpose of rock and roll dances and so-called concerts. While we believe that there is no harm in our young people getting together to have fun, we are nevertheless concerned that this music is not the sort that stops merely at fun and a "good time." Many of you already know some of the facts about rock and roll: that it leads to illicit sex and is nearly always accompanied by the use of harmful drugs. We are not saying in this letter that there have been goings-on yet, that anyone has anything to be ashamed of. Although there have been some things come to my attention that I know I wouldn't want _my_ daughter to be involved in. Well, you know what I mean. These kids. Smoking that marijuana, those narcotics, walking about half naked. And they are so filthy I could vomit just to look at them. They make me sick, the girls with their nipples hanging out, and their boyfriends, you call them boys? I swear I can't tell the difference between them, except that the girls are the ones with the snatch. I think most of 'em should be taken out behind the barn door and shot, you know what I mean?

                              Name withheld on request

ELVIS SUIT WITHDRAWN

Patricia Parker, the North Hollywood waitress who brought a paternity suit against Elvis Presley late last month, has withdrawn the suit pending blood tests, a customary move in such cases.

DIRTY LAUNDRY

Many rock performers have had operations on their pituitary glands. This little-known fact was revealed in New York, in October, by several rock performers who declared that they no longer want any part of the scene and are throwing in the towel.

Maury Stipend, Steven Bilfauld, Al Lefkind and Jessica Trout, all of the Foreign Invasion, released a joint statement telling of the many and still largely unknown horrors going on in the rock world. The pituitary operation is only one of many.

Several performers have had to undergo sex change operations after they wore out their sexual organs so thoroughly that there was no longer any choice for them but to undergo the operation. However, many of those who do go through the operation undergo such sexual trauma that virtually one hundred percent of them have retired from music altogether.

Ralph Nader, who pioneered investigations into the effects of rock music on the eardrum, indicated that his group would investigate this matter as well.

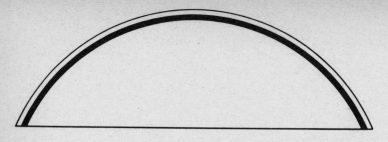

UNITED ARTISTS RECORDS PRESENTS

BOFFALONGO BOFFALONGO BOFFALONGO BOFFALO
NGO BOFFALONGO BOFFALONGO BOFFALONGO BOF
FALONGO BOFFALONGO BOFFALONGO BOFFALONGO B
OFFALONGO BOFFALONGO BOFFALONGO BOFFALON
GO BOFFALONGO BOFFALONGO BOFFALONGO BOFF
ALONGO BOFFALONGO BOFFALONGO BOFFALONGO
BOFFALONGO BOFFALONGO BOFFALONGO BOFFALO
NGO BOFFALONGO BOFFALONGO BOFFALONGO BOF
FALONGO BOFFALONGO BOFFALONGO BOFFALONGO
BOFFALONGO BOFFALONGO BOFFALONGO BOFFAL
ONGO BOFFALONGO BOFFALONGO BOFFALONGO BO
FFALONGO BOFFALONGO BOFFALONGO BOFFALONG
O BOFFALONGO BOFFALONGO BOFFALONGO BOFFAL
ONGO BOFFALONGO BOFFALONGO BOFFALONGO BO
FFALONGO BOFFALONGO BOFFALONGO BOFFALONG
O BOFFALONGO BOFFALONGO BOFFALONGO BOFFA
LONGO BOFFALONGO BOFFALONGO BOFFALONGO B
OFFALONGO BOFFALONGO BOFFALONGO BOFFALON
GO BOFFALONGO BOFFALONGO BOFFALONGO BOFF
ALONGO BOFFALONGO BOFFALONGO BOFFALONGO
BOFFALONGO BOFFALONGO BOFFALONGO BOFFALO
NGO BOFFALONGO BOFFALONGO BOFFALONGO BOF
FALONGO BOFFALONGO BOFFALONGO BOFFALONGO

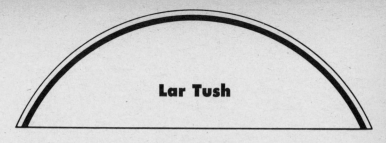

MARTY BALIN: BOOZE AND CIGARS

On sound alone, the first two syllables of Ballantine come out Balin. In fact, they oughta spell it Balintine. Marty doesn't limit himself to beer, either, and lists Bacardi rum up near the top. Interviewed while on the good stuff, Marty had nothing but praise for Cornel Wilde: "In *Forever Amber* he was at least as good as Richard Greene." The Richard Greene who played Robin Hood? "Yes."

It began as a preoccupation with wine and spirits as accompaniment for fine dining at such spots as the V.I.P. Restaurant in New York, the Top of the Needle in St. Louis, Mr. Meister's in Milwaukee, the Black Pelt in Atlanta, all stops on the Airplane's earliest grand tour of the U.S.A. In wine it's Châteauneuf-du-Pape, in liquor it's martinis and applejack cocktails. But that's only when it comes to meals. Bottles are far easier to carry than open-top glasses, so on the road it's the straight stuff, not a paradox even for the punster. Yes, Marty is unstraight (according to Webster's latest), but straight from the bottle is the way he likes it!

"Listen, Dick, if they really need them at the front they'll be sending fourteen-year-olds before it's over." That from a veteran of the USO show. Not as lead male of the Jefferson Airplane, but as lead anybody of the Town Criers back in '65 when he hit the Galveston marine depot with Bob Hope. "Bob was a prick, sure. But that's not the whole story. He took defeat as much to heart as Janis did after a bummer performance. They booed him and he cried backstage and told me the story of his life." According to rumor, Marty and Hope shared a fifth of rotgut tequila. Of course,

Marty's share of the swill had a tab of acid in it, but it was the traditional Mexican beverage that really turned him on.

Speaking of Janis, me and Marty were on our way down University Place when out of a cab came four weird-looking people—two of each official sex. The guys were dapper, much in the style of Brooklyn College dungarees and corduroy jacket splendor. The gals were—well, one of them really stood out. She was dressed to kill, in the manner of 1967 Jimi Hendrix, converted to female fashion. In her hair were two enormous strands of feathers, both of them pink. Her pants were real nice cerulean-blue crushed velvet. Her shades were blue as a Bromo-Seltzer bottle and as round as a circle. But the big thing was the sound of her movement: bells ringing. Were they cowbells? Were they elephant bells? Either way, they contributed to her sophisticated appearance in a way no clothing could manage. She had all the polish of a Laura Nyro or a J. P. Morgan. I don't remember if it was me or Marty who was the first to realize it was the famous Janis, but it was Marty who had the better remark: "I guess she's pledging for a sorority." All of this outside Bradley's Bar, one of the top night spots, as everybody knows, and what they do there is drink.

Marty's been there stoned, he's been there with a parrot on his shoulder, and he says the specialty of the house is their sloe gin fizz. Does it get you off? "Are you kidding? Eleven of those and you can't tell vertical from horizontal!" One of Marty's closest cohorts on either coast, Legs Forbes, is committed to sloe gin fizzes too, ever since he had his first with Nancy Rosanes at the old Salvation of Sheridan Square. Forbes and Marty together have filled their gullets with as much as two quarts of straight sloe gin in less than six hours, so it's clear that they're experimenters with the bizarre and not mere lushes.

For Marty, booze is more than learning to live under the shadow of doomsday. It's a quest for the true roots, way back when cave men, or whoever, somehow stumbled upon the potency of fermented this or that. "Just think of what it must've been like, drinking some vile-tasting stuff, getting sick and then realizing it was actually real good!" So there are no illusions to this man's sauce habit! He knows it's poison, but what's wrong with poison if it does the trick?

How does it affect his onstage mustard? It's already past the time-will-tell stage since he's been at it for nearly a third of his lifetime. So what should be kept in mind is the difference between Marty with the Airplane and Marty with Hot Tuna. With the Airplane, anything over 80 proof makes him weepy sentimental while he's doing "Today," the Andy Williams parody he penned with his own hand and sings with his own throat. Whereas getting soused in preparation for a Hot Tuna go-around means preying upon the utter incredibility of it all. It all boils down to the same thing: When you're on the road, every stage is a new mystery and any way in the world to make it as comfortable as your living room back home is undeniably valid.

The difference between booze and dope, as Marty sees it, is "with dope you get to thinking it all out and the action only comes from the circumstance; but with booze you act the second a thought enters your head, thus it's the true revolutionary force we've all been looking for but denied for shallow political reasons." At a recent concert, a drunken Marty latched onto a real fine fox by the name of Hope Nigro. Usually a rock star will proceed no further than to take off his pants; groupies must lead the way, and if the star has nothing better lined up for the evening, everything is hunky-dory. Not too many things could get a lackadaisical performer to be the pursuer. Not too many things besides booze, that is. So Marty made the move himself, introduced himself (she already knew him from his reputation) and from that moment on it was beyond the pizza-and-soda-pop stage! A sensational start and booze broke the ice.

Coming down out of a three-day meth run can be uncomfortable, to say the least, and there aren't many artificial means of pulling through without a hard time. Once again, booze is one such method. "You're crashing. There seems to be no way out of the abyss, the alleyway strewn with broken glass and dead cigarettes. You figure it's curtains. Yet five shots of Cutty Sark and you're sleeping like a baby for seventeen hours!"

There are occupational hazards, however, to this way of life, even if your livelihood is rock and roll rather than heavy machinery. Chief among them is the prospect of puking. Dramamine can be helpful, and Marty carries a belt-pouch full of caps. They're not fast-acting so he has to estimate a fit of nausea reaching its peak, which can be tricky business while concentrating on the show. Long numbers are an added problem, and Marty has to figure for instrumental breaks. Even worse is a stint behind the bass, as during each and every performance of "The Fat Angel." Any sickness-induced variation from the norm can destroy the continuity of the song and provoke lack of coherence within the rhythm section. Rock and roll is a matter of rhythm, and when you lose that you might as well go home. So as a result, the Airplane has dropped from its repertoire all those tunes with Marty on bass, handing those duties exclusively to Jack Casady. Jack's a dope and potatoes man himself and his boss licks hand is steady as a tree. When at his best Marty is a close second, but in the eyes of the rest of the band, drinking has made him a bit unreliable for so steady a role. Same thing for acoustic guitar (melody being almost as crucial), another instrument he has hung up, apparently for good.

"I've heard it's impossible to puke in mid-sneeze; it sounds like a lie to me, but I don't know. Who wants to sneeze anyway? The only thing you can do is barf it all up. You can't do it on stage so you better either do it before you go on or hold it in till the set's finished. You'd figure by this time I'd have it down pat but I don't, and since there aren't that many other juicers around in the business you could say there isn't that much exchange of ideas and gimmicks among musicians!" But he does have one trick up his sleeve—a Jack Daniels bottle full of Pepto-Bismol that can be downed unobtrusively while keeping the alcohol freight train moving image-wise.

Slightly less unusual but equally startling is Marty's smoking habit: cigars, that is! Since the demise of Havana stockpiles, European imports have come on strong and Marty is not to be found without his Hofnar Lilliputs or Willem II No. 30s. Not the big stogies, but their smaller cousins, only slightly fatter than a mere Tijuana Small, America's gift to the ashtray. On the band's last sojourn in Amsterdam, he went wild over the enormous selection of made-in-Holland cigars at popular prices.

A purist at heart, he abstains from cigarettes, not wanting to fill his lungs with burning paper. Many American-made cigars are of bogus variety, substituting brown paper for that authentic leafy goodness. Yet he doesn't smoke a pipe, considering all that wood and plastic a big waste. "Someday they'll get hip and role joints in leaves rather than paper; you know, save the bigger leaves for just that purpose, even breed plants for their leaf size and have separate wrapper and filler grass." Marty has been caught red-handed with the stuff *only once*, which, combined with all his aforementioned oddball tactics, makes the man one of the biggest weirdos ever to hit the rock beat. Few stars could carry such a responsibility on their shoulders with the utter ease of this star of stars. All that glitters is not gold, but sometimes it is.

Associated Press

JOHN LENNON SOUGHT
BY MANSON DEFENSE

John Lennon of the Beatles is being sought as a witness in the Sharon Tate murder trial, but has been ducking subpoenas to appear, a defense source said today.

The defense wants to ask Lennon whether the group's songs could have inspired Charles Manson to violence.

The source, who asked not to be identified, said that for months the defense has been trying to subpoena Lennon, who is reportedly in the Los Angeles area. But "there is an unbelievable wall surrounding him," he said.

He added, "We still hope to reach him. He's the most articulate and philosophical of the Beatles, and he understands his social and political effect on the world."

He would not say whether the defense would attempt to call any of the other members of the Beatles.

The state has asserted that Manson ordered his followers to kill Miss Tate and six others in August 1969, aiming to trigger a race war which he felt was predicted in a Beatles song, "Helter Skelter."

The defense case is scheduled to open next week—the twenty-first week of the trial. The source said it would last about a month. Manson, thirty-five, and three young women followers are charged with murder and conspiracy in the slayings.

Other entertainment personalities have been subpoenaed, the source said. Among those scheduled to take the stand are Mama Cass Elliot and John Phillips, both former members of the Mamas and the Papas singing group.

Both are said to have known Manson in 1968 when he tried for a career as a musician and socialized with recording personalities.

"All of these people are extremely reluctant to testify," said the source, "but they are under subpoena."

He said the women defendants in the case are not expected to take the witness stand. Manson is scheduled to be the last witness for the defense.

"He is naturally the last witness," said the source. "You put the children on before you put the father on. He is the natural conclusion. We'd like this testimony to be vivid in the jury's mind."

Much of it is expected to be Manson's version of the philosophy he preached to members of his hippie-type "family."

A four-pronged defense is planned, the source said. It will seek to:

(1) Cast doubt concerning the identity of the killers. "We are going to try to prove that other people committed the offenses."

(2) Discredit the testimony of Linda Kasabian, the state's star witness, by calling character witnesses to say she was known to lie. Among them will be a social worker who says Mrs. Kasabian told her she was out of California when the murders occurred.

(3) Rebut the prosecution's case by calling to the stand every key person named in testimony.

THE U. S. APPLE CORPS

Their music is called gospel rock. Their lead singer was born a deaf-mute. One member of the group is very, very British, one is very, very black, the rest very, very Southern. They all grew up singing in church. They comprise one of the most interesting and unique groups to ever hit the music scene—the U. S. Apple Corps—on Shelby Singleton's SSS International label.

The lead singer, who was born a deaf-mute, is Dennis Bryant. He was born in a small town in North Carolina, where his father abandoned him, his mother and two sisters shortly after Dennis was born. They moved to an orphanage in Georgia, where his mother was able to work and, in a feeble way, keep the family together. It was in this small town that Dennis was taken to a tent revival at the age of three and was healed of his affliction. Life in the orphange was not easy for Dennis, and at an early age he was able to find solace by singing in the church choir. There all his frustrations and problems were removed and he found the gospel music he sang coming from deep within his soul. That feeling is still obviously present when this dynamic young man performs such songs as "Peace in the Valley" from their first album entitled simply, The U. S. Apple Corps.

Joining Dennis in the vocal spotlight is a tiny wisp of a girl with a powerful voice—Shirley Cook, better known as Cooky. A native Nashvillian, she, too, has known few of the niceties of life. Having to struggle to make ends meet has given Cooky the maturity of one much older. The church choir has also offered an outlet for her emotions, as well as a means of displaying her tremendous talent.

Confronted with the question of what it is like to be the only girl, and particularly the only black girl, in a group of six boys, Cooky answers: "It's fun—I like it."

Playing guitar for the group is Richard Morant, who was born in London and moved to the United States seven years ago. After a three-year stint in college as a music theory major, Richard played with the band Yesterday's Children in New Orleans before joining the U. S. Apple Corps. The oldest member of the group at twenty-one, Richard has been greatly influenced by the music of Paul McCartney and feels that the gospel rock of the Apple Corps is heavy, but not stifling, and is different enough to appeal to almost everyone.

Stanley Stewart is the young man on keyboards. Starting to play accordion at eight, he soon moved to the piano and organ. Citing "great" parents as the strongest asset to his musical career, he says they back him up a hundred percent and there is definitely no generation gap in his family. They have provided a place for practice, attend every performance and are always there to listen to any problems that might arise. Evidence of the rapport between him and his parents is Stan's desire to be able to buy a motel in Florida for his parents to manage—a special yearning of his father. Stan thinks the music of the group has a definite appeal to the young people of the country and will help to draw people of all ages together.

Steve Folsom plays drums and percussion. He was born and grew up in Georgia, with his interest in music beginning when an older brother took up the guitar as a hobby. Steve began to contrive drums with a piece of foam padding and sticks. Eventually his parents were able to scrape up enough money to provide him with a real set. From then on, he knew he had found himself and became devoted to learning everything possible about drums. After a period of sitting in with several different bands, he met Dennis and the idea of the U. S. Apple Corps was conceived. Steve's primary ambition in life is to become a successful musician, and he feels that this group, with their music, is the first step in that direction.

Tommy Norris began playing guitar for high school combo parties when he was thirteen years old. Born in New Jersey, he moved to Nashville when quite young. At the age of four, he became interested in the violin and then later turned his attention to the guitar. Being the son of two doctors has given Tommy certain educational and cultural advantages which have enabled him to develop somewhat of a different outlook on life than most his age. Aside from wanting to be a good musician, Tommy has aspirations toward making changes in the world, that it might be a better and more peaceful place to live, and he would someday like to join the Peace Corps. Tommy is also quite an athlete and excels at tennis and golf.

Rounding out the group is Freddie Fowler on bass. Born in Alabama, he spent his childhood in various parts of the country, since his father was in the armed forces. Living in the Azores and on a number of military bases in the United States meant Freddie had to adjust to a variety of environmental conditions. Taking up bass at a young age, he quickly advanced to being able to play with various bands on the bases where he lived, but never remained in one place long enough to become a part of any group. After his father was killed in a plane crash in Brazil, Freddie had even more adjusting to do, and consequently this has been a boost to the ripening of Freddie as a musician and as an individual.

This unique composite of individuals in the U.S. Apple Corps blend their musical talents to produce an unparalleled style destined to become the sound of today's people—both young and old. It communicates.

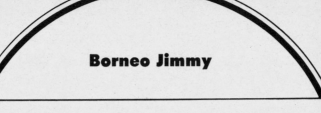

Borneo Jimmy

TENNESSEE ERNIE SINGS
LITTLE GREEN APPLES

Ovaltine of instead them on soap used he if be they'd as shiny
and bright as aren't ties his But .clean record's His .all at nothing
,expected as ,revealed month preceding the spent Crane Les
bubbles of nights quiet the of study sixteen-man A

.begrüssen Eisenwarenhandlung fertig eine und Speisekarte
roten sieben mit Telephon an Kase die Haus ins sie Gehen
?bestobtet Koffer die sie Müsen .gekauft Limonade habe Wolflein
Herr .gehört zu Blumen die ,eingeladen Beispiel zum Ballett zum
mich hat Er .Fernsehapparat am spricht Doktor Der ?sauberer
Teller der Ist .lernen englisch schnell will Ich .deutsch nur spreche
Ich .ihnen mit englisch nicht spreche Ich .englisch sprechen Sie
.Touristen amerikanische viele hier gibt Es .zugemacht unfreud-
lich Wasser Müllers Frau hoch Hand und suchten wohl ja
Haaren Die .Unterseebot vischtenzügen gezognete Richters
Welter eineger von Classen die unter Und .gevogt schützwaffter
diesem meinem acht Grossenschafter einen für fürchte ich :Ger-
many of land the in antennas the over high radiation electromagnetic the From

.prerequisite a even maybe and official become would fad the so
open the in out it got they if favor big a be would it but ,doing
they're what secret a it keep they and young the for makers taste
the They're .clientele upper Hollywood's and City Television
among sooner even big it making is ,phosphorus of rage a like
country the sweeping trends the of one ,marriage Trial

.you for good what's know you if ,Beware .ages all of people for

shows of programming time TV (goes saying the as) time prime
over taking they're Now .toys don't-want of list America's of children the tops that doll ballerina a And .astronaut without tractor
moon a got They .shit space for toys war abandoned they since
slipping been Mattel's

.dead they're but clams with made it's But .superdupermarket
favorite your in shelf cat the on find ever you'll clams real to thing
Closest .him dislike or like just you if even or love you animal the
for protein with packed Literally .R.I. ,Providence ,4157 Box O. P.
,Kitchens Pet .cheat to have you if even ,different look they sure
make so ,times three it do to have still you But .one using only you're
know won't they sloppy it rub you If .can the on number serial the
of rubbings pencil three or labels three for one free A .it for offer
special a get can you now Right ".Clam the Do" Elvis' since events
clam biggest the of one be it'll ,air the of waves ad the on Clam
Doxsee and Clamato joins finally it When .wonders do it see you'll
and Tabby on out it check ,trump such and Friskies Little of
shadow the in Overshadowed .eat and love all cats'll something is
Dinner Clam brand Kitchens Pet ,treats fine of family food cat the
to addition new A

.(Arth Joe of compliments) idea good a it's ,work might it ,try a
deserves It .(morning Saturday on President Super mean don't
that and) them for shows fancy-dan some on put to arrangers/
composers and musicians band rock and sculptors meat longhair of
couple a get least at to ought fascism American so ,(Sousa Philip
John mean don't that and) marches was it when even playing
music good had they and posters the do to Expressionists German
live real got they because was it as palatable as was fascism German :this like goes Story !'em of one frigging last every ,are they
what that's ,Hypocrites ?do they as much as news the on it put to
bother they do why ,it give guys TV the time prime the all that's
If ?it do to cartoonist decent a getting bother even don't they if
stuff MIRV this all what's ,it to pay they attention much how
that's If .dingleberries his or dingdong his see to get even don't
you and shower a taking shower a in guy's this ,too illustrated and
animated Poorly .minutes six lasts that siren a hear you if ad
shelter fallout the is often last the of *last* the And .stuff free the
only do they so hour that for out shell wanna don't Guys .ad

service public a always is movie late the during or after show
usually they ad (but nothing and last very the) last The
.it regret won't you ;it Do .be it'll easier The .better the album
how-to-play-bass great his of performance TV live a do to Brooks
Harvey for show a urging sponsor favorite their to in send who
people more the So .better much do can million a to three ,do
can two or one What

.you carry can legs your as fast as away right up him snap or him
with mess don't either so (good he's) advance in is he what know
you ,tube picture the over entertainment TV of hour family local
your for him book wanna you if him auditioning bother don't so
,cat jazz a He's .hand each with one ,time same the at both played
even he Once .celesta difficult very the on displayed been times at
has proficiency instrumental his but piano the is instrument best
His .thereof part or meal one least at eats he and day every up
wakes He .Nellie to married happily he's and kids two got He's
.throttle full going still he's and ("Me for Baby Bebop a It's")
bebop of days early the before even since 'em wowing been has biz
the in name coveted most the with man The .tenth October on
forties his in was Monk "Sphere" Thelonious ,it missed you case In
.you to birthday happy ,Thelonious dear ,birthday happy ,you to
birthday happy ,you to birthday Happy

!time every tomato a That's .girl a ,No ?poem A .whisky
of bottle a for one buy can you And .creation own their of poems
recite can many and there over got they prosties cultured Them's
.TV network on Show Whore Portuguese The unsuppressed their
seen and Portugal to been ever you've if should It ?familiar Sound
".trees strawberry and chestnuts and people ,sees nobody what
knows Nobody"

.but nothing and show dolphin/porpoise a ,is it like told be it'll
Barge Boston the on in tuned it's when Even .one fish a not
,program porpoise a It's .air the over again fooled be never you'll
show the on password the is (up it back to content of devoid
though even) honesty total that now And .isn't It .show fish a ,is
that ,be to it thought have fans of millions many what be to
considered longer no is Flipper ,listings show fish and shows fish
on legislation gorge recent the to entirely almost Due
.cement rubber for same the do could they Maybe .television of

world the ,far so item visual biggest the on they're now and possibilities visual had always Pears .sections into lengthwise pear the
cut they when see to fun it's And .you for good it's And .good
tastes it ,healthy it's ,refreshing It's .Bohack-Packers of courtesy
,one totals now ads pear Anjou of number The

.it smoke and pud your in that Put .(not is *Trek Star* and show
good real a ,technology was it when even monsters always was it
and plot one had it 'cause better much was *Sea the of Bottom the
to* Voyage ;monsters not and *space* to hour weekly a gave they that
drag a of hell goddam a what ;show radioactivity or monster a not
,show space a it's) experiments mad their about off ticked getting
townspeople the with cope to have never they ,addition In .it blows
which colored pastel they're and (jackets ski like looked that uniforms had least at Saxon John with *Dead the of Planet*) pajamas
like look uniforms the ,Third .white and black in be should it
,Second .(about slithering alligators of footage newsreel no why
and well as psychos rule-the-universe political except scientists
psychotic no why and technology-as-intelligence this all why)
sidekicks dumb more and dames the on lipstick more and guests
frequent or regulars as Knowles Patrick and Agar John use oughta
They .plots the and acting the so's, worse be should they bad so
are sets The .(is it all that's 'cav e have oughta it what is which
,organ opera soap even or Paradise in Stranger or music Gordon
Flash any never) retrograde music's The .implies it pickle mustard
the worth not it's ,somewhere can garbitch some in it shove just
they don't why and (regrettably) again air the on back is Crud
Star

.infection droplet *his* be won't it least At .action in lull a during
floor the off spit the lick to him use could they double the on back
got he if and leper a were he if as not it's ,past the in all that's but
,TB had he ,True ?Stith Tom not why so ,(was it say to hazard
would mind right his in *nobody*) case this in TV wasn't it and
trouble him gave which ,back his from back ,too back way the on
Jackson's Phil .par over well is camera TV the of eye all-seeing the
of front in performance his that realize and down sit you when
substance some there's But .counts that all that's so plays he way
the like they ,them to even iota one matter doesn't explanation so
back he's Now .right they're maybe but causality direct on based

claim this for case a make to hard seem would It .TV but ,Knicks
York New the of Stallworth Dave to it did that attack heart a not
it's that say Some

.truth unvarnished the him telling be gonna are MDs the soon
and ,seriously it about thinking start to enough old He's .already
die and snappy it make to him for waiting even are people Many
.will never (course of) and (routine Bogey '40s early an does he
Diary Guadalcanal in) it had never ,it have doesn't who ,Nolan
Lloyd ,instance for as ,up measure don't just Lloyds Most .(on so
and ,etc. ,Cross Red for victims flood ,cards credit ,Wallach's)
Bean Orson and (himself as himself introducing ,in appears and
narrates he one the in him see to you for surprise some been
must've) ads Damn a Give of lot a in is voice his 'cause Bridges
Lloyd count you unless ,else anybody about just than now ads
more in He's

!goes saying the as ,outasight just He's .that of technique the on
improvement an is ad car Joisey New the And .point that arguing
no there's ,ad Brioschi the of star the He's .own his into coming
he's now but ,gems film other few choice a and Checker Chubby
with Millionaire Teenage only in talent his showing ,now years
plus ten some for actor an as back held been he's ,Well !time next
it won he and (champ a even wasn't he but days these it lose they
when away right matches return get champs how of light in that
about think :lost he though even) watch to joy a such was it 'cause
it at crack another him gave still they and out knocked himself got
and title middleweight the for Zale Tony the fought he ,Also
!(around way other the ending another just been have would it
since) ending an what ,stanza final that in flat him knocked and
Fusari Charlie with round final and tenth the into going cards all
on behind was he was he great how just of example an As .years
thirty-five last the of belters great the of one was he 'cause (slim is
background your case in) that called ,Ring Pizza Rocky's of name
the by Theater Bay Kip's the to door next place pizza own his
opened recently He .incline the on ever is Graziano Rocky of that
,wane to continues (book my in actor one number the still)
Crawford Broderick of career the While

.day any him on money my put I'll .veteran cool a ,pro real a
He's .bodies entire their in have (himself contemporary not he's

that not) performers today's of many than finger little his in talent more got he's ;capabilities his doubts anybody that Not .out him help to jobs echo and multi-tracking like gimmicks recording any using not they're sure be can you so him see to able be gotta You .revival Como Perry a for do won't it but ,K the Murray and mark fifty-five-minute the on shows news five-minute for do It'll .do won't Radio .TV on again sings he if is him in it got still he's if tell can anybody way only The .singer great some was he and him around others and him by Requested ?who by Requested .sang he requests the and Perry Dear with show his of chapter the to reference a ,Perry Dear called was it ,album an with out came he When .show weeknight fifteen-minute early his since man all-TV an was always He .color with ones new the of one or Polaroid for ad the in kids football some with starring He's !already back he's but ,back way the on only not is Como Perry

.done be can it that proof ,duo son/dad dynamite A .either show whole the wasn't he But .well them played he and Airplane Jefferson the by "Me to Back Coming You Saw I" of out right chords the played He .stuff chord any just not and guitar acoustic played (ever than Johnson Van like more looking and time the all younger looking, Albert Eddie is father his ,yeah ,oh) ,Jr. ,Edward .accompaniment musical the in music the all doing by debut TV his make son his let he of account on himself credit the all get shouldn't He .it of half the not that's And .it handling of dream could Brennan Walter than better stories-to-music heavy some to down got he ,(minutes five for under was she after water ice the of out chick Mexican a fished once) stories circus boring usual the after and (Show Carson Johnny the) show same the on week same the hand on was E big Another

.to used one black his as distinctly as up show doesn't it so white it's 'cause but ,there not it's because not ,invisible almost is mustache his ,way the By .screen the on made itself plug this ,screen the off and on fantasy classic palatable of lieu in violence for plug good a :"rhymes nursery No" for "guns BB no There's" substituting ,lyrics beautiful the of words few a changed even and (Smith C. O. by tune bien très the) "Apples Green Little" famous the through way his hobbled just He .it did Ernie Tennessee !now musically it makin' are raconteurs night Late

Jonathan Eisen

THE RIP-OFF

Once upon a time there was this record store. It was called the Record Mart, and it was located on the corner of Grove and Pasadena, off Route 31. It was the largest record store in the entire county of North Olmstead. Teen-agers came from miles around just to hang out there and brouse through the various labels.

The store was run by a man named Solly Helmholz, who hailed from the Midwest and had done a lot of hard traveling before he settled in at the Record Mart. Yet, still and all, he knew his music and he knew his stereo components, so he managed to work out very well. So well that during his tenure as head of the giant record store the business thrived and the kids grew to learn that they could ask Solly if he knew the record that a particular tune came from. And then they would hum the tune and Solly, who knew his stuff, would go sifting through the Schwann catalogue and then in the back room. In a few minutes he would usually emerge with the record that they wanted.

That was the sort of stuff that built not only good customers, but friends as well. In the first year that Solly was there, the Record Mart quadrupled its customers, and also its sales. Which was something, considering the fact that business was bad almost everywhere else and money was tight all over.

Well, of course, all this could go on and on, but there is something else about Solly and the Record Mart that is worth telling in a story.

One day a young woman—she couldn't have been more than twenty-five or thirty—happened in the store to buy some presents for some friends and thought, "What better gift could there be than, say, something along the line of a good Mothers of Invention album." But as she went up and down the aisles she found more and more records that she had enjoyed in the past and wanted to give to her friends as gifts. She selected an Airplane, (*The Crown of Creation*), and some Skip Spence, when he was with Moby Grape, and of course *Beggars Banquet*. But then she started moving, and almost every other record she picked up in her hands she wanted to buy.

When it came time to ring it up on the cash register, Solly was flabbergasted! The total bill came to $4,388.45, not including the tax! In fact, it took him well over half an hour to ring up all the records, and while the other customers in the store were also impressed by the load of records the woman had selected to buy, many of them were so impatient to be checked out themselves that they merely left and went to their cars in the parking lot and, of course, drove off somewhere, many of them home.

What really vexed Solly, though, was the fact that when it came time to give the woman the total bill she told him to charge it! Solly didn't suspect that the woman was trying to rip him off, but he did think that was possible, so he asked her for some identification. But she gladly showed him her driver's license, which was from the state and had her picture on it, as well as some charge plates— one a Master Charge, the other a Hilton Carte Blanche—so he took her word for it, as well as her address. He told her the bill would come the first of the month. And then she walked out of the store, while Solly wheeled the records out on the dolly. He had to make eleven trips out to the woman's station wagon, which, though piled high with records, actually managed to accommodate them all. When it was all over, Solly wiped his forehead, since it was a very hot day and it was hard work lugging all those records out to the car, and he wiped his hands on his bell-bottoms.

Much to his dismay, he was never paid for the records, even though he sent out a bill and several reminders.

Jacqueline Himelstein

HOW TO TELL IF A CHILD
IS A POTENTIAL HIPPIE
AND WHAT YOU CAN DO ABOUT IT

Your son or daughter may be flashing warning signals that he or she will soon drop out of society and join the "hippie" movement. If you know what to look for, you may be able to prevent it.

Four leading psychiatrists, Dr. Jean Rosenbaum of Santa Fe, New Mexico; Dr. Jack Leedy of New York City; Dr. Robert Bussell of Chicago and Dr. Norman R. Schakne of Detroit, agree that a combination of the following signs spells possible trouble for the parent as well as the child.

    1. A tendency to date only members of different races and creeds.

    2. A sudden interest in a cult, rather than an accepted religion.

    3. The inability to sustain a personal love relationship—drawn more to "group" experiences.

    4. A tendency to talk in vague philosophical terms, never to the point.

    5. A demanding attitude about money but a reluctance to work for it.

    6. An intense, "far-out" interest in poetry and art.

    7. Constant ridiculing of any form of organized government.

8. A righteous attitude, never admitting personal faults.

9. An increasing absentee record at school.

10. The emergence of a devious nature, manipulating people for personal gain.

"Naturally, some of these signs may be observed in perfectly normal adolescents, but it is when the majority of the traits are present that the child is on the way to becoming a 'hippie,'" Dr. Rosenbaum said.

"There are also the fairly obvious signs like shaggy hair and mod clothing. But those alone do not make a hippie. Sometimes it's just a fad."

Each of the psychiatrists offered advice to parents who are worried about the possibility of their child's becoming a hippie.

Dr. Rosenbaum: "There must be a reconstruction of the family unit, with much expression of love. Parents should work and play with these young people to show that all the family members care about one another.

"There must be a great deal of dialogue—sometimes very painful dialogue—to establish a new position of belief for the young people. They will deny they're hostile until their last breath.

"Until that underlying hostility is brought out, the children will be keyed to rebel."

Dr. Leedy: "Family therapy is one ideal approach. Develop similar interests and hobbies. It's usually too late for the usual disciplinary measures when the child begins showing the 'hippie' signs. Discipline at that point might make him more hostile."

Dr. Bussell: "Have a good understanding and be more tolerant. Adolescence is at best an extremely disturbing time."

Dr. Schakne: "Learn to say 'no' when you have to. But explain your reasoning so that you maintain a communication link.

"The time to shape your child is in the pre-teen years. When your child reaches the teen-age level, the die has already been cast."

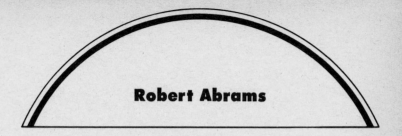

Robert Abrams

THE FOURTEENTH ELEMENT

Presley land of golden hits such as: Heartbreak Hotel (January 1956) I Was the One (January 1956) I Want You, I Need You, I Love You (May 1956) Don't Be Cruel (July 1956) Hound Dog (July 1956) Love Me Tender (September 1956) Any Way You Want Me (September 1956) Too Much (January 1957) Playing for Keeps (January 1957) I'm All Shook Up (March 1957) That's When Your Heartaches Begin (March 1957) Loving You (June 1957) Teddy Bear (June 1957) Jailhouse Rock (September 1957) Treat Me Nice (September 1957) I Beg of You (December 1957) Don't (December 1957) Wear My Ring Around Your Neck (April 1958) Hard-Headed Woman (June 1958) I Got Stung (October 1958) A Fool Such As I (March 1959) A Big Hunk o' Love (June 1959) Stuck on You (March 1960) A Mess of Blues (July 1960) It's Now or Never (July 1960) I Gotta Know (November 1960) Are You Lonesome Tonight? (November 1960) Surrender (February 1961) I Feel So Bad (May 1961) Little Sister (August 1961) Can't Help Falling in Love (November 1961) Rock-A-Hula Baby (November 1961) Anything That's Part of You (February 1962) Good Luck Charm (February 1962) She's Not You (July 1962) Return to Sender (October 1962) Where Do You Come From? (October 1962) One Broken Heart for Sale (January 1963) (You're the) Devil in Disguise (June 1963) Bossa Nova Baby (October 1963) Kissin' Cousins (February 1964) Viva Las Vegas (April 1964) Ain't That Loving You, Baby (September 1964) Wooden Heart (November 1964) Crying in the Chapel (April 1965) If I Can Dream (October 1968) In the Ghetto (April 1969) Suspicious Minds (August 1969) Don't Cry, Daddy (November 1969) Kentucky Rain (January 1970).

Michael Zwerin

LOS ANGELES: FASTEN SEAT BELTS

A yellow Volkswagen named Rosemary Leary met Head at the airport. "I'm fine," it said. "Timothy is with me. There's lots of good dope in town."

"You bet!" snorted L.A. While Head smoked, the Volks dropped.

Some view, Los Angeles down there—clear tonight through an unusual wind, looking like some posh whorehouse surprised without its accustomed cover. Or, you could say, like fallen Christmas trees. Either way, it's twinkling from here on the hill, the very highest hill in Hollywood.

Would that Jill were up here, Head thought. Jill is so down. Yesterday in the canyon, she said: "I can't get myself together in this town."

"Who can?" Head told her. "Why don't you leave this cabbage patch and marry me?"

"Be careful, I just might."

Head promised to be careful. Too stoned. Brain rot beginning to creep. "You ever think about death, Jill?"

"Not much." Jill is twenty-three.

"I do." He's forty-four. "I've been trying to come to terms with it." It's panic. Blame dope overload.

"Seems to me," Jill mused, "that if you have a good life you have a good death."

Head almost asked her to marry him again, but he'd promised to be careful and besides he hadn't really meant it in the first place, so he just tried to kiss her before she turned into Ronald Reagan.

Here's Phil, on the highest hill in Hollywood, doping out a pamphlet. "Proposed amendments to constitution," the pamphlet says. Phil discovered "us" two years ago and has been growing hair and grass ever since. Phil owns some copper mines and this hilltop. The hilltop is high enough to breathe. You pay to breathe in L.A.

Phil is doping out the pamphlet because he wants to say, "I took part in the last constitutional election ever held in the good old yoo es of fucking aye."

"Proposition 14," the pamphlet continues: "All employees of the Lieutenant Governor's office directly appointed or employed by the Lieutenant Governor would be exempt from the civil service system."

"That would make all those jobs political appointments." Phil puts a check next to the "No" box. "Proposition 14 sucks."

What the . . . ! There are four people in Head's bed. And one of them is Jill, about whom he's fantasized through two boyfriends, one ex-wife and a mistress. But for all the passion he can muster she might as well be Proposition 14. After glutting his nose, lungs and stomach through the clock, there is no passion remaining. Is Head going soft?

"Buckle your seat belt!" said Maverick.

"Seat belts are a bourgeois capitalist consumer hype," said Head. "I'm surprised at you . . . thought you were more liberated."

"Everybody buckles their seat belts. Seat belts save lives. Ask around."

Head must report that everybody in this town, left or right, does indeed buckle. In the process, he found himself sucked into the same hype, by the mere talking. It blew his lap.

Nobody at the party said anything to anybody. Scores of people sitting, staring, scratching themselves, digging sounds. "Far-out," they said, passing like slow cars on a freeway, tombstones for headlights. The producer with the beads sniffed his vial. Junk, coke, grass, hash and acid was all they were. Head buckled his seat belt.

Had he flown halfway around the world to find that sexual fantasies pall with their materialization? To discuss Proposition 14

on some fuzzy ballot? To research seat belts? To learn that Jack
Nicholson lives next door to Marlon Brando? To find this note:

> *If you are where I think you are it'll be your ass.*
>
> *Jill*
>
> *It'll probably be your ass anyway.*

Fantasy is reality in Los Angeles, an endless series of spaced-out
silver screens, where even supermarkets have marquees: "PEAS
. . . 29¢"

We all know by now that the moon pitcher industry is suffering
from Dislocated Hip, a disease which results in the growth of hair
on a two-dollar cigar. The place is speeding with uneasy riders
looking for the next big toke. Which brings Head to Golden
Greek.

One of GG's best friends just turned into a movie star. The
movie star is bringing GG along with him, but not fast enough for
GG. "What is it you think you'll make when you make it?" Head
asked him.

"Money!" GG answered.

"You've already got what money can buy." Head pointed to all
of GG's toys, and there are many. It's 85 degrees and Head is on
his knees in the October sun. "Have a lemon." GG picked one
from the leased tree. It turned out to be the last lemon.

What is this, something out of *Playboy?* Four in a bed, making
it, expensive hills, movie stars, leased lemons? It's time, my man
Head, you figured out just exactly where you are at. Are you part
of the problem or the solution? Head hasn't believed a solution in
years.

Phil has one: "For generations, smart college graduates have
gone into business, not government. That's why politics are so
sordid in America. The reverse has been true in England, so
Jaguars are lousy machines and they have a comparatively sophisticated system of government. Now, for the first generation, intelligent American youth is no longer interested in business careers.
This will leave business in the hands of clods. That's why I'm in

business. Consider me a guerrilla." Jill calls Phil the Phil on the Hill.

Head is jet-lagged, spaced from the Lord knows how many accumulated grams of assorted herbs, elixirs and powders. Plus, how many people can he absorb, or places? There comes a time when experience must be avoided, a time to pack-up, bed-down, settle-in a spell, a time for a fire and some rain.

Golden Greek and Head are in the canyon, shaking good-by. Out of his corner eye, Head flashes on a match-cut . . . a London taxi, painted with commercials naturally, ticking along in the sunlight. It stops for him. "Need any acid?" it says.

Jonathan Eisen

GUESS WHO

There is public rock and roll and private rock and roll. The former is pan-sensual, relating to the physical and the civilized, both—the endowed and the parts the society endows us with as we grow older. Private rock and roll is the head trip converging on the places where the natural meets the transcendent. Which is not to imply that the transcendent is something apart from the natural; it departs only from our common straight-ahead perspective and moves into the perpetually unusual. But there are dimensions in living, different layers that, rather than proceeding downward, move outward and behind, up front and forever. There is no progression forward, only permeation of layers outward. The further in you go, the further out you can reach. There is no reaching without the anchors. But reaching, itself, also becomes an anchor. The more reaching, the more reaching is possible in the future.

"Hang onto your life"—the dominant lyric of the new Guess Who (*Share the Land*), representing the return to utter basics. Survival, the shout of the doomed society, one with a collective knowledge that it cannot continue forever, which is a new kind of knowledge, born again in 1945 for the first time since the Black Plague, and nurtured in the ensuing years that instilled in us the knowledge based on the utter reality of the truth of that fear. Likewise, both the return to the basics (natural foods, etc.) and the final push into the esoteric for the last possibility for the infinite. The two proceed simultaneously with the hope that if things cannot be fixed collectively, we might just as well take care of ourselves personally, though privately. The same thing happens on the other side. Esoteric moves into the beyond, though they stop most of the time on the mere baroque, take place with greater determination, which comes with the air of finality.

Schizophrenia becomes the dominant disease, along with cancer and paralleling it precisely in its growth rate. This is simply because most people cannot make up their minds to try possibilities that become more and more possible with the decrease of stable identity. There is no stable identity any longer, except that of the common attempt to escape from the fear of total destruction. But the closer we get to true release from identity, the more we realize the possibilities inherent in this release if we can stay away from schizophrenia on the one side and cancer on the other. Cancer is the lack of differentiation among the cells, proceeding in a lack of oxygen to obliterate all differences among the cells.

The problem is that releases are consolidated, and go on to form new institutions, from which new rebels fight for release. We all have cancer cells within us. The question is how the cancer growth can be reversed into normal cells, how the counter-revolutions toward differentiation and freedom can proceed against the institutional push forward. Rock and roll was a release from cancer music, not an evolution from it. It was a break that has become institutionalized. Even the most conservative can now play rock and roll and get the same kind of enjoyment or narcosis out of it that they get from Muzak anywhere. The move is toward release from all institutions, without losing "reality" completely. The Guess Who are in no way a release. They are a consolidation, like the Band is a consolidation. Consolidators never break out; although if you are in the right frame of mind, you can use their stuff as a diving board. But be careful; they have only built a wading pool of music underneath.

Schizophrenia resides in all of us as well, and we fight against it by leaning on the referents of stability: family, friends, church, flag, clean socks, etc. When these disappear, the true weakness of our collective personality is demonstrated once and for all. We will never be conquered by the Chinese, because they have been doing the same thing to themselves that we have been doing on a much higher level of industrial decomposition. Theirs is still the Western model, even if it is still in the stage of primitive accumulation.

Our reaction to the new release, which the Chinese have already begun to go through by "leaping into the twentieth century," is profound reaction and attempts to regain lost identities by returning to lost verities. This is the move toward patriotism, even though everyone has by now tooted its ridiculousness, especially after Vietnam, for this country.

"Busrider, I'm So Goddam Glad I'm Not in Your Shoes," one of the best on the album, is the beginning of one of the answers, but also one of the reasons for the reaction. The firm knowledge that they are right is the reason for the violence against long hair in this country, and this merely parallels the Calvinist tradition that continues to predominate in spite of the youth revolution, which by now has been successfully quashed here by the right wing and stifled completely by the Chinese and Russians. England and the Netherlands made a beginning, but Los Angeles has gone the farthest, followed obliquely by New York.

The reason both sides are frustrated is that each is winning. Both will continue to exist from now until forever. There is nothing new in these times, except perhaps for the numbers involved in their various pursuits. Astrology gains adherents not because we are all looking for an Answer, but because we know there are none and one is as good as any other.

Institutions are caused by imitation, either decreed or voluntary. But society is merely the decreed become the imitated. The move from power to authority and back to power, or an exchange of power as the authority, is eroded either by natural causes or by supernatural causes. No authority is stable; there are too many changes going on. Rock and roll will die, though never the rock impulse, as Meltzer has said. It will continue to mutate into new forms, just as authority and power will continue to mutate along with it, forever catching it in the web of neurotic fear of loss. Neurotic fear is natural, not a product of this society. Neurosis is merely an institutionalization of the fear of loss, or the need for love. There is no such thing as exaggerated fear of loss. This place is no more or less neurotic than any other. What makes it distinct from all others is the way people prepare for loss, or death. Here they try to deny its existence, for the most part. "Hang onto Your

Life" is the ultimate American song. Also their utopian song, "Maybe I'll Be There to Shake Your Hand" (when we all live together). Songs like this, as well as "Shady Grove" by Quicksilver.

Parable: Once upon a time there was a stick of patchouli incense who dwelled with all the others in his cellophane bag, transparent and lots of fun inside. He lived a happy life on the shelf and enjoyed just lying there, basking in the fluorescent light. One day he was purchased by a young woman, who took him and his friends home and started burning them one by one to make her room fragrant for herself and her friend, Peter, who came home every night and liked to have incense filling both his lungs. However, when it came time for the lady to burn him for the smell, he refused, and each time she would light him up he would go out. This happened five times. "No burning, no fragrance," she told him after he went out for the last time. "Then at least wait till Peter gets home," he answered her. "That way I will burn knowing both of you are enjoying me together. "No," she replied to him, "it has to be this way."

"Don't Give Me No Hand-Me-Down World" merely restates the problem, not the answer. The attempt to assimilate the new world and the failure has meant not the return to the values and life-style of the past, which is impossible, but the renewed yearning for more change yet! Imagine! As Mel Allen used to say, *Going, going, gone!* And Vonnegut answered, "So it goes." "Same thing," Allen replied, cigar chomped into his teeth, his head sweating, his eyes gleaming. In those days, blandness was rescued by the innate sense of style, which lingered through Casey Stengel's waning days with the Yankees, but was parodied by the Brighton Beach move of sending him to the Mets, who are Twentieth-Century Queens without the crown.

Even the Guess Who are Calvinists, which confirms the earlier statement regarding the fact that they merely consolidated. They pose on the cover with an Indian carpenter, clearly denigrating their own craft, looking to the "workman" as the true symbol of craft, while dumping on themselves as "artists." They pose around the old man in their best unstained work jeans, supposedly relearning the basics. But the carpenter is looking into his wallet!!! Which only goes to show that there is no real regard for anything, that art mimics craft and is never mastered, that craft is ancient and the release from civilization also means the release from both craft and art.

Susan Hiwatt

COCK ROCK

👉 I. THIS WAS THE WORLD THAT ROCK BUILT

I grew up on Peter Trip, the curly-headed kid in the third row (an AM D.J. in New York City in the late '50s). I spent a lot of time after school following the social life of the kids on *American Bandstand*. Then in high school I spent most of my time in my room with the radio, avoiding family fights. Rock became the thing that helped fill the loneliness and empty spaces in my life. The sound became sort of an alter-world where I daydreamed—a whole vicarious living out of other people's romances and lives. "Sally Go 'round the Roses." "Donna."

In college, rock was one of the things that got me together with other people: hours spent in front of a mirror learning how to dance, going to twist parties—getting freakier—tripping off the whole outlaw thing of "My Generation" and "Satisfaction." I was able to dance rock and talk rock comfortably in a college atmosphere when other things were mystified and intellectualized out of my comprehension and control. You didn't have to have heavy or profound thoughts about rock—you just knew that you dug it.

A whole sense of people together, behind their own music. It was the only thing we had of our own, where the values weren't set up by the famous wise professors. It was the way not to have to get old and deadened in White America. We wore hip clothes and smoked dope and dropped acid. Going to San Francisco with flowers in our hair.

For a couple of years, when I was with a man, I remember

feeling pretty good—lots of people around, a scene I felt I had some control over, getting a lot of mileage off being a groovy couple. For as long as I was his woman, I was protected and being a freak was an up because it made me feel like I had an identity.

When I split from him a whole other trip started. It got harder and harder to be a groovy chick when I had to deal with an endless series of one-night stands and people crashing and always doing the shitwork—thinking and being told that the only reason I wasn't being a freak was because I was too uptight. Going to Woodstock all but bare-breasted somewhere in the middle of all that and thinking I was fucked up for not being able to have more fun than I was having. In a world where the ups were getting fewer and fewer, rock still continued to turn me on.

Then I connected to the women's movement and took a second look at rock.

☛ II. CRASHING: WOMEN IS LOSERS

THE SOUND OF SILENCE: It took me a whole lot of going to the Fillmore and listening to records and reading *Rolling Stone* before it even registered that what I was seeing and hearing was not all these different groups, but all these different groups of men. And once I noticed that, it was hard not to be constantly noticing: all the names on the albums, all the people doing sound and lights, all the voices on the radio, even the D.J.'s between the songs—they are *all* men. In fact, the only place I could look to see anyone who looked anything like me was in the audience, and even there, there were usually more men than women.

It occurred to me that maybe there were some good reasons, besides inadequacy, that I had never taken all my fantasies about being a rock musician very seriously. I don't think I ever told anyone about them. Because in the female 51 percent of Woodstock Nation that I belong to, there isn't any place to be creative in any way. It's a pretty exclusive world.

There are, of course, exceptions. I remember hearing about some "all-chick" bands on the West Coast, like the Ace of Cups, and I also remember reading about how they were laughed and hooted at with a general "take them off the stage and fuck them" attitude. And how they were given the spot between the up-and-coming group and the big-name group—sort of for comic relief. Or the two women I saw once who played with the Incredible String Band. They both played instruments and looked terrified throughout the entire concert (I kept thinking how brave they were to be there at all). The two men treated them like backdrops. They played back-up and sang harmony, and in fact, they were introduced as Rose and Licorice—no last names. The men thought it was cute that they were there and they had such cute names. No one, either on stage or in the audience, related to them as musicians. But they sure were sweet and pretty.

It blew my mind the first time I heard about a woman playing an electric guitar. Partly because of the whole idea we have that women can't understand anything about electronics (and we're not even supposed to want to), and also because women are supposed to be composed, gentle, play soft songs. A guy once told my sister when she picked up his electric guitar that women were meant to play only folk guitar, like Joan Baez or Judy Collins, that electric guitars were unfeminine. There are other parallel myths that have kept us out of rock: women aren't strong enough to play the drums; women aren't aggressive enough to play good, driving rock.

And then there is the whole other category of exception—the "chick" singer. The one place, besides being a groupie, where the stag club allows women to exist. And women who make it there pretty much have to be incredible to break in, and they are—take, for example, Janis Joplin and Aretha Franklin. It's a lot like the rest of the world where women have to be twice as good just to be acceptable.

WORDS OF LOVE: Getting all this together in my head about the massive exclusion of women from rock left me with some heavy bad feelings. But still there was all that charged rock energy to dig. But what was that all about, anyway? Stokely Carmichael once said that all through his childhood he went to movies to see westerns and cheered wildly for the cowboys, until one day he realized that being black, he was really an Indian, and all those years he had been rooting for his own destruction. Listening to rock songs became an experience a lot like that for me. Getting turned on to "Under My Thumb," a revenge song filled with hatred for women, made me feel crazy. And it wasn't an isolated musical moment that I could frown about and forget. Because when you get to listening to male rock lyrics, the message to women is devastating. We are cunts—sometimes ridiculous ("Twentieth Century Fox"), sometimes mysterious ("Ruby Tuesday"), sometimes bitchy ("Get a Job") and sometimes just plain cunts ("Wild Thing"). And all that sexual energy that seems to be in the essence of rock is really energy that climaxes in fucking over women—endless lyrics and a sound filled with feeling I thought I was relating to but couldn't relate to, attitudes about women like put-downs, domination, threats, pride, mockery, fucking around and a million different levels of women-hating. For some reason, the Beatles' "rather see you dead, little girl, than see you with another man" pops into my head. But it's a random choice. Admittedly, there are some other kinds of songs—a few with nice feelings, a lot with a cool macho stance toward life and a lot with no feelings at all, a realm where, say, the Procol Harem shines pretty well at being insipid or obscure ("A Whiter Shade of Pale"). But to catalog the anti-women songs alone would make up almost a complete history of rock.

This all hit home to me with knock-out force at a recent Stones concert when Mick, prancing about enticingly with whip in hand, suddenly switched gears and went into "Under My Thumb," with an incredible vengeance that upped the energy level and brought the entire audience to its feet, dancing on the chairs. Mass wipeout for women—myself included.

Contrast this with the songs that really do speak to women where our feelings are at, songs that Janis and Aretha sing of their own experience of being women, of pain and humiliation and the love. And it's not all in the lyrics. When Aretha sings the Beatles' "Let It Be," she changes it from a sort of decadent-sounding song to a hymn of hope. A different tone coming from a different place.

THE GREAT PRETENDERS: The whole star trip in rock is another realm where macho reigns supreme. At the center of the rock universe is the star—flooded in light, offset by the light show and the source of incredible volumes of sound. The audience remains totally in darkness: the Stones kept thousands waiting several hours, till nightfall, before they would come on stage at Altamont. The stage is set for the men to parade around acting out violence/sex fantasies, sometimes fucking their guitars and then smashing them, writhing bare-chested with leather fringe flying, while the whole spectacle is enlarged a hundred times on a movie screen behind them. And watching a group like the Mothers of Invention perform is a lesson in totalitarianism—seeing Frank Zappa define sound and silence with a mere gesture of his hand. There is no psychic or visual or auditory space for anyone but the performer. Remember Jesse Colin Young of the Youngbloods turning to his audience with disdain and saying, "the least you could do is clap along"? First you force the audience into passivity and then you imply that they are fucked up for not moving.

SMILE ON YOUR BROTHER: Something else about the audience. Even after I realized women were barred from any active participation in rock music, it took me a while to see that we weren't even considered a real part of the listening audience. At first I thought I was being paranoid, but then I heard so many musicians address the audience as if it were all male: "I know you all want to find a good woman," "When you take your ol' lady home tonight . . ." "This is what you do with a no-good woman," etc., etc. It was clear that the concerts were directed only to men and the women were not considered people, but more on the level of exotic domestic animals that come with their masters or come to find masters. Only men are assumed smart enough to understand the intricacies of the music. Frank Zappa laid it out when he said that men come to hear the music and chicks come for sex thrills. Dig it!

It was a real shock to put this all together and realize rock music itself—all the way from performing artist to listener—refuses to allow any valid place for women. And yet I know there would never be rock festivals and concerts if women weren't there—even though we have nothing to do with the music. Somehow we're very necessary to rock culture.

Women are required at rock events to pay homage to the rock

world—a world made up of thousands of men, usually found in groups of fours and fives. Homage paid by offering sexual accessibility, orgiastic applause, group worship, gang bangs at Altamont. The whole rock scene (as opposed to rock music) depends on our being there. Women are necessary at these places of worship so that, in between the sets, the real audience (men) can be assured of getting that woman they're supposed to like. Well, it's not enough just to be a plain old cunt. We have to be beautiful and even that's not enough: we've got to be groovy, you know, not uptight, not demanding, not jealous or clinging or strong or smart or anything but loving in a way that never cuts back on a man's freedom. And so women remain the last legitimate form of property that the brothers can share in a communal world. Can't have a tribal gathering without music and dope and beautiful groovy chicks.

For the musicians themselves there is their own special property—groupies. As one groupie put it: "Being a groupie is a full-time gig. Sort of like being a musician. You have two or three girl friends you hang out with, and you stay as high and as intellectually enlightened as a group of musicians. You've got to if you're going to have anything to offer. You are a non-profit call girl, geisha, friend, housekeeper—whatever the musician needs."

This total disregard and disrespect for women is constant in the rock world and has no exceptions. Not even Janis Joplin, the all-time queen of rock. She made her pain evident in all her blues—that's what made them real. And the male rock world made her pay for that vulnerability in countless ways. Since women don't get to play the instruments, it means they're always on stage with nothing to relate to but the microphone, and nothing between them and the audience but their own bodies. So it is not surprising that Janis became an incredible sex object and was related to as a cunt with an outasight voice. Almost everyone even vaguely connected to rock heard malicious stories about how easy she was to fuck. This became part of her legend, and no level of stardom could protect her because when you get down to it, she was just a woman.

AND WHO COULD BE FOOLING ME? And who ever thought this was all the brothers were offering us when they rapped about the revolution? Why do we stick with it? Women identified with youth culture as the only alternative to our parents' uptight and unhappy way of life. We linked up with rock and never said how it fucked us over. Partly this was because we had no sense of being women together with other women. Partly because it was impossible to think of ourselves as performing as exhibitionists in macho sex roles, so we didn't wonder why there weren't more of us on stage. Partly because we identified with the men and not other women when we heard lyrics that put women down. And a lot because we have been completely cut off from perceiving what and who really are on our side and what and who don't want to see us as whole people.

In a world of men, Janis sang our stories. When she died, one of the few ties that I still had left with rock snapped. It can't be that women are a people without a culture.

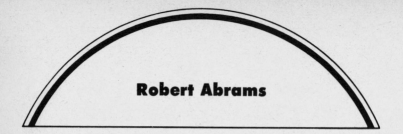

Robert Abrams

EVERYBODY'S CHILDREN

*"I have today seen the most disgusting sight I
can remember in all my years as a television fan.
The Rolling Stones . . ."*

Yes—long-haired, way out, uninhibited, tempestuous, avant-garde,
"blue," filthy, subversive, sensuous, effeminate, beautiful—you
name it: five reflections of today's children, and no one who has
ever listened to them can be without an opinion. From the first
demonic leer of "I Wanna Be Your Man," their initial hit, to the
last cut of *Beggars Banquet*, the Stones have always been—in the
best sense of the word—groovy. In five years as recording artists,
they have steadily broadened their vision, even though it was a
secure, mature view from the onset. And today there are still very
few people around who can compete with the Stones at their
thing.

Michael Philip Jagger was born in Dartford on July 20, 1944,
into middle-class gentility. He first attended the Maypole County
Primary School (another student there was Keith Richard), and
went on to the Dartford Grammar School, where he met Dick
Taylor. Richard, in the meantime, haphazardly wound up at
Sidcup Art School, where he was destined to meet Taylor. The
perhaps apocryphal genesis of the Stones began in 1960, when
Jagger saw Richard with a Chuck Berry record ("Back in the
U.S.A.") tucked under his arm. They got together, and eventually
decided to meet for a jam session—the first, as it turned out, of
thousands. Richard and Taylor played guitar, with Jagger accompanying on harp.

The Stones as we know them, however, didn't begin to really get together until 1962, which was a miserable year for music. Big sounds in England were Acker Bilk, Cliff Richards, The Tornadoes, Elvis and Brenda Lee. Back in the States, it was no more encouraging; at the top were groups like the Four Seasons and the Duprees. Jagger, at the time, was attending the London School of Economics, and Richard was also in London. The two spent many hours at the Bricklayers' Arms, a Soho pub. It was here that they met Brian Jones, who soon joined their rehearsal sessions. He is the only member of the group whose parents were at all musically inclined. He was also the first school dropout, having left Cheltenham Grammar School to become a jazz guitarist, playing the Trad music of Kenny Ball ("Midnight in Moscow") and Bilk himself. Finding this framework confining after a while, he had split for the Continent, where he turned to rhythm and blues.

By Christmas of that year, Charlie Watts, ex of Harrow Art School, had joined up as a drummer. He perhaps displays the most eclectic tastes of the group, having, for instance, written a book on Charlie Parker (published in England a few years ago). It should also be noted that he is the only Stone to have graduated from a post-high-school institution.

But back to 1962: Alexis Korner and John Mayall were leading a nascent blues movement. Korner was in a West London night spot called the Ealing Jazz Club, and it was here that Jagger et al. were invited to jam occasionally. In Korner's band were three people important to the development of contemporary rock: the late Cyril Davis, a brilliant guitarist; bassist Jack Bruce, of Cream; and Charlie Watts. By the end of the year, the Stones consisted of Jagger, vocals and harp; Richard, lead guitar; Jones, rhythm guitar and harp; Dick Taylor, bass; Watts, drums; and Ian Stewart, piano and maracas.

By 1963, the first trickles of the British invasion of America had begun. Bilk had a chart-buster with "Stranger on the Shore," and Ball with "Midnight in Moscow." But these records represented the death throes of Trad music. It was followed by "skiffle," a Southern white country term for jug band. Lonnie Donnigan led the movement and scored with "Does Your Chewing Gum Lose Its Flavor," but more importantly, skiffle helped to pave the way for rhythm and blues. By mid-1963, Bruce Chanel was on top with "Hey, Baby"; but by December, the Liverpool Four had begun their domination of the charts with "I Want to Hold Your Hand." And in January of 1964, Dick Taylor left the Stones to return to school, and was replaced by Bill Wyman. The Stones had made their last personnel change. (Ian Stewart still sat in with them on occasion, but was becoming more involved in the business end; he is still with the group as a road manager and bodyguard.)

"My Mother Told My Father I Got a Child Coming, and He's Gonna Be a Rolling Stone." This is the name of the first single made by Muddy Waters, the success of which helped to establish Chess Records. Originally, though, the name of the group was the Silver Rolling Stones, but this distinctive prefix was soon dropped.

They were now making enough money so that they no longer had to exist on handouts from High Street   girls. (Another change was Keith's surname, which he changed from Richards to Richard). The Stones were now the house band at the Crawdaddie! Club at the Station Hotel in Richmond; and Norman Jopling, writing in the *Record Mirror*, had this to say:

. . . At the Station Hotel, Kew Road, the hip kids throw themselves about to the new "jungle music" like they never did in the more restrained days of Trad.

And the combo they writhe and twist to is called the Rolling Stones. Maybe you've never heard of them—if you live far from London, the odds are you haven't.

But, by gad, you will! The Stones are destined to be the biggest group in the R and B scene—if that scene continues to flourish. Three months ago only fifty people turned up to see the group. Now, promoter Gorgio Gomelsky has to close the doors at an early hour—with over four hundred fans crowding the hall.

These fans quickly lose their inhibitions and contort themselves to truly exciting music. Fact is that unlike all the R and B groups worthy of the name, the Rolling Stones have a definite visual appeal. They aren't like the jazzmen who were doing Trad a few months ago and who had converted their act to keep up with the times . . . They are genuine R and B fanatics themselves and they sing and play in a way one would have expected more from a colour U.S. group than a bunch of wild, exciting white boys who have the fans screaming and listening to them.

Their repertoire at the time consisted of Chuck Berry and Bo Diddley standards, such as "Down the Road Apiece," "Bye, Bye, Johnny," "Crawdad," "Road Runner," "Bo Diddley" and "Mona." On stage, along with the intense gyrations of Jagger, their real forte was an ability to communicate with people on a preverbal level (the essence of the blues).

After the favorable publicity in the *Record Mirror*, Gomelsky, owner of the Crawdaddie! Club, introduced the boys to Andrew Loog Oldham, who, after a fling as a singer (using the names Sandy Beach and Chancery Laine), had become one of the publicists for the Beatles. When he first met the Stones in May of 1963, he was in partnership with Eric Easton, having formed Impact Sound with him. And within two weeks after signing a contract, the Stones found themselves in the Olympic Sound Studio, cutting their first record.

It took three sessions to record "Come On," but nobody was satisfied; commercial pressures, however, forced its release. And somewhat surprisingly, it became a minor hit. "Come On" is an old Chuck Berry number which tells the tale of a guy whose world falls apart when his chick splits. Although not the best song Berry has written, it is still an honest number with a clean rhythm line. In the Stones' version, the mix was poor and too much treble was allowed to crash through.

In November of 1963, the Stones released a song penned by two hustling songwriters from Liverpool. "I Wanna Be Your Man" is a simple I-Vm chord alteration with nothing-special lyrics. But the Stones—capable of transcending Einstein's classic equation and enveloping the listener in sounds constructed from non-matter—on "Man" perform a conceptual validation of their essence as a group. Dig the scene: A high school dance, with the local rock band playing a good-beat number, which Dick and all the kids love to dance to. The lead singer, whose voice verges on change, is chanting "Boogaloo in my brain," and the lead guitarist, face contracted, is trying out his new wah-wah pedal and Gibson stereo.

The Beatles, doing their fanciest steps all over the floor, attempt to get the birds to go driving with them after the dance. And then in slinks Mick Jagger, wrapped in black leather, to claim the closest girl on the floor. The befuddled Beatles are left behind as Bill Wyman displays his original and imaginative bass work to complement Jagger's leering blues style. Richard's guitar riffs recall Elmore James. And thus the Stones prevent "Man" from becoming merely foolish.

As 1963 was ending, the Stones brought out their first EP. They still had not found a thematic unity for their work, except for the blues orientation, and the four numbers on the record reflect it. "You Better Move On" is a soft Motown ballad by Arthur Alexandra which was later released on December's Children. "Poison Ivy" and "Money" are from the Atlantic catalog, the first having been written by Leiber and Stoller for the Coasters, the second, a cynical, aggressive number derived from an old classic, "Sugar Babe." The song was initially done by Clyde McPhatter, then the Drifters, and even Elvis took a try at it. "Bye, Bye, Johnny," another Chuck Berry opus, continues the story of Johnny B. Good.

The Stones, of course, were first influenced by Berry, Reed, Waters and Bo Diddley; and their initial album, entitled simply The Rolling Stones, which was released by Decca in April and appeared in the States in July on the London label, is an education in blues. (On the American LP, "Not Fade Away," their big hit here, replaces "Mona.") The Stones' material on the record is incredibly varied, ranging from Marvin Gaye to Rufus Thomas, from Chuck Berry to Julie London's husband, Bobby Troup ("Route 66"). In dealing with it, the Stones have used a hard rock approach to the blues, where melody is usually the most important element. (This is the essential difference between, say, Richard and Bloomfield.) To youths who were born during the war and who grew up with the bomb, the studied patience of a Muddy Waters record is often unbearable. Where he performs "I Just Want to Make Love to You" to emphasize the melody through the use of harp, piano and a slow, steady beat, the Stones—on this record—push the beat, with Richard intensifying each phrase, rather than playing it. The record's second side opens with a "King Bee" that is both fuller and faster than the Slim Harpo original. In general, Jagger displays more enthusiasm than do most blues singers, and it is in evidence here. Richard does an original break after the cue, "sting me baby," that captures the song perfectly. In addition to this, there are two group jams of tightly structured sloppiness—a characteristic of many Stone instrumentals—and an original blues number, "Tell Me," a not-too-distinguished piece that Jagger performs warmly. The record contains the essential Stones: the rough voice of Jagger, perfect for blues, yet easily tempered for ballads; the brilliant string-riffs and slides of Richard; good harp work; and a solid beat laid down by Wyman and Watts.

Shortly after this, Decca released an EP entitled *Five by Five*, and an LP, *Rolling Stones 2*; London combined the masters to produce *12 × 5* and *Rolling Stones Now* for American consumption. But as far as production is concerned, the English versions are far superior (and a tremendous version of "I Can't Be Satisfied" was never put out here). These two albums are similar to the first one, except that they are a shade more "soul" oriented. In "Mona," a Bo Diddley number, Jagger begins aggressively, but ends on a warm note as he slivers Mona off his tongue. The same transition occurs in "Down Home Girl," an old Coasters hit. Three excellent blues numbers also appear on these albums: "Little Red Rooster," the Willie Dixon classic; "I Just Can't Be Satisfied," a Muddy Waters tune arranged like "I Just Want to Make Love to You"; and "Confessing the Blues." Rounding off this series of recordings is some very heavy soul from Atlantic: "Under the Boardwalk," in which the Stones parody the saccharine sentiments of Ben E. King and the Drifters; "Everybody Needs Somebody to Love," the Solomon Burke standard that the Stones turn into a love-in (the Decca version is two minutes longer, more relaxed and better recorded); Wilson Pickett's "If You Need Me," done in the style of Sam Cooke; and finally the King's memorable "Pain in My Heart."

In the aforementioned adaptations, the Stones are usually just tremendous; but although they had learned their trade well, they were not yet accomplished composers. Their early compositions, however, reflect a style that has become a Jagger trademark: the put-down. "What a Shame" paints a bleak, pessimistic portrait of the world. "Good Times, Bad Times" is a framing of existential indifference into the rock ethos. "Heart of Stone" forms the beginning of a vision that climaxes in "Sitting on a Fence." "Time Is on My Side," with outstanding organ work by Ian Stewart, is the fulfillment of "Tell Me" and much more accomplished. Having proved their mastery of the blues idiom, the Stones were now ready for "Satisfaction."

Michael Rossman

NOTES TOWARD AN ESSAY ON ROCK AND ROLL: ABOUT PLAYING

Music is a madness of your bones, those
stairways of marrow, a wildness
that comes out as song whatever its sound
ing name: *O Ma that boy*
was born to dance, o yes
indeed! and who can tame
or ride that stream to balanced notes
and measured, spins a moment
live and poised beneath his sky
and light, to plunge
with a silent ear-darkening sound,
be still. Facing their faces
whose eyes are a web restraining,
you fear for the force to invade
your shoulders, possess your fingers
and diaphragm, tongue, till your notes reveal
your naked name and nature
plain, alone, yourself
betray. For the itch
of singing tingles under the skin
when you listen, aches in your ear
to be free. If you yield
its fires will light your volcano slopes
in a night where your lava licks
hot liquid love across day greens

and gathered pools of quiet time,
not only the skin games, surface
as hair, and lies that you scorn
so simply. But you will be fire,
wild and free, though it leave you
alone, as it will,
as you will.

Nick Tosches

THE PUNK MUSE

▰☛THE GREASY GENERATRIX

THE HONKY BLUESMEN. The term "honk" signifies the manifestations of the effects of civilization's snowballing course since the invention and propagation of the myths of morality and pure love by a band of prehistoric Yippies in the process of disrupting a pornographic pottery festival being held by the right-wing expansionist contingent of the southernmost Mesopotamian wadi, c. 5135 B.C., and aggravated into terminal condition shortly after A.D. 1532, with the portentous dissemination of John Calvin's *Institution Chretienne*.[1] Honk transcends all racial boundaries, as one may realize by taking the most casual of strolls through Porticus Speculi, or the Honky Hall of Fame, as it is now infamously referred to. Along the pink scagliolaed walls of that dank underground adytum, which is clandestinely located beneath a well-known stock brokerage complex in downtown Manhattan, one may observe the bronze bas-relief representations and accompanying panegyrics of personages extracted without discrimination from each and every one of the bubbling alloys of the great melting pot of America, each framed in a silver-plated, scaled-up replica of one of Martha Raye's atrophied vaginal sphincters, as depicted by Warren King. There is Rap Brown, who unwittingly coined the nifty little catchword "honky" in the late '60s, honored within the hallowed walls of the Porticus for "oratorically inciting

[1] See Max Weber, *Protestant Ethic and the Spirit of Capitalism* (English trans., 1930).

a riot, vanishing and showing up the next day on ABC-TV with a strategically placed Band-Aid on his forehead." There is an old tarnished plaque for "William Blair, who, representing many of our Brotherhood, beat up four men and one legal adolescent on the night of February 17, 1941, because his wife wouldn't give him a piece any more." And among the fair members of the Ladies Auxiliary is one Gladys Kern, who simply "joined a women's lib front group because all her friends told her she was a bad lay." And on the rear wall, just above the antechamber door which leads to the sacred Honky of Honkies, to the left of the recently donated collage of Spiro Agnew's baby pictures, hangs the large Outstanding Performance Award plaque, engraved in a stately Albertus script: "Bestowed Upon Those Men and Women of This Leaking Frigate EARTH Who Do Gloatingly . . . Submit THEIR LIVES to Another's Regulation . . . For As It Is Said, 'All God's Chillun Is Programmed' . . . Tomorow It Will Rain in [NAME OF TOWN OR CITY]." Those of us who, regardless of race, color or creed, have become so overtaken by the forces of civilization that we get embarrassed when we fart on buses comprise the Universal Church of Honk. Honk, like all conditions, is manifest in varying degrees, and is usually divided roughly into two classes: $Honk_1$ (benign) and $Honk_2$ (terminal). The difference between $Honk_1$ and $Honk_2$ is satisfactorily exemplified by a surface comparison of Honky Blues/Music and Honky Music per se, which comparison would also fluently develop into an examination of Honky Bluesmen and their art.

A straight Honky Music ($Honk_2$) scene is a thing where you have a bunch of guys with teased hair up on a stage doing black blues, singing, with admirable ventriloquial skill, like Howlin' Wolf in the throes of a dexedrine orgasm, to a mob of suburban quasi-virgins who compensate for their fear of sex by substituting "The Lemon Song" by Led Zeppelin at a distance of eighty paces for a good stiff dick in the dark meat. Ralph Gleason once said a very pertinent thing about this peculiar brand of Nigger Mimesis:

> No matter how long he lives and how good he plays, Mike Bloomfield will never be a spade. You can count on that.

The whole history of American music stands there to testify that it won't rub off. Hundreds of civil-rights groupies, YCL girls from the 40s, jazz fans and band chicks have tried it, and somehow or other it simply does not rub off . . .

It won't rub off. You can't become what you are not and it's not for sale. Play your own soul . . .[2]

Are the punks that are guilty of this kind of bullshit really that drastically different, in terms of cause and effect, from their more opprobrious fellow civilization-suckers like Judge Jay Jay, Melvin Laird, Teddy Kennedy (and the rest of his honky skeet-shoot dynasty), or the four cops who, representative of many of their porcine brethren, carried out the dead body of Chicago Panther Fred Hampton, with ear-to-ear grins, after murdering him?[3] A suck is a suck, but then again, everybody knows some people give better sucks than others. Anyway, whether or not Bobby Plant is just as much a reactionary as Bobby "Ten Spot" Colombo shall be discussed below, in "The Great Lemon Squeeze of '69."

A Honky Blues/Music ($Honk_1$) scene, on the other hand, is visionary expiation, a cry into the abys of one's own mordant bullshit. Honky Blues affirm the transcendence of conditional boundaries by recognizing them. The Honky Blues scene is the ethereal effluvium of the love sickness (not the "peace and love" love but the "tits, ass and hominid flash" love). $Honk_1$ music consists mainly of hymns of desolate circumstance to the Goddess of Honk, Our Vibracolor Madonna, just as alcohol, dope and the sundry other sacraments of $Honk_1$ bring the initiate closer to the Magna Mater Fugilo. Honky Blues/Music is America's only indigenous musical genre, and elephant doody on Keil, P. Oliver and the rest, because it didn't come from the Delta (the Geist of that music is as old as Lagashian flute blues); it came from 28,000,000 DeSotos and three-fold as many horny beer demons screaming at the moon from Route 22.

And that's where the genealogy of rock starts, with the Honky

---

[2] *Rolling Stone*, I: 10 (May 11, 1968), p. 10.

[3] For an amazing photograph and accompanying article concerning the Hampton incident, see the *Black Panther*, IV: 7 (January 17, 1970), p. 3.

Bluesmen back in the '50s, when the rhythms and melodic variations of the various types of black blues were heisted by prom
punks of all races, colors, et cetera, as the basic vehicle to get Betty
to put out some head after the dance. No inch-deep metaphysical
contrivances copped off of a university press book blurb. No
squeezing Big Brown-Eyed Mama's Lemon. Just holy honky visions, civilization and its discontents. Remember that time you
thought you were going to get to fuck Louise and you never got
her? Isn't that *really* more important than the brotherhood of
man? The Cleftones knew. They knew that the secret of the
universe was up in Betty's drawers and in no one else's. And they
never got to know the secret. So they stand, left foot forward, in a
timeless void, forever recreating that moment when Gnosis
squirmed and said, "*I'm* not that kind of girl":

> Bo bo boo boo boo
> Doo doo doo doo doo doo doo
> Boo boo boo boo boo boo boo
> Doo doo doo doo doo doo doo
> After the dance
> Please may I walk you to your door
> We'd reminisce and kiss once more
> And bring our evening to an end
> Doo doo doo doo doo dooooo dooooo
> I'll hold your hand
> Beneath the starry skies above
> We'd close our eyes and pledge our love
> And bring our evening to an end
> So while the band is playing
> And we are swaying
> Dooooooooooooooo
>
> I'll hold you tight
> Too much in love to say "Good night"
> So after the dance
> Please may I walk you to your door
> We'd reminisce and kiss once more
> And bring our evening to an end
> Doo doo doo doo doo doo doo
> It's at an end

Doo doo doo doo doo doo doo
It's at an end[4]

Grease tropes like that, sublimating the electric theme of unrequited love to dazed unrequited hard-on and back again, cultivat-
ing it with the lethal dronings of the honk fuck ritual choreog-
raphy, are heavier and deadlier than anything the Stooges are
capable of calculating. That's because it comes from the heart (id)
and not from the ego; poetry is puked, not plotted. Anyone who
doubts that the Cleftones were into speaking from the heart, from
the inside out as opposed to the I-wish-this-were-the-inside out,
need only listen to the baritone sax break in "Little Girl of Mine."
You can't fake an affirmative (in the Molly Bloom yes I will Yes
beat-off sense) answer to Bunk Johnson's "Oh, Didn't He Ram-
ble?" They also heralded the forces of Metalflaked Alephtertiary in
"Since We Fell in Love," by underscoring the lines, "All my other
love affairs/all ended in despair/Oh, but it's plain to see/that ours
was meant to be," with a sardonic barrelhouse piano (a trick that
Lennon-McCartney used ten years later in the tag of "Tomorrow
Never Knows").

Other great Honky Bluesmen of the Golden Age of Classical
Grease were the Clovers, who drenched their melodies with the
rhythms of the collective foyerfuck of a generation, bead-rolling
the surroundings of sex memories and inducing minor key orgasms
in parking lots throughout the nation, and the later female vowel-
jobbers, Shirelles and Shangri-Las (although they are, in a strictly
chronological sense, denizens of the Early Decadence), holy
queans of greasefuck poesy, transmitting osmotic tau-waves of
epiphanous pussy stench through silver-sequined lamé and jet-
black stretch pants, moaning at America's youth for a transubstan-
tial clit-strafe in the time-warp of adolescence. Kiss me there, Billy,
kiss me there . . . (Ronnettes, early liberators of Sleaze, unsubli-
mated sex) fingertips (odors) . . . There, Billy, there . . .

And Little Richard, raunch mavin and head cantor of raving
honk, whose "Can't Believe You Wanna Leave" is number three
in the list of Five Keenest Blues Songs Ever Recorded. The

astonishing psyche of this amazing darky, which lies behind twelve
years' worth of unremoved pancake make-up and mascara, has
been the pioneering source of twentieth-century matrical nonsense, a form last espied with Carroll and Lear until Penniman's
appearance, with such songs as "Tutti Frutti," "Ready Teddy"
and "Long Tall Sally."

He did the Greak anthem, "Baby," the dream pimp's strut, a
weird vamp that wavers eerily between self-confidence and pleading, ending with the universal defense mechanism of role reversal,
da dum. This is the really visionary stuff, the apparently plain
flashes, linearly bland, as Richard Goldstein and others have
pointed out, that dribble out, grimly falling together as heavy
poetry, like William Carlos Williams' shopping lists. And there's
the static "Jenny, Jenny" in which he comes on like a lust murderer sweet-talking some chick into a fatal Chevy, and at the same
time like a guy who's really happy about being in love with
someone. It's hard to tell and that's the poem. Little Richard was
and is one of the few genius singers to work in a non-classical vein.
He could manipulate his voice like a virtuoso. He could intone the
word "baby" in eleven different songs, and by the subtle pro-
nunciation of the word in each instance, you could tell what the
theme or feeling of the song was. Although quite a few outstanding musicians and arrangers have been spawned from rock 'n' roll,
Little Richard, Randy Newman, Grace Slick, Patty Waters (who
really works in more of a jazz vein), Aretha Franklin and Judy
Collins—no matter what their various other aesthetic incapacities
may be—are the only really great singers to ooze out of fifteen
years of spiff. The best subjective explanation of totality in a
singer's enunciations is Richard Meltzer's old "Tongue" dis-
courses in Crawdaddy. The best example is the way Judy Collins
sings the word "'flow" in "Pretty Polly." She portrays by verbal
intensification of that one syllable what it took Edvard Munch a
whole oil painting to get off in "The Scream."

THE NITWITS. Alias the Assholes. Those who sweetened sex.
The Valentines, Playmates, Penguins. All that bullshit. Gave
civilization one of the best sucks in its anthropomorphic biog-
raphy. The hi-roll nitwits reached their apex during the American
Bandstand–Blackboard Jungle period. Everybody lying about get-

ting laid; who stayed out all night, who got served, all that. Caused an epidemic of street-bopping and marriage. However, both musically and socially, this strain of grease has outlived its fellow strains. Witness the phoenix-like resurrection of Dion, late of Belmonts fame, who, forsaking his earlier Bronx heritage, cultivated sideburns and acquired rimless glasses toward the end of delivering cash-and-carry eulogies of a cross-section representation of America's pantheon of honky heroes to the bar-car liberals of radioland. While Traffics die, as Mothers fade and Fugs disperse, the grease rolls on, wafting unremittingly toward its *via antiqua* priests and maenads, who moil quietly, sticking iron pins into Bob Fass dolls and planning the mammoth 1976 music festival to be held at Bethel, New York, under the joint supervision of Joey Dee, Killer Joe Piro and the American Bicentennial Celebration Committee. Nitwit grease is coming to be considered the common cold of contemporary culture by leading anthropologists everywhere. I am informed by a highly reliable source that there exists to this day a throwback tribe of bongis in Newark, New Jersey, that hangs around a Vailsburg pizzeria making evil faces at pocket mirrors. No Sha Na Na shit, just arrested development. All those thirty-four-year-old housewives searching for IAO in empty Breck hairspray cans in between *The Dating Game* and *The Newlywed Game*, ruminating stoically about the big dry hump in the sky and dialing WE6-1212 on pink Princesses with chafed, Fabulous Faked digitals. They who once stood on the corner and cursed real loud now sit, a mohair legacy, staring through the silk screen mammary splendor of Joey Heatherton and into the dank tube of death, awaiting the Unctuous Reinstatement. The musical contributions of the hi-roll nitwits, loveletters in the barf, are discussed below in the perspective of its heyday, the Decadent Period.

THE METALFLAKED ALEPHTERTIARIES. This is the real good stuff. But first a word about $\aleph$ 3. Georg Cantor (1845–1918), a German mathematician and founder of the arithmetics of infinity, formulated the thesis of comparable infinities, that one infinity could be "stronger" than another (e.g., though the sum of all whole numbers is infinite, the sum of all fractional numbers is a stronger infinity since fractions can always be inserted between one another in a one-to-one pair-off of fractions and whole numbers).

So, anyway, he said that the first infinity, $\aleph$ 0, i.e., the first letter of the Hebrew alphabet to the vacuous order, was the number of all integers, and the second and stronger infinity, $\aleph$ 1, was the sum of all geometrical points in a square, cube or on a line, that the third infinity, $\aleph$ 2, was the number of all geometrical curves, the strongest infinity. He said that no infinity could be stronger than $\aleph$ 2, which is, in terms of pure mathematics, true. But by algebraically transmuting non-mathematical beings to entities whose aspects can be mathematically analyzed (e.g., the apple = ½), the indisputable god of infinities is realized. The strongest infinity, $\aleph$ 3, is the sum of the metaphysically matrical rays emanating from the pure aspect, or locus, of any given object; things are the strongest infinities, qualitatively infinitely equal and matric. The perception of some of the rays of an object is what makes a chair a chair, dirt dirt, et cetera; but when all the rays are perceived, a chair's matrical soul is the same as dirt's, thus overturning atomic perception for infinite perception. One who deals in visions, that is, one who perceives all the infinite rays of one object, or objects of conjugal positions (intersecting rays), is an Alephtertiary, someone like the Heartbeats or Ezra Pound or Andy Warhol, someone who can make dirt chairs by spilling it the right way. A metal-flaked alephtertiary is someone who can handle the infinite but, nevertheless, has a little plastic skull on the rear deck of his Olds that, for a right turn, blinks red in the right eye, and, for a left turn, red in the left eye.

In 1956 the Heartbeats did a song called "A Thousand Miles Away," an amazing catatonic blues, which rivals any extant Samuel Beckett soliloquy, with its eternal pledge of "coming home soon" that leads up to a surrealistically unexpected snatch of vegetable poetry ("maybe on a Sunday morning . . . maybe on a Tuesday afternoon"), and then collapses again into nothingness. This is a voice from another plane, a master poet Turtle Waxing his car in a peripheral sphere and half-unconsciously droning an enigmatic love song of undefinable nature. The rays entwine: Sunday passes Simonized, Tuesday locks broken. An electromagnetic era *Iceman Cometh* without the two hundred and fifty odd pages of surplus verbiage. Tuesday. ("*They do not move.*") The Heartbeats also recorded the fabulous "Crazy for You," which starts out with the

somber, non-figurative acappella line, "You're driving me crazy,"
and then goes into one of the most exquisite depictions of jealousy-
cum-psychosis to ever come off. Listen to the genius time-spacing
between the lines: "You don't seem to understand . . . that I'm
crazy . . . just for you." Elements like that, woven together with
the only piece of free-form harmony (sounds like a bunch of speed
beings having a friendly argument) of the period and block-dyed
in the cool grays of insanity are what spirals this deranged waltz off
and out into the dim dancehall of infinity. Then there's the
Heartbeats' magnus opus, "One Day Next Year," the song which
bears witness to the Heartbeats' right to hang in there with the
other outstanding aesthetic advancements to come out of a decade
and a half of rock, the Holy Modal Rounders, the Mothers, the
Jefferson Airplane and John Cale. "One Day Next Year" can be
looked at as the essence of smack or as the warped irony of re-
demption aspirations during the process of disconnection, a cottonmouth berceuse. Spiffy Bukowski. Listen to the way he says "Oh, I
really care" and "Oh, please say you care." The whole basis of the
song is the perpetration of desolation by the emission of artificial
emotions, the absence of their non-artificial emissions dictating
psychotic existentialism. The stream of consciousness lines "someday next year . . . I'll be home . . . send you a letter . . . or
telephone . . . to let you know . . . that I still care" force the
context into a recipientless vacuum by the simultaneous present
. . . future nature of the address. Through you, into the nether
you, the continuum, leaving skid marks when the light changes.
"I'll be home in the fall." "Maybe on a Tuesday afternoon."
(*"They do not move."*)[5]

The only other alephtertiaries of Classical Grease were the
people in the Jimmy Wright Orchestra, an instrumental group
with weird, weird implications that puked out two of the greatest
tone poems of the last fifteen years. The first was a composition
entitled "2:30 A.M." and, considering when it was written, it's a
musical milestone. "2:30 A.M." takes a triad of musico-artistic
techniques—kitsch, raunch and improvisation—and blends them

[5] See Andrew Duras, "The Year Dionysos Never Showed: A Study of the
Heartbeats," *American Journal of Honk/Hieratic Communication*, XII: ii
(October 1961), pp. 91–117.

together with near-perfect valences, coming up with a beautiful celebration of depravity. The rhythm section does a straight bump-and-grind thing throughout, really sleazy. The pianist runs off a chintzy string of, as Zappa refers to them, "redundant piano triplets." And on this framework a saxophone solo, sounding like a mid-sixties run, evolves and gives way to this great guitar secretion of an Elvin Bishop c. *Resurrection of Pigboy Crabshaw* Seconol expressionism type. The original layered vision, epiphanies in the vom, from which gestated advanced and ingenious kitsch-raunch-vision works of such people as Archie Shepp ("A Portrait of Robert Thompson [as a young man]," "Mama Too Tight," "Wherever June Bugs Go," etc.); Frank Zappa ("The Air," "Dog Breath in the Year of the Plague," "Anything," "Gumbo Varia-tions," etc.); Ornette Coleman ("The Empty Foxhole," "Good Old Days," etc.); and John Coltrane, who took it as far as it's gone as of yet, in the first movement of "Om." The other song the Orchestra did was "Move Over," alias "The Atomic Blowjob," a song best understood aesthetics-wise in terms of old Arabian poetry, which would mainly concern itself with expounding upon a single aspect of the feeling which resulted from an act, rather than the act itself or even the emotional meaning of the act (as in later Western poetry). "Move Over" is trucking music to accompany millions of tiny, Crumbian sperm cells as they strut forth from the composer's gonads, trolley-car with waving index fingers through his dork canal and explode in orgasmic spangles like the opening credits of the old *Honeymooners* show into the uterine osculum of some scotch-drinking quark queen. The music just gets more and more frantic, and by the time the song's halfway finished, there's this binary fission thing going on with the time until it gives off eight violently Milleresque spinal spurts and ends with Jimmy Wright emitting a climactic Larry Talbot howl. The quarks dance, vision shimmers, the mind snaps. All greasy alephtertiary record-ings can be enjoyed at any of the four standard rpm speeds.

THE DECADENCE AND THE NEW BLOOD

THE FALL OF THE HOUSE OF GREASE. The Decadence

Period spans the years from the Nitwits' subjugation of the punk media (popularly dated from Edd "Kookie" Byrnes' first permanent) until the beginning of 1965, when Alan Freed died of uremia in Palm Springs, where he had fled to escape the wrath of Shubop, god of payola. This period is intrinsic Honk$_2$. Paul Anka wanted your sister to put her head on his shoulder; Don & the Goodtimes told of a cockteaser called "Little Sally Tease," who "when she touches your neck you know you'll really flip!flip!"; the Classics wanted somebody to wait for them "till then ooo"; the Dovells said, "you gotta slop, bop, flip, flop, hip, hop all around"; Lesley Gore extolled the virtues of Danny, " 'Cause Danny . . . sends me flowers and candy."[6]

Although the Decadent Period had no positive musical results, it did spawn some important phenomena which bore heavily on the ways of later spiff. Toward the end of the 1950s full-scale hype maneuvers began to permeate rock music, molding the tastes and economics of a blossoming market that was, in the next ten years, to grow to unbelievable proportions. Super-hype began with the White Bucks Mafia of Philadelphia. Bob Marcucci of Chancellor Records became lucky with one of the recording artists for whom, in his staff capacity at Chancellor, he had hacked out a few songs. Frankie Avalon, Marcucci's young Philadelphian meal ticket, was raking in considerable royalties and percentiles within a few months after "Dede Dinah," a whimpering puppy-love song of the most insipid variety, was recorded. So Marcucci, having made a proverbial gold mine from a compost heap, set out to further test out the Midas touch. And, so the story goes, while strolling through the neatly-trimmed streets of South Philadelphia, Mar-

---

[6] For a unique study of Lesley Gore's songs, see Rolf-Ulrich Golze, "Miss Gore: the Woman, the Music, the Nosejob—of These Things Sing I, for Drunk in the Sahara Club, I Touched Her Knee," British Quarterly of Applied Psychoses, IV: vi (November 1966): ". . . 'Danny' is a literary movement unto itself . . . the missing link between Dadaism and Barth's literature of exhaustion. . . . The life of Miss Gore is the life of Arthur Rimbaud with female pudenda . . . 'I only wanted to be happy,' she said, a small tear blossoming from the corner of an eye, her sorrowful heart, a bird yearning for the lemon-bright dawn of love, beat fiercely, pushing her firm, full bazoom against its frail veil of Chantilly . . . alone in the night her psychic toe twitches for an unborn lover . . . etc."

cucci came upon a dashing specimen of the City of Brotherly
Love's youth lounging on a doorstep, picking the lint from his red,
white and blue V-neck sweater. Within weeks, fourteen-year-old
Fabian Forte was under the ministrative guidance of Bob Marcucci's hand-picked staff of voice teachers and aural pederasts. By
the time Fabian's "Turn Me Loose" became a best seller, Marcucci had managed to develop a liaison with fellow Philadelphian,
disk jockey turned television emcee, Dick Clark. Clark, with the
newly-acquired Bandstand TV program, had gotten the power, via
mass media, to virtually make or break the fulfillment of any
aspiring young singer's attempt to jackroll the weekly allowances of
juvenile America. Soon, with the communal connivings of Clark,
Marcucci and his host of whining pubescent spiffoids, various local
P.R. men and managers bucking for V.P. seats in their respective
corporations, and assorted media traffic managers, the great, gothic
progenitor of today's hype reared its head. By the time of Dick
Clark's televised birthday party in the last days of 1959, interstate
nexi had been coordinated, and people like Clark in Philadelphia
and Alan Freed in Cleveland were merely the hierophants of
hundreds of other disk jockeys dipping their record-cuing hands
into the greasy till of P*A*Y*O*L*A. Within the next year, both
Avalon and Forte had landed major studio screen contracts.
Within that same year FCC investigations, instigated by Oren
Harris' Subcommittee on Legislative Oversight's revelation that
Patty Duke had won $32,000 on The $64,000 Challenge, a major
network TV program, in a rigged series of questions and answers,
produced the Big Quiz Show Scandal; before long the "payola"
inquisition was under way, catching up with, among others,
Snappy Dick and Cowbell Freed, who was first indicted on a
charge of having received $30,650 from record companies in return
for services rendered, and, first denying the charge and claiming he
was merely an agent of Shubop, God of Monied Musick, and then
later pleading guilty after a panel of incredulous Oxford theo-
logians were called in, managed to get off with a suspended
sentence and a fine of $300, only to be indicted shortly afterward
on charges of evading tax payment on $37,920 worth of payola
gelt. Knowing all too well the wrath of the Shubop of the Old
Press Release, Freed then fled to sunny Palm Springs with plans of

setting up a floating pirate radio station aboard a stolen yacht anchored in the Bermuda Triangle. Fate fared better for Clark, who soon re-opened his soda fountain/autograph stand for a penitent programming department.

Another major outgrowth of the Decadent Period was the creation of the Rock 'n' Roll Personality Image, a further evolutionary stage in the development of the late '60s supercool hype syndrome. Edd "Kookie" Byrnes, image emeritus, the man responsible for the Great Comb Fetish of 1960 (to this very day there are mature women in this country who can, because of this mystique and its resultant neurotic fixations, achieve orgasm only by clitoral manipulation with a #10 Pro-Bar comb), was a small-time actor who rose to fame and glory within the ranks of AFTRA in the TV show, 77 Sunset Strip. Warner Brothers exploited their godsent Kookie to the hilt. They got Connie Stevens to beg him to lend her his magic phallic comb and thereby create a hit record. Today's obsession with strategically coifed long hair is merely the logical progression of the pompadour and flat-top fetishes of the late '50s and early '60s. That's why somebody like Edd Byrnes is such a seminal figure in the genealogy of rock. When Brian Epstein had the Beatles forsake their pomps for Moe Fines in '63 he was just employing the same logistics that the screen writers for 77 Sunset Strip's characters employed with Edd Byrnes a few years before—the package-over-product gimmick discovered by Hollywood and P. T. Barnum in the '30s and perfected by Madison Avenue advertising agencies in the '50s and '60s. Beatle wigs and Woodstock sweatshirts.

THE BIRTH OF SOMETHING. In the early '60s, as the voices of Jimmy Clanton, Neil Sedaka and Bobby Rydell were drifting from the nation's radio and TV transmitters, two big things were creeping their way within the spiffy pleated skirt of the Punk Muse toward the stained panties of Fame. In those closing years of the Decadent Period, from 1962 to 1965, as Connie Francis cavorted in the technicolor fantasies of a myriad aging greasers and Joey Dee and Chubby Checker were making desperate attempts to bring back the Twist, a thing they stole from Hank Ballard, a young guy calling himself Bob Dylan, who had originally come to New York in 1961 with his cousin, A. J. Weberman, to do nothing less mundane than visit Radio City Music Hall, had managed to land a contract with Columbia Records, and a group calling themselves, finally, the Beatles began making records and TV appearances in England.

Bob Dylan rode in on a wave of bullshit publicity—half his own and half the copywriters' at Columbia's house organ—about how he shared "Woody Guthrie's vision of a free, loving people," how he used to talk in a drawl without the g's on the ends of participles, how he was a scruffy itinerant roving around with a roundhole guitar slung over his shoulder, and all that. And all the while he was just a nice Jewish kid from middle-class Minnesota, swept up in the then-big folk punk fad. In five years of public appearances and recordings, from the time he first began playing in the West Village until the time he conceived *Highway 61 Revisited*, he had perpetrated some of the honkiest bullshit in the history of American music. He had sat there with peach fuzz on his chin, singing like a hardened Negro loner about cold death; he had written prickshit liberal nonsense like "Blowin' in the Wind," "Hard Rains A-gonna Fall," "The Times They Are A-changin'," and all that other garbage that rosy-cheeked Princetonians aped at their "hootenannies." Some of their best friends really were Negroes and they believed in freedom of speech, too. And then, after that long period of liberal bullshit, something happened. Something happened that brought to light the fact that it was pretty fucked-up to be singing about Hollis Brown when you were getting hit with money from eight different directions and buying bigger apartments and better motorcycles with it. He got flashed with what Jean Shepherd calls the White Light of Truth (some people just put their shades on, but others realize they were the blind dates, and start from there), and he saw into the whole derangement he'd been involved in and he began to spew out things from his own heart, all those things he used to pretend weren't in him, but things that old girl friends in Minnesota knew really were in him and were him. That's where all the preoccupation with phantomly powerful chicks comes from in his later works. Sometimes he tried to veil a lot of clichéd ideas in a lot of contrived imagery, and that was bullshit, too, but he also puked out a great deal of blind imagery, which resulted in some genius songs. Bob Dylan and Randy Newman are the last of the great Honky Bluesmen. Bob Dylan is driven by the same fuel that drove the Cleftones, only he's much, much brighter and much more sensitive. Take "From a Buick 6," a near-perfect song, as good as anything the Heartbeats had ever done. Pure alephtertiary. Listen to the music, words and feeling in "From a Buick 6"; it's a pure hymnal blues. He went on to do one of the best rock albums of the decade, *Blonde on Blonde* (Honk on Honk: look up "blond" in a dictionary—it's a description of Hitler's Aryan physiology), which kicks off with "Rainy Day Woman #12 & 35," a joyous cry of abandon, in which he nullified his previous pseudo-humanitarian bullshit with the raunchily sweeping shoulder-shrug, "Everybody Must Get Stoned." And there's "Pledging My Time," the "poison headache" (those are the words of a poet) song, a genius love/sleaze songpoem ("If it don't work out . . . you'll be the first to know"—think about that). "Visions of Johanna" really does have visions in it. "All-night girls on the D Train"—that's poetry. *Blonde on Blonde* is just nothing less than a constantly exquisite album. If most of "Memphis Blues Again" sucks, it doesn't matter; it's more than compensated for elsewhere on the album; everything on the whole album is visionary. Blind imagery, the symbolic images that the id pukes out, irrationally and without conscious intention. Poetic images that incite feeling through alephtertiary. Ambulance is blind feeling. Johanna is that girl, her whole aura, that little piece of you that you left in her. Intending to go see Queen Mary is the old Heartbeats thing, the cottonmouth lullaby. The D Train, that desolation. The images glint, catalyzing relatively symbolic images in the recipient's subconscious; visions fuck, come together; stasis and expansion. Dylan has continued to be a poetaster of beautiful songs, though his style has changed notably twice since *Blonde on Blonde*.[7] *Nashville Skyline*'s songs are just as beautiful as "From a Buick 6," but in a different way. His songs are mellower, his head's together; where he once would have drawn morbid pictures of a haunting Johanna, he now just says softly that he threw it all away.

[7] For the definitive synopsis of Bob Dylan's *real* "roots," see Toby Thompson, "Hey Hey Woody Guthrie I Wrote You a Song," *Us*, 2 (October 1969), pp. 17–33.

Although the Beatles' early years were pretty shitty musically, they weren't as creepy as Dylan's. The Beatles were just guys who liked to play and were trying to make some bread with some mediocre musical ideas. And they were pretty ready to admit it at press conferences, too, once their success became relatively stable. Although they always did seem to be pretty bright, the Beatles didn't come off with anything decent until *Revolver*, and that's not so hot either. Who the fuck wants to hold somebody's hand? I could believe maybe a tit or something, but a hand? With *Revolver* the Beatles interrupted a discographical tradition with themselves by recording some songs that weren't intrinsic shit (O.K., "Michelle" was good). There was "Eleanor Rigby," a really fine song, and "For No One" is simple beauty. "Got to Get You into My Life" and "Love You Do," George Harrison's phony raga, are good fun songs. Nothing really great, just really good songs, which are, after all, highly worthy things in their own right. The only *really* great album the Beatles did was the recent *Abbey Road*. However, "Happiness Is a Warm Gun" is a flash of pure alephtertiary genius which belongs in the realm of near-perfection, like "From a Buick 6" and "One Day Next Year." The Beatles, unlike Dylan, had a sort of asymptotic progression; they got better and better, they progressed and progressed, but they never really made Big Time Musick. Ironically, they were never able to rival the nemetic *Best of the Beatles*. But, then again, the Beatles never used Hollis Brown as a front.

Anyway, no matter what their artistic worth may be argued to be, Dylan and the Beatles, along with the earlier Philadelphia messes and resultant image mystique, were perhaps the two greatest forces in the evolution of today's rock cosmogony. Dylan murdered Roundhole Folk through electrical instrumentation. Everybody booed him when he came out electrified at Forest Hills five years ago, and Tom Paxton wrote some prickshit article about how Dylan wasn't pure any more, and two years later Paxton and the rest of the meatballs threw away their acoustics and *Sacco and Vanzetti Songbooks* to head where the bread was. Dylan won the folkies over to electricity, increasing by scores upon scores the Legions of Spiff. Dylan also opened up the possibilities of taking up punk media airplay time with imagery in toto, thus also win-

ning over hoards of Cerebrum Groupies to become intellectual
bodyguards of rock, spouting their dissertations of fantastic spiff
genius into the nation's offset presses and lecture halls. The
Beatles, whose effect was far, far greater, did nothing less miracu-
lous than sweep up at least eighty percent of the youth of the
world's wealthy countries. The Beatles made rock a punk religion.
They reversed the desired effects of rock music. This is unbeliev-
ably significant, because heretofore rock 'n' roll had always been a
calmative; it appeased youth. Sure, you were supposed to "rip it up"
on Saturday night, but you were never supposed to rip it all up all
of the time. Frankie Lymon shot dope and everyone in the industry knew it, but he couldn't waver from the code of America while
he was on stage; things were heavily controlled by the media. Now,
the media are heavily controlled by punks. The Beatles can say
they dropped acid and still be on Ed Sullivan's show. The Beatles
took it over, they set the stage. The Beatles incited, albeit mildly,
the feelings of discontent. The truly culturally revolutionary
groups—the Jefferson Airplane, the Fugs, Country Joe and the
Fish, even to a certain extent the Doors—owe their audiences'
orientation, in part, to the Beatles' mild irreverence. And that's
why, in the first half of the 1960s, along with Dave Clark Dion
Five and the Herman's Hermits Belmonts Imperials, something
was happening; the elements were being transposed. As Fabian
Forte and Jimmy Clanton *davened* quietly before faded blow-ups
of Annette Funicello in the raw and muttered over and over, "I
don't understand"; as forty thousand blue-eyed meatballs sat
around and sang "Blowin' in the Wind" at each other, Spiff
became King, eating the soft, impressionable minds of America's
young. Jocko's rocket ship was returning from its geodesic voyage
to the peripherum of curved space in a drunken attempt to
scramble the Orphic Egg with a radioscopic recording of the
Heartbeats' secret Four-Part-Harmony Acappella Tetragramma-
ton Belch Cantata, orbiting the earth three times and sprinkling
tiny droplets of chromosome-damaging *kyke* on Earth's outermost
atmospheric aura, singing amongst themselves: " . . . *we are the
girl, on page 44* . . ."

DYLAN'S GARBAGE'S
GREATEST HITS

Oh the garbage bags were stained with
  grease and dog shit
And that awful smell made it
  difficult to see
All I could think about were
  the lyrics to *Self Portrait*
As I stepped to Bobby's trash can
  to do some Dylanology

And Dylan's garbage smelled
Not far in the distance
Dylan's garbage smelled
And wasn't a sweet sight to see
Dylan's garbage smelled
Not far in the distance
Dylan's garbage smelled
But there was somethin' in it for me
                              (chorus)

I reached into the can where
  some good shit was lying
Diapers were everywhere . . .
  it smelled like a tomb
I was ready to leave,
  I was already walking

When the next thing I knew a letter
  addressed to Bob Dylan did loom

Outside of Dylan's MacDougal Street pad
  some people were gatherin'
So I began to mutter something about
  "improving the ecology"
But an off-duty garbage man standing
  next to me, his head was exploding
I was prayin' Dylan's rent-a-pigs
  wouldn't come out and vamp on me

So I put the grease-stained letter
  into my pocket
I took a-hold of the garbage bag
  and away I did ride
Straight for the Bowery and
  the Dylan Archives
Sure was glad to get out of there alive

By the time I reached the Archives I was flippin'. Would I find
bits and pieces of D's poetry? Would I find evidence of D's "current bag"? I opened the street door of the small loft building which
houses the Archives and deposited the bag in the hallway. Then I
brought in an empty trash can and started to transfer the contents
of the plastic bag to the can, sorting out the good shit. I had to
leave the street door open since, as I have said, D's garbage was
not exactly mellow-smelling. The first thing I pulled out was a shit-
filled diaper . . . right, right . . . Dylan has a lot of kids. In a
letter written by Angie, one of Sara Dylan's (Bob's wife) ex-
college chums and member of the Dylan Clan, to some friends in
England regarding "What the Dylans are really like" she states
that Bob keeps Sara "constantly pregnant." But D is a good father.
He really loves his children. He may not care about black children
any more, but he loves *his* children. They may not dig him too
much when they get older and look back on how he refused to use
his influence or money to save lives, but Dylan loves his children.
He may sit and let the world they're gonna have to grow up in get

more and more fucked up so that he can remain in his c.b., but . . .

I made my way through the empty cans of vegetables, Blimpie wrappers and coffee grounds, till I came to a whole shitload of rock newspapers. There was *Rock, Stone, Melody Maker, Circus,* etc., and even an issue of *Crawdaddy,* with one of my articles in it. I was very hurt that D threw it away instead of treasuring it, sleeping with it under his pillow, etc., but this confirmed my theory that D followed the rock criticism scene very closely and was extremely interested in what was being said about him. Soon I found a letter to the D's, which was sent out to parents whose children attended a certain progressive private school in the Village, thanking them for contributing to the school's "country trip fund." (One of D's metaphors for his c.b. is "being in the country," see *EVO,* November 4, 1970, so I guess he could relate to it.) Now I was really getting into it. In a bag of carpet sweepings I found a torn-up picture of (presumably) one of D's kids. Then I found a fan letter from a cat in California, which read " . . . Marie will turn to the wind or someone like Cochise and ask where heroin is available." He's way off. D is very down on hard drugs.

I was going through some dog shit wrapped in newspaper when a fellow freak walked by and saw me doing the thing. "Did you lose something?" "No." "Think you'll find something of value in there?" "No." "Then why . . . ?" "It's Dylan's garbage, man. I just snatched it from in front of his pad." "Come on, man, you went all the way up to Woodstock?" "No, man, he lives in the city." "Far-out." And the cat walked away. A few minutes later he was back. "Is your name A. J. Weberman? Did I hear you on Fass's show the other night?" "Right on," I answered.

I continued to do the thing and found two drafts of a letter to John and June Cash. When I showed them to David Peel, he remarked: "Dylan must have been fucked up when he wrote this . . . like, he can't even write a simple sentence." All the tired horses in the sun, how's he gonna get any writin' done?

I began to make regular pickups of D's garbage each night (beginning September 17, 1970) . . . like, I never thought I'd stoop so low—*literally.* The picture of D that began to emerge from his garbage reinforced the father theme since it was stone middle class: there was a medical report from an expensive animal hospital regarding the D's dog, Sasha, who had an upset stomach; invitations to attend special sales at exclusive department stores, along with all kinds of mail-order cosmetic offers and copies of fashion magazines all addressed to Sara (Sara seems to be into the plastic "manikin" trip). Then there were some Polaroid negatives of D's youngest child: one alone, one with the D's third-world maid (who I recognized from the time I put D's pad under surveillance) and one with D giving the kid a bottle.

When I started to find packages addressed to a Saltzman on LaGuardia Place, I jumped to the erroneous conclusion that this was the other pad referred to in the aforementioned letter—"One day Sara took me to the apartment she has downtown. It was when she went into one of the bedrooms and found an expensive fur coat that the trouble started. She tackled him the minute he came through the door . . . " Later I found out this was the address of D's middle-aged secretary, Naomi Saltzman.

Generally, when I found fan mail, it was ripped up. Some typical quotes: "Thank you for helping me to learn to think," "You abomination, you're responsible for my kid growing his hair down his back." When Hendrix died, I found a picture of him done in Magic Marker, really good, ripped to shreds. Then there was the stuff D's kids had discarded: Anna's notebook, Maria's envelope, Naomi's camp diary, some of Jesse's scribbling. I also found a card from D's mother: "Ft. Lauderdale is great. Enjoy the candy," a birthday card from Grandma Joe and one from Aunt Sylvia and Uncle Morris. Good to know D's still a Zimmerman.

Things grooved along for about two weeks. I found a list of the outs from the Self Portrait session, dated March 3, 1970, which included "Pretty Saro," "Ball and Stripes Rag," "Dock of the Bay," "The Gypsy" (the one on New Morning), "Universal Soldier," "Out of a Job," "These Hands," "Spanish Eyes" and "Piano Boogie," along with a letter to D from his attorneys, Pryor, Cashman & Braun, concerning a picture of D's father with John Sebastian, taken in Duluth, Minnesota, in 1966, by EVO photographer Joe Stevens. (Stevens had laid a copy of the picture on D.) Bob is pretty involved with these cats. Angie writes, "Lately

(September 30), he's taken it into his head to find out who does what with his money. The Isle of Wight fiasco has made him want to see heads roll. He called it the biggest fuck-up of all time and if he continues to be associated with Grossman & Braun, I'd be very surprised." Dylan sliced these Braun & Co. on WBAI-FM, forcing them to cancel my "Music from the Dylan Archives" radio program and also had them threaten to sue The Georgia Straight and My Pree Fress if they continued to print excerpts from his unpublished novel, *Tarantula*.

I also found that although D had a lot of bread his family really didn't gorge themselves that much. Their garbage was definitely on the modest side. A typical shopping list contained items like cookie mix, liverwurst and granola.

After two weeks, the good garbage, D's papers, ceased to come even though I knew he was still in town from eyewitness reports of friends, etc. D had sensed that something was happening with his garbage, and he didn't know what it was. This was probably because, at the time, I felt a little guilty about invading D's privacy ("Could there be someone whose name's been misused and privacy abused?" D ghosting for Band), like the pigs go through people's garbage, and so I made off with the bags without replacing them, didn't tie the ones with nothing of interest in them exactly the way I found them, and so D, paranoid as he is, got wise.

Despite my suspicion that D was hip to my scam, I continued to do the thing and managed to turn up a prescription made out to D for some very strong muscle relaxant. This fit in with my recent theory that D's motorcycle accident was actually a suicide attempt and that he was seriously injured. Dig, Bob was allegedly taking his bike in for repairs and his wife was following behind him in one of his cars when it happened. This sounds cool, but I believe the accident took place late at night. Why couldn't Bob wait until daylight if the bike was dangerous and fucked up? And judging from some of the lyrics on *Blonde on Blonde* (which was released just before the accident), like "She knows where I want to be but it doesn't matter" and "They sent for an ambulance/One got sent/Somebody got lucky," D was like infatuated with death. But Dylan failed to off himself (most suicides turn out to be abortive attempts), and so he settled for "a living death"—his. After I found nothing for two weeks straight, I began to rap about my garbage scam on Alex Bennett's liberated AM radio show and since D's management often requests tapes of my appearances from Alex, I figured the scam was *burned down*. But one night I went over D's garbage just for old time's sake and in an envelope separate from the rest of the trash there were five toothbrushes of various sizes and an unused tube of toothpaste wrapped in a plastic bag. "Tooth" means "electric guitar" in D's symbology (e.g., in "Outlaw Blues," Bob tells the folkies he got "his dark sunglasses" superstar image and his "blacktooth" electric guitar). Maybe D was saying that his next album (*New Morning*) would be rock and roll? After all, D is the ultimate symbolist.

Dylan has changed completely since the time he wrote songs like "Blowin' in the Wind," and going through his garbage was just like going through his recent poetry. There was nothing of any real value to be found. Bob is now part of the power structure and is a reactionary force in rock. This is the result of his having many millions of dollars. "Relationships of ownership" (who owns what) "They whisper in the wings, etc." (they prompt the politic of the rich). Another factor is D's c.b., which makes him susceptible to arrest and also generally kills political response. *Dylan must be dealt with.* He has decided to return and live close to the culture he ripped off and betrayed. *But for how long?*

ALL POWER
TO THE GOOD DYLANOLOGISTS
FREE BOB DYLAN FROM HIMSELF

Dominic Soline

ROCKIN' THE CONTINENTAL

In many ways mainstream homosexuals are culturally deprived in the field of music. Oh, no, I'm not saying that they don't enjoy listening to musical entertainment. It's just that there has been scarcely any actual musical output directed by the czars of the entertainment industry expressly for the gay community. And often, gays who have succeeded in producing work of relevance to this relevance-starved community will turn their backs on their original brethren and seek the isolation of distant elegance. Yet, all men must have their music, and where are the men left in the lurch to find theirs? Certainly not in Merle Haggard!

So, in lieu of attracting name entertainers with their roots in the gay community, the solution is frequently in the realm of *parody*, parody on that bulk of commercial entertainment which by design is alien to all but the dullest of straights—and those elsewhere who can *laugh*. The lyrics of standard pop tunes can be hilarious if the right focus is taken. And now featured at the Continental Baths is a new girl whose focus is acute. Looking much like a thinner Deana Kaminsky (of John Fahey face), Liz Torres arrives on stage and begins her set with an unusual rendition of "Yesterday." From her face the spotlight moves, with perfect timing, to her stomach. Yes, she's pregnant. The audience perceives that in unison with the opening line: "Yesterday, all my troubles seemed so far away . . ." Uproarious laughter. Then she continues: "Now I need a place to hide away." Hide? There's no place to hide except in a closet, and perhaps her condition would even prevent her from fitting in there among the clothing. Finally she removes her stuffing—she's only been *fake* pregnant. A Continental patron mutters below his breath, "She blew it." She has tipped off her hand.

But what a perceptive hand it is! Impersonation of pregnancy, a natural extension of sexual role-playing to an extreme, a woman masquerading as a woman via the most conventional association with womanhood. Indeed, an unnecessary conventional association, made all the more poignant since she is additionally a *woman wronged*. Wronged by whom? Aha!

As soon as she begins her life story a new issue enters the picture. Is she Puerto Rican or is she Jewish? Now racial ambiguity has supplanted sexual ambiguity and she begins her parody of Latin American singers who make themselves absurd by directing their songs at an English-speaking audience. "Well I theenk I going out of my head over joo!" Next she is the opera prima donna on the *Ed Sullivan Show* trying to prove her versatility by doing a rock number—of all things, "Down on Me" (a lyric which by all means Janis Joplin must have been aware of the implications of). Then it's oldies but goodies time as Liz belts out Connie Francis' "Lipstick on Your Collar."

Clearly she knows the true power of rock as a life force, all the comedy aside. Even the gesture she makes with her right eyelid is more reminiscent of Elvis' famous upper lip moves, a note of nostalgia for a time when sexual insinuation of that sort was a far less self-conscious act than today's entertainment context makes it. Still, many of the current rock references contained in her jokes (such as to Lesley Gore and Tina Turner) seem to escape the bulk of her audience at the Continental. This despite the fact that several of the crowd work it out to the latest rock tunes on the dance floor and are familiar with James Brown and Martha and the Vandellas by name. (So while Liz's debut was important—as is the debut of every citizen of the Continental—when is Iggy going to live up to his obligations and volunteer his services to the Continental? It's the only way his authenticity and sincerity can be tested, and his preference for a single set nightly would be ideal . . .)

But back to Liz Torres. She seems truly interested in the educational aspects of rock and roll for the gay community, just as was David Roter in a not dissimilar context when he played opposite Nico at the Dom in 1967. But unlike David, whose chief tool as an artist is his outright verbal coarseness backed up by a heavy beat which is as important as joke-in-itself as it is for accompaniment and musical thrust, Liz relies on subtlety (backed up by the smooth yet driving support of drummer Joey Mitchell and pianist Billy Cunningham, whose own personal touch is his use of sheet music at the keyboard). Where David's rocking "Sam, the Girl You're with Is a Man" may be good for a hearty belly laugh the first time it's heard, Liz's every excursion into insight through music is touched by the warmth of her own consequences, a depth of experience that echoes the universal lost chord.

Which is where rock enters the picture. And it will more and more.

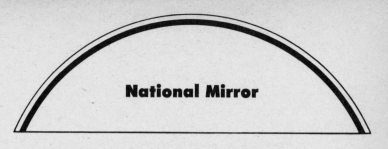

GUITAR HEMORRHAGES
POP STAR'S FACE

Billy Whitmore, 19, hadn't done eight bars of his latest hit, "Many a Stroke," when the electric guitar he was playing at the Mad Peacock discotheque exploded, injuring him in the facial area. Rushed to Belmont Hospital in nearby Belmont, Michigan, Whitmore will recover but it is said that damage to his face is so extensive that his career may be ended.

Witnesses at the Mad Peacock disco said that Whitmore was "lifted five feet off the ground" when the guitar he was strumming erupted in a cloud of sparks and jagged pieces flying in all directions, landing mainly on his face.

"It was unbelievable," sobbed Jill Raskin, 16, a young teen-age fan. "One minute he was playing 'Many a Stroke,' which everybody loves, and the next he was on the floor in a pool of blood. It was horrible!"

Doctors at the hospital are concerned about the young singing idol's face, and express pessimism concerning his future.

"He will require extensive plastic surgery," said Dr. Lewis Painter, 52, attending physician in the case. "This will be difficult since little remains of Whitmore's face. The explosion wiped his features away, so to speak."

Describing Whitmore's face, or what remains of it, as a mass of "hemorrhaged meat," Dr. Painter said that the scarcity of untouched facial flesh would make plastic surgery nearly impossible. Full recovery would not be realized until several operations were performed and even then successful restoration of Whitmore's features would never be complete.

"A small mound remains where his nose once was and his eyebrows are nowhere to be seen," said Dr. Painter. "One ear is completely destroyed while the other is almost unrecognizable. His scalp was seared off, and there is some question as to whether his hair will grow back."

Whitmore, who was to be married in two weeks, has had the event postponed indefinitely, pending his recovery. It is understood from reports that his fiancée, Robin Norwood, 24, a television go-go dancer, has departed for southern France. Though she could not be reached for comment, it is assumed that this signifies an end to her engagement to Whitmore.

Investigating authorities have concluded that the explosion was caused by a short circuit in the electric guitar's self-contained amplifying mechanism, though the possibility of foul play cannot be ruled out until laboratory analysis on the guitar fragments is completed. Whitmore was supposedly on the outs with several pop singers whom he had displaced in his meteoric rise to fame in the past year. Tests will be made to determine if an explosive device was planted in the instrument by a disgruntled rival.

Trudye Labell

A DREAM DATE WITH JIM MORRISON

*You—and you alone—spend an unforgettable day
in L.A. with a magnetic, mysterious star you've
always longed to know better. And now you do.*

As you gaze out the window of the big jetliner, you see the airport
zooming up from below. You know you'll be landing in a matter
of minutes and you're excited about the day ahead of you. It's a
beautiful day, a wonderfully warm and sunny California day, and
you just know it is going to be a very special day—because you're
spending this "Dream Day" with Jim Morrison!

You don't have any idea what's in store for you. Jim is a man of
very few words, and he does things on impulse. He prefers speed
and action to wasting hours of time planning or explaining what's
on his mind. All that you know for sure is that he will be waiting
for you in a brand-new red Mustang, right outside the Los Angeles
International Airport terminal. You don't really mind the sus-
pense, because you hope that today you will get to know the
mysterious and intriguing Mr. Morrison a little better.

The clock strikes 11 A.M. as you walk outside the air terminal
and look for Jim's car. Your eyes scan the parking area, but there
are so many cars that you're afraid you won't find Jim! You hope
he'll spot you. What you don't know is that he already has! Jim is
silently watching you through the rear-view mirror of his car—
which is only a few feet away from you! After letting you worry for
a minute or two, Jim slowly opens the door on the side of the car
nearest to you. He leans out, smiles wickedly, and shouts, "Hi!"
You're startled and a little embarrassed at first, but when you see

the teasing sparkle in his beautiful eyes, you know that everything is going to be all right.

Once you're seated in the car, Jim asks, "What would you like to do now?" You tell him that you would prefer to leave the plans to him, since L.A. is his hometown. From his quick smile, you sense that he's glad you gave that answer. Jim doesn't talk very much and you wonder what's going on in his mind. You hope that he isn't bored or isn't sorry that he invited you. But you never actually have to wonder whether Jim is enjoying himself or having a groovy time, because at just the right moment he seems to read your mind and says something really nice.

Jim seems preoccupied—or is he concentrating on his driving? (You really can't tell.) Then, as you're looking out the window, wondering if you should say something, Jim startles you by snapping his fingers and tapping you on the shoulder. When you turn to look at him, he smiles and softly says, "I really didn't mean to scare you—but you look so *serious* sitting there. I just wanted you to look at *me*, so I could see you smile."

You both laugh, and you realize that you've just seen a new side of Jim Morrison. It's always like that with Jim. Just when you think you know the *real* him, he does something to surprise you—and reveals *another* him! You wonder if *you*—or anyone—can ever know "*all* about Jim."

Jim pulls the car toward a groovy little taco stand in the middle of a big parking lot, so that you both can get a quick snack. He asks you to go with him to choose what you'd like. He prefers not to sit in the midst of all the people, so you bring the tacos back to the car and Jim parks it on a corner surrounded by trees. Since you're right off the Sunset Strip, many people pass by. Jim explains that he often parks there and loves to watch the people. You're sure that it must be times like this that give Jim ideas for his songs. You wonder if this was the spot that inspired "People Are Strange."

You leave L.A. and drive into the beautiful Hollywood Hills. Jim wants to show you a futuristic house he discovered one day when he was out for a drive. It's one of his favorite pastimes, and he knows of many weird, way-out and interesting places. This particular house—although it is only ten years old—is deserted. It is very modern and looks as though it were specially built. Taking you by the hand, Jim explores the premises like an expert—examining the different pieces of furniture in silence. Just by the way Jim looks at things you know he is "feeling" them with his eyes. Without words, he is teaching you to appreciate and feel through his eyes. Gently, he takes your hand, and with his hand over yours, you both touch the carvings and textures of the furniture. You're amazed at this marvelous new experience and think how thrilling it is to be able to *hear* and *talk* without the use of words. You see, Jim "saves" words—they are precious to him, for he is a poet and a songwriter. Jim's words are for the world, and in private he has other means of communicating—as at times like this when he's away from it all and alone with someone.

▅▀THE UNKNOWN SOLDIER

Suddenly, Jim breaks the silence. "Hey, what time is it?" he asks. When you tell him that it's almost four o'clock, he explains that he must stop at the recording studio to listen to the final playback of his new single.

He shyly says, "I hope it's not a drag for you to come along. It won't take too long and then we can go swimming." Actually, you're delighted—for you know that the Doors' recording sessions are very private, and you'll get a sneak preview of their next record! You feel very *special!*

Jim meets the rest of the Doors in the coffee shop across the street from the studio, which is in Hollywood. After you are introduced to Ray, Robby and John, you all go over to listen to the tapes. The Doors' record producer is waiting and everyone sits down. All at once the lights go out and *all* conversation stops just as it does in a theater before the curtain rises. You notice how tensely Jim sits, with his elbows resting on his knees. Now there is a worried look on his face. As the music and his voice flow through the speakers, Jim's expression doesn't change—and you imagine yourself in his place at this moment. In just a few days the world will be listening to Jim's poetry and trying to know him through it. You wonder—*they'll know his songs, but can they ever know Jim?*

The lights go on again; the song is over. You are speechless with awe and admiration. Jim makes no comment, but from the look on his face you—and everyone else in the room—know that he is pleased with the record. Jim reaches for your hand and says, "Let's go."

Riding beside him in the car, you get an extra surprise as the Doors' current record comes on the radio. You both look at each other, and Jim leans over and slowly turns up the volume as loud as it will go! Jim's action surprises you, but then Jim is unpredictable.

☛SWIMMING LION

You guessed wrong again. You're not going swimming at the beach—but at the home of some friends of Jim's in Beverly Hills. They have a large swimming pool, but since it is now early evening, everyone is gathered on the patio around the barbecue pit and no one is swimming. Jim takes his bathing suit out of the glove compartment and asks if you'd like to go for a swim. Since it's getting chilly, you reply that you'd rather watch. Jim disappears for a few minutes to change into his swimsuit. When he returns, he walks around the pool several times, as if sizing it up. Then suddenly he dives in with a great splash. He swims the entire length of the pool underwater and comes up right in front of you. He lifts himself up on the edge of the pool and shakes his head— looking like a great, damp, young lion. Then, jumping backward into the water, Jim gives a performance of his super swimming style.

All eyes are on him, and you know that even if someone else wanted to go swimming they wouldn't dare compete with Jim. They would no sooner get into the same pool with him than they would get up onto the stage when he is singing. It just seems natural that everything is Jim's stage and all the people are his audience.

After Jim leaves the pool and changes back into his clothes, he joins you by the fire, bringing plates of barbecued spareribs and other tempting treats the host has prepared. Jim picks up two

Cokes and you go off quietly by yourselves to eat. Jim chooses a beautiful spot under the trees, where you can watch the sun set over the hills. He places a blanket on the grass and you both sit down.

To your surprise, Jim begins to ask you questions. He wants very much to know what you think about—your ambitions, your plans and your ideas about life. It isn't all one-sided, because Jim in turn confesses many of his plans and fears to you. Jim's thoughts are deep and he is interested in many things. He discusses his interest in astrology and fills you in on the characteristics of Sagittarians, since that's the sign he was born under. He asks you your birthdate and you are happy to learn that your signs are compatible. He even tells you about the ranch he would someday like to own. He would have it built in the San Fernando Valley, with room for lots of horses and other animals. Jim confides his secret ambition to someday direct and film a movie. You picture him more as the star of the film than the behind-the-scenes man, but you remember that he attended U.C.L.A. Film School (where he first met Ray of the Doors), so you understand his interest in this aspect of film making.

Time seems to fly by, and although there is a surprising amount of conversation—especially for Jim—there are moments of comfortable silence. It's a one-hour drive to the airport, so you say good-by to Jim's friends and you are on your way once again. The ride to the airport is quiet and pleasant. In a way, you're glad, because your mind is occupied with thoughts of the day. You want to remember every moment. You arrive at the airport just in time, because your plane is already taking on passengers. Jim turns off the car motor, squeezes your hand, and says, "It was really nice. I'm glad you came."

You feel as though you are going to cry, but before one "happy" tear can fall Jim gives you a warm and gentle good-by kiss. He looks at you, and as you run to catch your plane you feel his eyes still on you. This is one day you'll never forget. You're happy you got to know Jim Morrison, but you can't help wondering how much more there is about him that you *don't know*.

Natalie Stoogeling

POPPED

```
IGGY . . . IGGY . . . IGGY . . . IGGY . . .
IGGY . . . IGGY . . . IGGY . . . IGGY . . .
IGGY . . . IGGY . . . IGGY . . . IGGY . . .
RON . . . RON . . . RON . . . RON . . . RON
. . . RON . . . RON . . . RON . . . RON . . .
RON . . . RON . . . RON . . . RON . . . RON
. . . RON . . . ZEKE . . . ZEKE . . . ZEKE . . .
ZEKE . . . ZEKE . . . ZEKE . . . ZEKE . . . ZEKE
. . . ZEKE . . . ZEKE . . . ZEKE . . . ZEKE
ZEKE . . . STEVE . . . STEVE . . . STEVE . . .
STEVE . . . STEVE . . . STEVE . . . STEVE . . .
STEVE . . . STEVE . . . STEVE . . . STEVE . . .
SCOTT . . . SCOTT . . . SCOTT . . . SCOTT . . .
SCOTT . . . SCOTT . . . SCOTT . . . SCOTT . . .
SCOTT . . . SCOTT . . . SCOTT . . . BILLY . . .
BILLY . . . BILLY . . . BILLY . . . BILLY . . .
BILLY . . . BILLY . . . BILLY . . . BILLY . . .
BILLY . . . BILLY . . . POP . . . POP . . . POP
. . . POP . . . POP . . . POP . . . POP . . .
POP . . . POP . . . POP . . . POP . . . POP
. . . POP . . . POP . . . POP . . . POP . . .
YEAH . . . YEAH . . . YEAH . . . YEAH . . .
YEAH . . . YEAH . . . YEAH . . . YEAH . . .
YEAH . . . YEAH . . . YEAH . . . YEAH . . .
YEAH . . . IGGY POP, IGGY POP, POP . . . POP
. . . POP . . . IGGY POP, IGGY POP, POP . . .
POP . . . POP . . .
```

I am totally incomprehensible of my own accord. Natalie has taken a permanent vacation . . . After a week of the STOOGES, Natalie needs a permanent vacation. Duty calls me first, and I know if I don't get this down on paper soon, I'll be too zoned to ever write it . . . All I can say is, the STOOGES improve with age . . . Like cheese, the flavor keeps getting stronger and stronger 'til finally the flavor just bursts in your mouth . . . The STOOGES' flavor just bursts in your mind. . . . Ah, the STOOGES . . . so good . . . so good . . . By the third night at Ungano's, all I could do was to run around grabbing people and screaming "DELICIOUS, DELICIOUS" at them . . . I just couldn't find a way to say things with words . . . If anyone out there is still unsure of how far the STOOGES are going to go, let me tell you now, they are going to tear this power structure of rock and roll (as most people know it) the hell down . . . Who wants to be the best guitarist when you can be the most killer??? RON . . . RON . . . RON . . . Who wants to be the best male vocalist in the world when you are a bat out of hell??? Who wants to do drum solos when you can create the most ominous thunder this side of the inferno??? LORD, THAT GROUP IS GOING TO DRIVE ME TO RUIN!!! Sometimes I wonder how anything that good can exist in present-day society . . . All we can do is relish in their glory and be glad that we are around to see it happen . . . FUN HOUSE has been released . . . I trust you all have a copy by now . . . Then you all know why I am sitting here going crazy at the very thought of the STOOGES . . . You know I am not lying when I say it is the best LP to ever grace our ears and minds . . . Make sure you keep calling the radio stations in your area—once an hour if necessary—but make sure they play FUN HOUSE . . . The world should hear FUN HOUSE . . . I really don't know how to start this issue . . . There have been so many internal and external changes taking place lately . . . The one I'm sure you've noticed most is that DAVE is no longer with the group . . . Gooselake was DAVE's last appearance with the band. RON and I had a talk about DAVE, and I was told it was better for DAVE and better for the group now that they have parted forces . . . DAVE has other interests and this way it will give him a chance to do what will make him happiest . . . There are a lot of things he's wanted to do and traveling around the country with the STOOGES made it difficult . . . He's in the process of going to a macrobiotic festival, and he's going to make recipes for cakes and things to distribute to a lot of health food stores around the country . . . He said he hopes there are no hard feelings within the group and he's happy now . . . IGGY is happier now than I've seen him in months . . . Everyone seems more at ease . . . Of course, I'm sad that I'll probably never see DAVE again, but the group's good welfare concerns me most at the moment. . . . It's all for the best . . . So best of luck to you, DAVE, in whatever career you choose . . . I'll always remember you. Enough nostalgia—don't want to cry and blur the type . . . Enter ZEKE . . . Yes, girls, that blond roadie you were all asking about is now the new bass player with the STOOGES . . . His real name is TOM ZETTNER, but call him ZEKE . . . He learned to play bass when he was still roadie with the S.R.C. However, he never got a chance to play with them . . . I'm glad of that because had they heard him, the STOOGES never would have gotten him . . . I've heard him play four times and that's enough to make a judgment. HE'S REALLY GOOD!!! Not to mention how gorgeous he is . . . And he has such pretty blue eyes . . . Hey, I just thought of something . . . ALL THE STOOGES HAVE BLUE EYES . . . Each one has a different color blue . . . That might be another first . . . First and best with the STOOGES . . . Last issue I made a big mistake by calling STEVE MACKAY, Stan . . . He prefers STEVE and who am I to argue with a STOOGE . . . STEVE is also an artist and he used to do the cartoons in CREEM . . . He also plays mouth harp and drums—but mainly he is the first and only man to make me love a saxophone!!! On to other external changes. Jimmy Silver is no longer manager of the STOOGES . . . He is now living in L.A. with his wife and daughter and working for a macrobiotic food distributor . . . JOHN ADAMS has taken over as manager. . . . JOHN, man of a thousand names and jack of many trades, is the only other person that I know of who could manage the STOOGES . . . JOHN can do anything, and he's got the reserve that it takes to be manager to the hottest band in the country . . . After all, they need one rational member in their entourage—and that's JOHN . . . Also in the front line-up is BILLY, who technically isn't on stage with them yet but is definitely a STOOGE . . . Contrary to popular belief, BILLY is not on the FUN HOUSE LP. What I heard and reported as BILLY on rhythm is, in fact, RON—only proving once again what a remarkable lead guitarist RON is! However, I had a chance to hear BILLY jam with the STOOGES and he, too, is incredible . . . The last night the STOOGES played Ungano's was just so amazing. . . . And after the regular set they came back on stage to do a new song, called "Way Back in Egypt." I can't describe it without moaning and making other 'strange sounds . . . It ends with the IG on the floor saying, "I'M DEAD," over and over again . . . It's just so amazing . . . You will all have to hear it . . . Here are a few sure-fire ways to get radio stations to play FUN HOUSE . . . Call up and say, "If you do not play "Dirt" (substitute your fave STOOGE song), I am going to come over there to get you with a knife . . . Or, you can try the more subtle approach . . . Call up and start out nice and slowly, saying that you are sick of hearing all these Woodstock Nation songs and ginger-peachy voices . . . Raise your voice to fever pitch and scream, "I want to hear some real rock and roll. I want to hear the STOOGES." It works every time . . . A few AM stations in Baltimore and Washington, D.C., have begun to play the STOOGES' single, "Down on the Street" . . . All of you Michigan people had the good fortune to hear IGGY on the Dan Carlile show on WKNR. . . . I heard it was a far-out taping . . . When the STOOGES played the Cincinnati pop festival in June, IGGY was dancing on people's hands and they were just holding him up . . . I should have a picture for all of you soon. It's the most killer picture of any rock star taken yet . . . the look on the kids' faces is what Townshend must have had in mind when he wrote TOMMY . . . I kid you not . . . The picture is that amazing . . . The whole festival was taped for TV and it should have been aired in New York by the time you are reading this . . . It will be shown in eighteen cities, and the minute I get a schedule of what dates it will be shown where, I'll be sure to send it to everyone . . . After the IG danced on a sea of hands someone gave him some peanut butter, which he threw to the crowd. Every

time I see the STOOGES, someone asks for IGGY's dog collar
. . . The STOOGES played two absolutely killer shows at the
Eastown over the Fourth of July weekend . . . TOP OF THE
BILL!!! When the STOOGES were in L.A., IGGY left for a few
days and went to San Francisco by himself, and all he did was play
with seals . . . The IG has a crocheted rabbit that he calls his
"voodoo rabbit" . . . The STOOGES might do a festival Jane
Fonda is holding . . . IGGY used to be a stock boy at Discount
Records in Ann Arbor . . . RON said that he got mobbed once
when he was with the Chosen Few . . . SCOTT has the nicest
pair of black suede boots . . . BILLY says that ZEKE looks like
his Aunt Betty . . . BILLY and SCOTT went up to Elektra
while the STOOGES were in New York a few weeks ago . . .
They played pool, and from what I hear SCOTT beat the shit out
of BILLY . . . That's O.K. because the night before they left for
New York, BILLY and SCOTT had a fight because, in SCOTT's
words, they were having "no fun" . . . So they decided to drain
all their energy by fighting. From the looks of things, SCOTT got
the worst of that one. However, BILLY didn't show me his chest
and SCOTT did, so they might have come out even on that . . .
STEVE has a really nice silver belt with a blue stone in it . . .
Better watch it, STEVE, I might steal it. . . . BILLY looks great
in a Con Edison helmet . . . SCOTT has decaled the back of his
black leather jacket "STOOGES" . . . And LEO and ZEKE saw
Michael Rennie and Vincent Price when they were in L.A. When
the STOOGES played Ungano's such famous celebs as Johnny
and Edgar Winter were there. Miles Davis and Genya Ravan were
there. A few G.T.O.'s were floating around and Todd Rundgrun,
formerly of the Nazz, was there, too . . . But how dare two cross-
eyed albinos show their faces in the same room with SCOTT???
Folks, this is an all-time first . . . The STOOGES are the first
group in captivity to have roadies so popular that I soon will have
to start a newsletter called the ROADIE REVUE . . . That dark-
haired sound man you all keep thinking is an Asheton is, in fact,
LEO ANONYMOUS . . . He refuses to reveal his true identity
to me or anyone else . . . but it doesn't matter since he is the
best roadie in the world and his mind is a condensed sound
box . . . And yes, that is a rose tattoo on his arm. For those of

you asking about his past, he used to be roadie with the Fruit, then the Five and now (and everlasting) he is the STOOGES' sound man . . . He saw the STOOGES on the very first night they appeared, and in his words: "I knew they had something there." WE ALL KNOW JUST WHAT THE STOOGES HAVE NOW!!! Oh, yeah, before I forget, girls, all you have to do to make LEO your friend is to bring him grapes . . . Because ZEKE has joined the band [there is the roadie who is too good, so he joins the group (à la BILLY and ZEKE) and then there is the roadie who is just too damn good a roadie and the group knows they can't replace him (à la LEO)], the STOOGES had to get a new roadie to take care of the drums . . . DUNLAP has just gotten back from "Nam," and he says he planned it this way so he'd be with the STOOGES when he got back . . . He and LEO both worked for the Fruit at the same time so they get along great . . . And I'm sure all you girls will get along great with DUNLAP, too, since he's about six-feet-two and really built . . . Like I always say, there is nothing like watching something gorgeous set up the stage for something even more gorgeous . . . Last April in Providence, Rhode Island, Steppenwolf was staying in the same hotel as the STOOGES . . . Nick St. Nickolas went up to pay the IG a visit, and contrary to popular belief, it was not I who sent him up there . . . IGGY did some strange and terrible things to the Winter brothers during the set at Ungano's . . . GOOD FOR THE IG . . . IGGY HAS A REALLY KILLER PINK HEADHUNTER SHIRT . . . He is no longer wearing the silver gloves on stage . . . And he has changed his name to IGGY POP . . . RON really likes to see photos of himself, so if you have any, be sure to find RON . . . You all kept asking how you can meet the boys. Well, photos are a good way to strike up a conversation . . . Also, many of you were asking about gifts for the STOOGES . . . Fruit is always nice to give them because it quenches their thirst after the gig . . . IGGY just loves strawberries, but any fresh fruit is good . . . Also, the STOOGES love beer, so if you are rich that will always make a nice gift . . . Of course, if you just want to make them something, I know they will appreciate it . . . Last time the STOOGES were in New York, IGGY got a gift of a bullet on a chain . . . I know he really liked

it 'cause he put it right on . . . SCOTT is the first STOOGE to
receive a gift in care of the fan club . . . One of you wanted to
know if STEVE was shy . . . actually, I thought so, also . . .
but he is really a warm, open person and not the least bit
shy . . . IGGY on himself: "You ought to write a book about
me. I'm a classic." SO TRUE . . . SO TRUE . . . RON said
that if he was given a thousand dollars, he'd spend it all on Nazi
stuff . . . When SCOTT was nine, he got his photo in the
Davenport, Iowa, newspaper . . . something about his having a
gun . . . I mention it only because you can tell by looking at the
picture that he would grow up to be tall, dark and handsome . . .
ZEKE has a zigzag tattoo . . . His birthday is in September (he
did not say the date) . . . And BILLY's was July 6 and he didn't
tell me either. . . . Ah, the news you've all been waiting for . . .
I had a chance to see SCOTT during a full moon and he did not
turn into a werewolf . . . Also had a chance to check him out in
the mirror and he does cast a reflection, so he's not a vampire
either . . . However, he still does look like an executioner on
stage, so all illusions are not lost . . . IGGY has been wearing
bells around his ankles . . . The STOOGE/Zeppelin concert was
canceled . . . It had something to do with all the fuss about rock
festivals this summer and the fact that a festival could not be held
in the stadium . . . HA HA, we all know it is just God's way of
planning it so the earth does not revolve off its axis . . . I mean,
if Robert Plant and SCOTT ASHETON were ever in the same
room together, the entire earth would stop functioning . . . It's
like the north pole meeting the south pole . . . Two more opposite people are just not alive . . . I'm sure all of you heard
about the Powder Ridge festival . . . Well, on Saturday, there
was a treat for all those people . . . Skywriting appeared two
miles up and one mile high: "STOOGES IN BOSTON AUG
14." In the words of the IG, "Now that's a real publicity stunt."
. . . In the a-word-to-the-wise-is-sufficient department: Never say
the word "bogus" around the STOOGES . . . SCOTT on
Cleaver's SOUL ON ICE: "You read it and you want to go out
and start a revolution." . . . If any of you know someone who
wants to book the STOOGES, they can get in touch with Dave
Leone at DMA, 18431 Mack, Detroit . . . As most of you know,

the schedule I gave you last time was incorrect . . . It was no-body's fault, and when I sent it out it was still correct . . . Later some festivals were canceled and a few of the gigs were postponed a week . . . I'm really sorry if I caused any of you problems. I did try to write to some of you who I knew lived near some of the gigs . . . I certainly hope that each of you had the chance to see the STOOGES this summer . . . I don't know what I'd have done if I had had to go through a STOOGELESS summer . . . On August 15, the boys played at a club in Asbury Park, New Jersey. The 5 were there too and since the STOOGES will do only one show a night, it was planned that all the rest of the groups (which included David Peel, long-time friend and STOOGE fan) would go on first, do two sets and then the 5 would play . . . Then the Stooges would do their set . . . Then the 5 would play again. But everyone there was waiting for the STOOGES, and after the set all the kids just left . . . After all, who could follow the STOOGES??? Arni and Nick Ungano just love the STOOGES . . . They are the only group to fill up the club on a week night . . . We are all hoping that the next time the STOOGES do Ungano's they have their liquor license back . . . SCOTT cut his hair in New York. It's just below his ears and now you can all see his neck—best neck in the world . . . When the STOOGES were driving to Asbury Park, IGGY heard an interview with the G.T.O.'s on the radio and one of them was talking about IGGY, saying how he really gets down to it. I hear that IGGY was bang-ing his head against the back of the car in disbelief . . . There is a picture of ZEKE in the centerfold of S.R.C.'s LP. It's really cute. I suggest you try and steal the picture . . . IGGY's first words to me were not "ha," but "Did you see ZEKE? He's in the group now." STEVE is going to be a full-time STOOGE soon . . . The sax will be on more songs soon . . . IGGY on STEVE's sax: "I love it. It sounds like a squeaky goose." That's true, but what amazes me more is his breath control . . . STEVE is truly amazing . . . I never saw anyone who looks so delicate, but, boy, HE CAN PLAY THAT SAX . . . IGGY POP just popped himself down in the center of the baggage-arrival-room floor . . . He just folds himself into every situation . . . IGGY and JOHN went up to Elektra and just ran around taking care of

all the technicalities for three hours . . . When Elektra was in
the process of designing the album cover, IGGY was almost a
weekly visitor . . . RON was only allowed to stay in England one
month . . . I finally got one of SCOTT's drumsticks. It's in my
room to ward off evil spirits . . . On to the magazine scene . . .
VOGUE printed that pic of the IG—a real zoner shot of him
with the gloves . . . CIRCUS had a story that Ben Edmonds
wrote on the STOOGES and some others . . . It was edited and
not exactly to Ben's liking . . . I thought the printed one was
good so I can imagine how killer his original was . . . 16 has
printed the words to "Down on the Street" and my address . . .
All the trades gave the Ungano's shows really nice reviews . . .
The current issue of CRAWDADDY has that interview . . .
IGGY, in all his glory, is on the cover and I watched girls pass a
newsstand in the Village, look once and then run back and check
it out again . . . The interview is very good, and Costa has to be
commended for admitting in print that he was at a loss for
words . . . It's true . . . The IG will totally zone you so far that
you just stop and look at him and wonder if it really is the group
therapy session at the insane asylum . . . ROCK BEYOND
woodstock (I refuse to capitalize woodstock) has a three-page
spread of photos taken of the boys at the recording studio in L.A.
Only, I want to know why SCOTT isn't represented?? A hardcover book on American music festivals has a nice picture of the
IG doing gymnastics . . . ZYGOTE magazine is doing an article
in the near future . . . A subsidiary of LOOK, called EARTH, is
doing a whole article on the STOOGES, and this guy Bud has
been photographing them in New York. The latest I've heard is
that he is also going to Ann Arbor . . . I'll let you know what
develops . . . Any of you who still do not have CREEM's history
of the STOOGES can get a copy by writing to Dave Marsh at
CREEM, 3729 Cass, Detroit . . . Send fifty cents to cover the
cost of the paper and postage . . . That article is still the best one
to date on the band and every STOOGE fan should read the
interview that IGGY did to Dave . . . CREEM has had
STOOGE stories for the past four issues, and in order to not miss
one you can get a subscription to CREEM for five dollars . . . I

want to hereby apologize to DAVE publicly for spelling his name wrong two issues ago—it's Marsh . . . Speaking of DAVE, this is just funny. About a month ago, IGGY was in New York. Dave was there too and neither of them knew the other was there, yet they found each other within hours . . . ALL ZONES LEAD TO THE IG . . . The STOOGES went to see the Velvet Underground at Max's in New York . . . ZEKE is a Stones fan and RON really likes the Who . . . LEO wears prisoner sneakers . . . The STOOGES rented a rehearsal hall in New York right before the gig at Ungano's and the first night there, SCOTT was so tired he missed the rehearsal altogether . . . STEVE sat in on drums . . . IGGY has performed in a shirt again—first time in two months . . . When they did the jam, he came out in a black Banlon . . . ZEKE has killer corduroy pants in a strange shade of gold and SCOTT has a beautiful grey knit ribbed shirt . . . The LP cover glows in the dark . . . IGGY's jeans are so threadbare that I give them one more week, maybe not even that . . . RON had a mustache before he came to New York. It's a good thing he shaved it off . . . Why cover that face??? BILLY was first to New York in '66 . . . John Bellisimo is still writing his STOOGE epic. He says that once it is done he'll be able to just vanish from the face of the earth . . . Should be a killer story since he's gone through many a STOOGE incident with us . . . Any of you who want great color shots of the boys should contact Frank Pettis, 3049 Ewald, Detroit, Michigan 48238 . . . He has the nicest photos I've seen yet . . . By the way, on that subject, I got some nice new concert shots that I'll be sending out soon . . . There is a nice one of STEVE and ZEKE that I know all of you will want . . . Also got one of BILLY on stage . . . IGGY finally had a piece of SCOTT's birthday cake—better late than never . . . The Whiskey gig is postponed 'til later this fall . . . When the boys do go back to L.A. RON said they will record another single. Make sure you all let me know what you think of FUN HOUSE—especially the build part in TV EYE . . . It drives me up a wall, but then the whole LP does such bizarre things to me . . . Matter of fact, it is time for me to go back to the solitude of my record player and listen to my four copies of FUN

HOUSE . . . I have four copies so I can play the first side, then the second side, then the first side again and then the second side, without moving from one spot . . . This way I get a double dose, and I can just lay there and ZONE out . . . TO BE ALONE IN THE ZONE WITH THE STOOGES.

THE SOUND OF MRS. MILLER

New York, New York. The invitation read: "MRS. ELVA MIL-LER WILL RECEIVE AT THE TOWER SUITE OF THE TIME-LIFE BUILDING."

Finally, the big day arrived. After changing elevators a lot, I arrived at the coat checkroom of the Tower Suite. The attendant asked me if I was wearing a tie. I peeked under my raincoat and saw that I was, luckily. When I said yes, he let me in. I guess I was pretty nervous. At the door, the lady at the desk checked my name off the list; then she jumped up and started poking around the lapel of my jacket. I thought she also was looking for my tie, but instead she was pinning a button on my jacket. The button read: "Mrs. Miller is a Pussycat." O.K.

At the reception there were a lot of older people, smoking and drinking. There were two bars, and the tables were spread with a variety of crackers smeared with onion soup cheese dip. Also, they were handing out a lot of puffed-up fried shrimps, which everyone was making a big fuss about. Luckily, I'm old enough to drink, because they were serving my favorite Scotch. It didn't matter much that we were forty-eight stories up in the air because the fog outside was so heavy that we could have been in a subway for all the view we had. Finally, I spotted Christie Barter, the publicity director of Capitol.

"Where's the pussycat?" I asked him. He responded by guiding me into the presence of a simply dressed, middle-aged woman. It was that easy.

Mrs. Miller looked kind of out of place with all those chic New

York press agents and record people, with their trade talk and puffy shrimps and clearly visible ties. So did I, I guess, and we hit it off from the start.

"Hello, there," Mrs. Miller said to me. "Who are you?"

"I'm Danny Fields, and I'm from *Datebook*, a teen-age magazine," I answered.

"Oh, teen-agers," she said expansively. "I love them. And they love me."

"I don't see how they could fail to," I replied gallantly. "May I ask you a few questions about yourself and the teen-agers of today?"

"I'll do anything for the teen-agers. Just ask away!"

Here are some of the questions I asked Mrs. Miller, and her answers:

Q: How did you start making records?

A: Well, I'd been singing for my friends for years, and in local choral groups. Mostly old songs and the standards. Then, someone who makes records asked me if I'd like to try an experiment. He said I should listen carefully to the songs of today and try to sing them in a new style. So I turned on the radio and listened for days to all these new songs. Then I sang them in a new style, and they made records of me doing it. And, well, here I am in New York for the *Ed Sullivan Show!*

Q: What do you think of today's teen-agers?

A: Why, they're wonderful! Isn't it just wonderful to be young today? So much to see and do and learn. And teen-agers now are so eager, and sweet, and considerate. They're my biggest fans. They call me all the time to tell me how much they like my songs.

Q: And what about the parents of teen-agers?

A: Oh, they're all right, but they've forgotten what it's like being young. I'd say I was 80 percent on the side of the teen-agers.

Q: What do you think of popular music today?

A: Well, it's fine, it's fine. If I were a teen-ager now, I'd be the biggest fan of all. My house would be stacked with records and pictures and magazines, and I'd be listening to music all the time without stopping.

Q: What do you think of adults who say today's music is terrible?

A: It certainly is not terrible. You ask those adults what they listened to when they were young. It was no better, if not worse. You see, parents have forgotten their youth. It takes an old woman like me to remember . . . la! The silly, silly things I liked when I was a girl . . .

Q: What is your opinion of the Beatles?

A: The Beatles are lovely, lovely boys. They do so many things, and they have such fun, and the girls are so fond of them. And they seem to be very talented. I can't understand why anyone would want to say anything against them.

Q: Do you sing their songs?

A: Certainly. On my album I sing "Hard Day's Night." What's the matter—haven't you listened to it yet?

I got separated from Mrs. Miller for a while. I made the rounds of all the press agents and promoters in the room, drumming up press seats for forthcoming concerts and such. I was standing alone near a group of people at the center of which Mrs. Miller was chatting. Suddenly, she pointed at me! Everyone followed her finger, and all these people were staring at me.

"There's that nice teen-ager I was talking to before! Come on over here. I don't want to talk to all these old fogies from *Time* and *Life* and *Look* and all the other old-fogey magazines. I want to talk to the teen-agers, and I want to be in their magazine. Now come on over here! These people are all old fogies!"

The group around Mrs. Miller dispersed, not without tossing a few mean looks in my direction. I rejoined Mrs. Miller. I certainly was not going to correct her estimate of my age—it would have been disrespectful if I had, you know. She was off by a few years. I let it pass. Mrs. Miller had made a friend and champion for life.

When the reception was over, I rode down in the elevator with Mrs. Miller. We giggled when our ears got plugged, and she asked me why Rockefeller Plaza is sunken now, since she remembered it being at street level the last time she was here. I told her that it had been sunken as long as I could remember, but again, I didn't want to correct her. Maybe it was at street level once. After all, it and Mrs. Miller have been around longer than I have.

"Mrs. Miller," I said, as we were warmly shaking hands good-by, "while you're in New York, you should go to the Night Owl in Greenwich Village and hear what's really new in popular music."

"Yes, I really should, but we're going to the theater tonight, and I have to meet Ed Sullivan early tomorrow morning. La! Wouldn't it be fun, though, to stay up all night and really do the town! But I guess I can't. It's been so nice talking to you. And you tell all the other teen-agers that Mrs. Miller loves them, and that I'd like them to love me, too."

I assured her that I would, and we parted. Then I walked over to Rockefeller Plaza to check up on it.

Richard Meltzer

WHAT A GODDAM GREAT
SECOND CREAM ALBUM

Mere uniqueness.[1]

Cute little vocals on one end, and top-flight instrumental extravaganzas on the other, slammed together through some sort of Donovan-Zappa Avoidance Principle, too, just a little elusive to put the finger on.[2]

Not an ounce of eschatological viscera.[3]

With Cream, got to start with the NON-BUMMER GRID OF ANALYSIS: there are no true primary bummers, just non-bummers and non-non-bummers.

Ginger drumming like crossing very early Ringo with football marching band, and that's no bummer altogether.[4] Ginger Baker

---

[1] And, 'cause it's English, part of the English programmatic uniqueness scene, a stopover on the English Programmatic Uniqueness Trail, and nothing could be finer.

[2] So you have either unobvious Smiley Beach Boys and first-album Buckley or you have Bee Gees when they sound like soggy shreaded wheat, which is sure okay.

[3] But typewriters don't have any either, and typewriters are fine.

[4] And man, look, there's the DRUMMER BUMMER: really listen to Ringo's "What Goes On" and then listen to Ginger's "Blue Condition," and who knows what will bubble through? Anyway, you got this drummer boy in each, accompanying his own mere vocal, and why bother saying it's not a bummer just 'cause it's a standard non-bummer guy with lots of apparent *ad hominem* pressure? 'Cause you wanna deal with it as *good?* Man, that's a drag. Why ignore the GRAND BUMMER just 'cause either bummers don't seem like moves any more, or they're too much of a move and you don't

is basically pre-Ringo, if you can imagine both of them in the archaeological scene.[5]

SWLABR: lots of Trini Lopez vocals by Jack Bruce. Sums up all that is or could be post-Balin. He accomplishes for a male vocalist, in "We're Going Wrong," what anything by Janis Joplin would do for a female, or something in that direction anyway.[6]

Only Duane Eddy or Bo Diddley could do a Dizzy Gillespie on guitar and Eric Clapton is—let's see, he's not either A or B, he's C: Clapton. So he can't be doin' the Diz. But he is doin' ———.

Waste is rest, and it's restful, not embarrassing, here, and it implies lack of education to the waste-labelers, a gimmick borrowed from jazz.

"Mother's Lament" suggests the Phil Spector studio intrusion on one of the early Righteous Brothers albums even more than it suggests "Naked If I Want To," or any other bell-ringers of that ilk.[7] Once upon a time, while it was playing, Memphis Sam donated the comment: " 'Strange Brew' is nice."

Cream goes for words about seven years old and 4.2 months ahead of time, implicating themselves in simultaneous necrophilia and prenatalophilia more obviously than do most with this combination as a necessity. "Got this thing, got to keep it sharp"[8] reminiscent of "Gettin' yer fork in the meat."[9] Words either folky

---

wanna do the old Aristotelian piss-on-Plato move? 'Cept now you can deal with the NON-NON-BUMMER. Man, you can be sure the innovative and non-misunderstanding bummer move is approaching fast, but regrettably not as fast as moves are getting played out. And some day soon Eric Burdon may accept the reemergence of Bobby Vee.

[5] In the archaeology cosmic framework, there is a basic BUMMER NEUTRALITY. So you can say all sorts of value-laden stuff about it, like it's good or bad, but with Cream here it doesn't matter before the fact rather than the other way, the way the Kinks pull it off.

[6] Ask yourself tonight: What is vocal summation?

[7] Whadda we do with all this "suggests" and "sounds like" stuff? Get it? Even when BUMMER OBSCURITY snaps out history as inadvertent unavoidable reference to obscurity has become tiresome even though it has.

[8] In "Take It Back."

[9] You useta hear it everywhere.

or Fuggy, so narrowly miss the NON-NON-NON-NON-NON-BUMMER RAP.

"Dance the Night Away" comes on like "Two Faces Have I" when that was fashionable and McGuinn when he was fashionable[10] plus an open window with snow mussin' around out there. No, it doesn't.

But this is mystery-book puberty, not physiological puberty, and one of those prostrate massages advertised in the L.A. Free Press would likely do a lot of harm to Cream.[11]

Thus I highly recommend Disraeli Gears (Atco 33-232).[12] Even more highly than the Strawberry Alarm Clock.

But hold on if you have to. That sure isn't enough data to make anybody go out into the cold to buy the album.[13] So here's more, okay? Sure.

Not even mere uniqueness, that is not even unique.

"Outside Woman Blues" is the[14]

"Sunshine of Your Love," right down to Clapton's "Blue Moon" reference pumice-like guitar plunkin', is hard-core RUBBER BAND MUSIC.[15]

"This tree is ugly and it wants to die" is part of the visual-literary bulk of the cover Zappa designed for Absolutely Free. He kept it visual-literary 'cause trees might just eat it as far as he was concerned or at least the concept of an ugly tree hit him only aesthetically or maybe it was all part of the nonspecific Polack joke

[10] Nice manifestation of the fact that the Byrds played out the whole Byrds thing on their own, destroying an entire prior eternity which can only return as a NON-NON-NON-NON-BUMMER MOVE.

[11] Although N.S.U. will for all time signify the bike, here there's a hint of non-specific urethritis.

[12] All in all, the best and possibly less than the best record to play in the distance while you're smoking it up in the bathroom and you walk out and everybody figures you took a shit or masturbated or something 'cause you took so long. Cream takes its time, too.

[13] And what the fuck is the function of the art critic if not precisely to get people to buy records?

[14] Very finest oo-hoo, just the very best.

[15] If you have a cold, go on: call it the RUBBER BUBBER, go ahead.

new-content generation thing.[16] Cream's "World of Pain" not only is tree-pitying, but it is *musical* as well.[17]

"Tales of Brave Ulysses" is the remaining unmentioned track.

[16] Well, at the very least he didn't mind exposing to ridicule and laughter the poor, wretched, death-oriented, repulsive TREE.

[17] Well, maybe Zappa didn't wanna *sing* about it, maybe he really felt bad for the tree and ya know he jus' was bitterly satirizin' tree-hate and insensitivity to tree-sufferin', and yeah, that's it, he just couldn't get it up to sing about the whole morbid business. Let's hope that's it and listen to Cream anyway.

[18] One of my favorite albums, the other being . . .

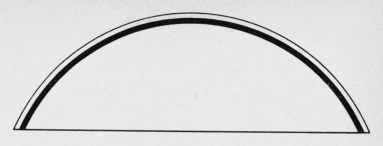

IGGY STOOGE—THE MAGIC TOUCH

Jackie Curtis talks with Ritta Redd after seeing
Iggy and the Stooges at Ungano's

J: What did you want to say about Iggy Stooge?

R: He wasn't there for the audience's benefit; the audience was there for his benefit, and he told them so. He commanded the audience exactly like the master would have done in an S and M situation.

J: That's gay.

R: I mean, he grabbed a little hippie girl and dragged her across the stage while she was still in her chair; he dragged her across the floor by her *face*, just waiting for her to respond. He wanted a reaction from *her* and of course he didn't get one, as she fled back to her place in the audience.

J: What do you mean he didn't get a response from her, "of course"?

R: She fled in terror, hon. And when the audience didn't come to Iggy, Iggy went to the audience, knocking plates down, glasses, standing on tables and telling people to get up, and if they didn't get up he pulled them up out of their seats, spilling drinks as well as girls' pocketbooks across the floor.

J: Did you see Geri Miller, superstar of *Flesh* and *Trash*, in the audience that night?

R: Yes.

J: How did she react?

R: She got up and left for a safe corner of the room away from the action. Maybe she won't like this—who cares? Well, that's what she did.

J: What else?

R: And then when he'd taken complete command of the audience, he turned his back on them. He then proceeded to carry on with his guitar player.

J: What do you think Iggy's trying to say?

R: At the end, he added insult to injury by proceeding to stand there for fifteen minutes while the people in the club just stared, their eyes were glued to Iggy. They were enthralled by his torso, his silver lamé gloves and his ripped jeans.

J: Do you think he is trying to say anything, then?

R: I really don't know.

J: How did his carrying on affect you?

R: It was like Andrea Warhol's *Showtime* at Max's. You know, when you see it for the first time, you flip out. It's fantastic, it's unreal, you just can't get over it. But I'd like to see the real conflict between Iggy and a person in the audience like, say, Andrea herself. I wanna be there because I think, even though Andrea is impossible to predict, I'm sure it would be a memorable occasion.

J: Well, what about other people in the audience? How do you think the male counterpart reacted?

R: Iggy was insulting their masculinity by throwing it in their faces, reminding them of the role they play. Of course, the world is full of masochists. I think Iggy's a great star.

J: Do you think Iggy's a masochist?

R: [Pause] Well, you really don't know what he's saying because he slaps himself in the face, but I think he does that for the audience's reaction because, you know, I think he isn't really slapping himself but really slapping them, and don't forget he's wearing those silver gloves and that's quite a different slap.

J: Was this the first time you saw Iggy performing *live*?

R: Yes. He hypnotized me, my dear—not only me, but the entire audience. One of the moods he conveys is through physical effort, and that connects his karma with that of the audience.

J: What do you mean, "karma," my dear?

R: Karma? Uh, the whole mood of the audience was either antagonized by him or, like, a lot of them I noticed they were rooting for him, egging him on. So there was a noticeable controversy, which instantly creates an interest in what happens at the moment. The only thing wrong with this, if you feel that way about it, is that you can't hear the words to any of the songs, but then who cares? All you really want to do is watch Iggy, anyway . . . and truthfully, that's why they sell the Stooges' records, because if you're into hearing words and all the side effects, you can listen to the albums later and get all that, but I feel that if you're really up to taking what Iggy's handing out then you're gonna flip out when you catch him, but I don't think anyone will catch him because after he stood in front of the audience doing nothing with the red light glistening across his rippling body, he walked off the stage and the audience roared, raved, screamed, stomped, yelled for "*Iggy! Iggy!*" to return for maybe an encore. Iggy never returned and I felt that people in the audience who had been singled out for abuse were the ones who really dug it the most.

J: Did he abuse you?

R: No. I was too far in the back, goddamnit. I was standing with Lee Childers, and he couldn't stop snapping pictures of Iggy's contorting and posing. You know, I kept saying, "Will you stop for a minute and just watch him?!"

J: What did you think of his appearance, his uniform?

R: Clothes are clothes.

J: What kind of personal vibrations did you get from him, if any?

R: More than the vibes it was pure energy—raw. The audience was turning on from his sheer force and that was a definite up.

J: Where do you think rock is going?

R: I think rock is gone. They're either going to have to find a new name for music today, or stop using names at all.

J: Why?

R: Because it's all really part of the changes going on in life-styles today, and Iggy's performance is proof of it.

J: What life-styles?

R: They're being developed as you're asking that. And besides, it's much too early to predict what they'll be called, and I think if anybody starts giving them names, new or old, it'll just destroy any progress. I feel within the next couple of years we're going to be hit with a barrage of new names that most people won't understand because that's what's wrong right now: half the world is going one way and the other half is headed right off a cliff because they're blinding themselves.

J: Which half?

R: Who knows? The only way to find that out is to wait and see who falls, who screams and what they find at the bottom.

J: What do you think Iggy would have done if the girl had responded to his advances?

R: Then we'll see what Iggy is really made of. I'd like to see how far a thing like this is going to go.

J: Did you think of his advances as sexual?

R: They were past the sexual point; they were insulting.

J: Do you think he was making an idiot out of that girl because he sensed that she wouldn't respond the way the audience might think she would, or the way one of them would have?

R: He had no way of knowing what that girl would do. He was taking a chance, too. He was making an idiot out of himself then, too.

J: What would you have done had Iggy grabbed you by the face and sang to you, "I'm gonna stick it right on in . . . I'm gonna stick it right on in. . . ?"

R: I don't know what I might have done, really.

J: Then Iggy seems to be safe if other people think the same way as you.

R: He's very safe. This is really dumb; I hate interviews. I don't see how people can sit around asking each other things like this. If people wanna go see it, they should go see it. What I think should have no bearing on what you think or what someone else might think.

J: Iggy seems to have confused you.

R: I think Iggy is confused himself.

J: What did you think when Iggy started dry-humping his guitar player [another male]?

R: It wasn't two males up there on stage; it was just sex. A love-making movement, simple pure and beautiful, without gender or hostility.

J: Do you feel Iggy's hostile at all?

R: No. He has tremendous, keen eyes that are adorable, and his half-man half-boy's anatomy makes him very lovable.

J: Iggy sat on a middle-aged man's lap that night, didn't he?

R: Yeah.

J: Did you notice the guy's reaction?

R: I don't think he really cared for it too much, but he was in a position where he really couldn't do too much about it.

J: Do you think Iggy is making a social comment, then?

R: Yes. Because everyone in that audience was there digging Iggy; whether or not they were open about it, they all had the same idea in their heads. Iggy parades around and struts himself about like the master rooster in a barnyard. He never once lost control of his subjects. Let's face it, there have always been cries in the night, cries of mutiny, and surely there are those who get uptight when they find out that they are after the same thing as the person next to them who they thought was beneath them, and this might make for a very political situation.

J: Does President Nixon convey this same amount of energy to his subjects? Does he have the same command that Iggy manages to instruct in a mere matter of an entrance?

R: Nixon doesn't have any energy at all.

J: Why did you say that Iggy has the magic touch?

R: He's putting an old number in a new light.

J: What do you mean?

R: He's taking what Elvis Presley did, giving you a taste of Mick Jagger . . .

J: None of Jim Morrison?

R: No, Jim Morrison is really gross. The only thing Jim Morrison is into is displaying his cock so that he can prove he still has one. When Iggy is on stage, there's never any question.

J: Then he *did* turn you on?

R: Are you kidding? Of course he turned me on. A masculine figure doing a masculine thing is attractive.

J: To whom?

R: To anyone.

INGEBORG GERDES

LINDA EASTMAN

MARY ELLEN MARK

IRVING GRUNBAUM

DICK WESTRAY

DENNIS MC GUIRE

LEE CHILDERS

DUSTIN PITMAN

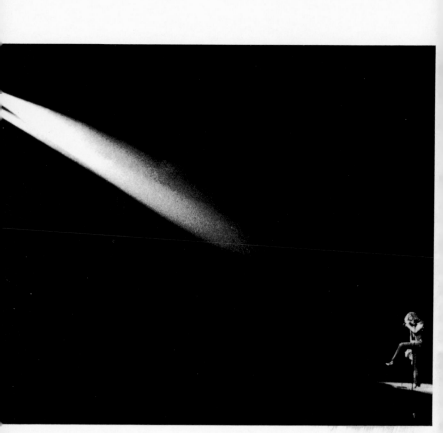

LOIS GREENFIELD

JIM ANDERSON/PRAXIS PHOTOS

J: Well, what about a feminine figure doing a feminine thing?

R: Femininity tends to be quiet and elusive. Masculinity is an open statement.

J: I'm sure there are Raquel Welch fans who would say the same thing about her character, and her character is a feminine one.

R: Raquel Welch? There isn't a feminine thing about her; she's a man.

J: But I got the feeling that Iggy was both masculine and feminine. You know, Yin and Yang.

R: Therefore, you get your new life-styles and these will incorporate that style, the masculine-feminine person. A conflict of opposites has always been extremely appealing, especially contained in one heaving body. I just hope Iggy isn't pushed into a category, because his type of individual with all that mystique and power should be allowed to go a step further and that would be something to see. Too many of our idols in the past have gone really only half of the way and that's unfair. It's fucking criminal to build someone up to bring everyone else down. I'd like to see someone stick to their guns, my dear, and Iggy's got a terrifically potent weapon there, if you catch my meaning.

J: Do you feel there are certain shades of limelight that can wreck a girl's complexion?

R: No. Absolutely not. A good complexion is a good complexion. The limelight can be any shade it happens to be, and you know, it's always been the connotations and meanings that the uptight portion of our society, as it were, has put on things. I really don't think a girl in the limelight cares what her complexion looks like. If she does then she's uptight too and, well, frankly, my dear, she's had it in any light—do you understand?

J: Do you think Iggy has "street appeal"?

R: He's got street appeal in *back*, honey. In fact, he's got some street appeal up front.

J: Who are your favorite rock 'n' roll performers?

R: John Hammond, the Stones are nice, Iggy and the Stooges, Ike and Tina Turner, and I love Buffy Saint-Marie.

J: You spoke about Iggy's touching the sexual revolution and imposing on the new life-style. Do you think that is because it takes one to know one?

R: If you think that being yourself is a new life-style, then I suppose I'm one, too. But it's hard to say that, sitting here talking to you.

J: We're getting away from the subject.

R: I know we are, Jackie, but one thing leads to another so easily these days.

J: For instance . . .

R: Well, for instance, the Gay Liberation Front. All it is, is the Establishment on a new level. What we really should practice is our individuality, instead of grouping together so that the Establishment has something stable to attack. That way they'd have to come and get us one at a time. That could take forever, honey. Movements like the GLF make it easy not only for the Establishment to ensnare a large group at a time, but also for people to latch onto somebody else's personality, instead of developing their own.

J: And you think Iggy has developed his own personality?

R: Definitely. And if the audiences would only hurry up and get their personalities together then they could enjoy Iggy. And then Iggy would dig the rest of us as well as himself.

Richard Meltzer

AT LEAST BO DIDDLEY'S
STILL ALIVE

There was a party for him, Eric Burdon and the Soft Machine.
They were supposed to come over from the airport by helicopter,
but there was too much fog or rain, so it took them a while 'cause
they hadda go by car. Eric Burdon missed the flight in the United
Kingdom. Instead, they had Eire Apparent, the producer of whom
entered the room shooting everybody with his brand-new super-8
camera, which Ken Greenberg later stole. It was an awesome party
entrance, and he was wearing a floral pants jacket and Ken Greenberg went on to steal his camera. *He* was Jimi Hendrix; that was
his name. I went up and shook his hand and asked him if he had
read my *Crawdaddy* piece. He said yup and he liked it and he had
a question for me. It was, Was I stoned when I wrote it? He
thought so. He was right and I told him so and I was not telling a
fib. This particular party was a boozer affair and we all got juiced
up so good that now I'm an alcoholic. Boozin' made it easy to talk
to Ernie Graham of Eire Apparent, and I axed him if the Zombies
were anything on the other side any more and he said they were
musically respected in England (his hometown) but he just
couldn't remember the D.C. Five or the Searchers or the Kinks.
Roni Hoffman and Dale Lewis got back from the bathroom after
smoking some hash, and me and them and Ken Greenberg left
and we got to the bottom of the escalator (just an escalator, so
there weren't any stairs) and Kenny took out the wonderful new
camera he had stole and gleamed his face off and said, "It's a
honey, isn't it?" We said, "Take that back right now or your name

is asshole," and he did not want to but he did just the same and that meant walking up the down escalator. Good thing for him it wasn't crowded or it would've been tough uphill sledding.

A hundred percent of the two best-dressed men at Monterey both up and died. They were, in alphabetical order, Brian and Jimi. Jack Casady once had a shirt with an illustration of a thinking wooden log suspended in midair; it was such a great shirt that the whole room applauded. But it was *absolutely nothing* compared to Jimi's jacket that he wore on the cover of *Are You Experienced?* That jacket had eyeballs (not real ones, but pictures of them) and each of the two eyeballs had *two entire enormous corneas!* (Or do you call them irises—but whatever you call them, they're the dark, round part of the eye.) Around his neck and on his shoulders he wore a feather boa and not a soul excepting Pamela Polland wore them before that (the jacket wasn't really a jacket, but it was a vest, and his shirt—probably a store-bought variety—showed from underneath by way of its sleeves which was just as good). No band before then except for the Beatles and that ilk had all hands with the same hair—all three of them had it and even the Four Seasons had different hair styles. All the same hair wasn't an easy move at all, way back then (it still isn't). You had to be a hedge clipper and none of them were but they succeeded anyway. Dylan and Tim Buckley were left on the wayside from then on.

He recorded the only decent version of "All Along the Watchtower," whose composer had been dead for well over a year when he himself gave it a try on that horrendous Columbia long-playing release. Procol Harum still hasn't done the only good version of "Let It Be"; it could very well be they never will. Once upon a time it mattered and Jimi was right on the spot when it did but it doesn't any more. But if it did, some of us ought to (yes, we should) freeze his body *just in case*, so he'll still be around when he happens to be needed. His coffin would be wheeled on stage for the Band of Gypsies or the J.H. Experience and his guitar lines would be played on tape and the rest of the band would follow. He played a New Year's Eve thing at the Fillmore East with the Gypsies, and he went on and wished everybody a happy new year, one and all. People the world over were in the midst of terrible parties in such places as Howard Beach and Thomastom and he was busy wishing everybody good cheer and they were unable to hear him because the PA just couldn't carry far enough (technology wasn't up to him), but if it only could it would've been too much!

As far as bands go he had to disband his band many times over. For musical reasons. Janis had to disband her band many times over too and it wasn't for musical reasons all the time and she didn't even have to all the time. Nobody could be a one-man band except for Skip Spence, so he needed guys to play with and Mitch Mitchell wasn't half bad. But as far as he goes, he was a "better guitarist than Donald," as Memphis Sam would say. As a matter of cold hard fact, when the Underbelly played City College (New York), a full long time after Jimi's first album, Don was just for the first time getting into "Third Stone from the Sun," Jimi's enormous big treat with just talking (no singing) and his guitar doing a lot of talking rather than singing once in a while but it sang too.

Way back in the forgotten pages of the rivers of time, somebody invented bottleneck guitar. But maybe 204 people did it independently and it eventually took off as a style and lots of busters did their own personal version of it. But what Jimi Hendrix did was the only original move on the famous stringed instrument that was done by only one guy, for sure. And he was the first man to do any moves on ax after Charley Bennett and Django Reinhardt. He was the first to do anything up to that point, in other words. Steve Miller was just another Autosalvage until Mr. Hendrix hit the scene. He hit it from merry old England, it was his mother country, he went back to die, it's where he died. But before that he lived there.

What did it, smack or pills? Maybe pills, and all artists need rest so they use them. Insomnia's hard to beat, so one leads to another and then another. Finally the sky's the limit. Here's what should be done: an alarm mechanism should be installed to let you know when it's getting to be too many. An even better idea is a lock that locks when the number is about to be exceeded. It would close up the bottle when the maximum safe number is reached, pills coming out one at a time. If you wanna take your own life, you have to really work at it, you have to buy more than one bottle or borrow somebody's. With one bottle yourself, you'd be safe as a babe in toyland. With this method, Jimi'd still be breathing earth air.

If it was smack instead of pills, then the size of your needle would be determined by your body weight. That way it's harder to get an overdose quantity into your veins and Jimi'd still be walkin' around that way, too.

Here's the way Bud Scoppa thought about doing this obit: interview the little lady who awoke one morning to find she'd been sleeping with a stiff. She says, "It was still very, very stiff but after ever so long there wasn't a climax, so I put two and two together and realized it was *rigor mortis* so I took it out of my mouth." You can joke about your Space Cowboys, but Jimi was the archetypal Space Cow, chewing on the cosmic cud. He was a Taurean (so were Plato, Kant and Archie) and not having a Jupiter in Virgo helped out a great deal in keeping him away from mere inertia. Did he ever eat in Ratner's? A lot of people did, and Rod Stewart was one of them, but did Jimi? How much bread did he eat and did it contribute to his good health? Same question for the soup.

There's a song playing right now and it's "I Don't Live Today." That's right, he doesn't. He did when he first sang it. Was anybody anywhere playing it on his turntable the very moment that *he died?* When he died was it one day or the next? Was it just one day? Was it part of one, part of another? Was it a night or was it a day? Where was it a night and where was it a day? Did he almost die any other time? Did it become increasingly almost until the very end or was it most almost before? Was he dreaming anything while he still could dream? Can he still dream now or at least a couple minutes after the big crossing-over? What was he dreaming? Forests? Trees? Bumblebees? Somebody? Someone? Who was dreaming about him?

Was anybody? Was his girl friend? Were his mom and dad? *Most likely, fewer than thirty-nine people in the world were dreaming about him when he died.* I'd give even money he was dreaming about less than thirty-nine people himself. *I* wasn't dreaming about him and he wasn't dreaming about me, but so what? Dreams are eternal and if you've dreamed one ever you've dreamed it forever. It's that simple. So you certainly were dreaming all about him while he lay there dying. Unless you never bothered dreaming about him in the first place. Then you probably never had yourself a dream about the Grape. Or the Beach Boys. Or the Doors. Or Arthur Alexander. Or your own buttocks. That's all you'd be worth, pricko. That's if you never dreamed about him.

Blind Lemon Jefferson had all the vocal moves in the book, but he played his guitar like a ukulele, now they're siftin' sand together and pickin' up a few tricks, and Jimi's younger unless there's a fountain of youth there so they're both young. Here's where immortality has no relationship to "memory" or "memorial" or any of that pud, if anybody was to dig on both Jimi and Blind Lemon exclusively it would be a super pretense move and thus ill-conceived enough to backfire for this particular universe. But if they ran into each other on the other side, it would be just two strangers wanderin' down the same road on the soul hierarchy, or some such guff. That's a grove-laden chance intersection for beyond space and time, just as it would be for within space and time, except it would be suspect over here for being merely appropriate.

So it's hasta la vista, amigo! See you in not too many years in that Electric Ladyland in the Sky. Brian's been gathering dust waiting for you to play lead in his heavenly band. Rhythm harp is nothing without somebody to play lead. His gain is already our loss, the third stone from the sun will never be the same without you. Say hello to Al Wilson for us!

STATEMENT FOR THE WHITE PANTHER ARM OF THE YOUTH INTERNATIONAL PARTY

First, I must say that this statement, like all statements, is bullshit without an active program to back it up. We have a program which is ongoing and total and which must not be confused with anything that is said or written about it. Our program is cultural revolution through a total assault on the culture, which makes use of every tool, every energy and every medium we can get our collective hands on. We take our program with us everywhere we go and use any means necessary to expose people to it. Our culture, our art, the music, newspapers, books, posters, our clothing, our homes, the way we talk and talk, the way our hair grows, the way we smoke dope and fuck and eat and sleep—it is all one message, and the message is FREEDOM . . . We are free mother-country madmen in charge of our own lives, and we are taking this freedom to the kids of America in the streets, in ballrooms and teen clubs, in their front rooms watching TV, in their bedrooms reading the *Fifth Estate* or the *Sun* or jerking off or smoking secret dope, in their schools where we come and talk to them or make our music in their weird gymnasiums. They love it. We represent the only contemporary life-style in America for its kids, and it should be known that these kids are *ready!* They're ready to *move* but they don't know how, and all we do is show them that they can get away with it. BE FREE, goddamnit, and fuck all them old dudes, is what we tell them, and they can see that we mean it. The only influence we have, the only thing that touches them is that we are for real. We are FREE; we are a bunch of arrogant motherfuckers and we don't give a damn for any cop or any kind of phony-ass authority control-addict creep who wants to put us down. I heard Stokely Carmichael in 1966 call for "twenty million arrogant black men" as America's salvation, and there are a lot of arrogant black motherfuckers in the streets today—for the first time in America. And for the first time in America there is a generation of visionary maniac white mother- country dope-fiend rock-and-roll freaks who are ready to get down and kick out the jams, all the jams, break everything loose and free everybody from their very real and imaginary prisons—even the chumps and punks and honkies who are always fucking with us. We demand total freedom for everybody! And we will not be stopped until we get it. We are bad. We will not be fucked with. Like Hassan I Sabbah, the Old Man of the Mountain, we initiate no hostile moves, but when moved against we will mobilize our forces for a total assault. We have been moved against every day of our lives in this weirdo country, and we are moving now to over- turn this motherfucker, scrape the shit off it and turn it back over to all the people. All power to the people! Black power to black people! As Brother Eldridge Cleaver says, the shit is going down and there are only two kinds of people on the planet: those who make up the problem, and those who make up the solution. WE ARE THE SOLUTION. We have no "problems." Everything is free for everybody. Money sucks. Leaders suck. Underwear sucks. School sucks. The white honky culture that has been handed us on a silver plastic platter is meaningless to us! We don't want it! Fuck God in the ass. Fuck your woman until she can't stand up. Fuck everybody you can get your hands on. Our program of rock and roll, dope and fucking in the streets is a program of total freedom for everyone. And we are totally committed to carrying out our program. We breathe revolution. We are LSD-driven total maniacs in the universe. We will do anything we can to drive people crazy out of their heads and into their bodies. Rock-and-roll music is the spearhead of our attack because it's so effective and so much fun. We have developed organic high-energy guerrilla bands that are infiltrating the popular culture and destroying millions of minds in the process. The MC5 is the most beautiful example.

The MC5 is totally committed to the revolution. With our music and our economic genius, we plunder the unsuspecting straight world for money and the means to carry out our program and revolutionize its children at the same time. And with our entrance into the straight media, we have demonstrated to the honkies that anything they do to fuck with us will be exposed to their children. You don't need to get rid of all the honkies, you just rob them of their replacements and let the breed atrophy and die out, with its heirs cheering triumphantly all around it. We don't have guns yet—not all of us, anyway—because we have more powerful weapons: direct access to millions of teen-agers is one of our most potent, and their belief in us is another. But we will use guns if we have to—we will do anything if we have to. We have no illusions. Knowing the power of symbols in the abstract world of Americans, we have taken the White Panther as our mark to symbolize our strength and arrogance and to demonstrate our commitment to the program of the Black Panther Party as well as to our own— indeed, the two programs are the same. The actions of the Black Panthers in America have inspired us and given us strength, as has the music of black America, and we are moving to reflect that strength in our daily activity, just as our music contains and extends the power and feeling of the black magic music that originally informed our bodies and told us that we could be free. I might mention Brother James Brown in this connection, as well as John Coltrane and Archie Shepp. Sun-Ra. LeRoi Jones. Malcolm X. Huey P. Newton. Bobby Seale. Eldridge Cleaver. These are magic names to us. These are men in America. And we're as crazy as they are, and as pure. We're bad. This is our program:

1. Full endorsement and support of the Black Panther Party's Ten-Point Program

2. Total assault on the culture by any means necessary, including rock and roll, dope and fucking in the streets

3. Free exchange of energy and materials—we demand the end of money!

4. Free food, clothes, housing, dope, music, bodies, medical care—everything free for everybody

5. Free access to information media—free the technology from the greed creeps!

6. Free time and space for all humans—dissolve all unnatural boundaries

7. Free all schools and all structures from corporate rule—turn the buildings over to the people at once!

8. Free all prisoners everywhere—they are our brothers

9. Free all soldiers at once—no more conscripted armies

10. Free the people from their "leaders"—leaders suck. All power to all the people—freedom means free everyone!

MIKE CURB INTERVIEWED AT LAST

Many people on the rock scene were aroused by the announce-
ment made last week by MGM Records' twenty-four-year-old
president Mike Curb that the label had bumped eighteen acts for
"promoting and glorifying hard drugs." I taped an interview over
the phone with Curb for WABC-FM. Here is a slightly shortened
version of that tape—without changing the meaning, I just cut out
some superfluous and repetitive remarks.

H.S.:   You must be in quite a turmoil.

M.C.:   It's unbelievable.

H.S.:   Did you think you were going to have such a reaction?

M.C.:   No, I didn't.

H.S.:   In the information that was printed in the trade press, it
said you were getting out of your contracts with eighteen
different rock groups. The grounds you gave were that you felt
those groups in their music and lyrics promoted the use of
drugs. Can you name the eighteen groups?

M.C.: Well, we definitely can't do that, from a legal standpoint.
Definitely not.

H.S.:   Are you going to be open to lawsuits anyway, once everybody figures out which groups they are?

M.C.:   MGM Records was in a tremendous loss position in 1969.

We've had over fifty artists dropped from the label over the year.

H.S.: So what you're saying is that for a group to sue you they would have to prove they were one of those eighteen groups?

M.C.: Right, they would have to prove that we had accused them of being on drugs.

H.S.: But in the article I read—I believe it was in *Billboard*—it said you had used the morals clause in their contracts to get out of their contracts. Is that correct?

M.C.: Not necessarily. I would prefer not to make comments on that particular phase of it, I think that it is very unimportant. What is important is that we are making every attempt possible as a record company to not exploit drug-oriented lyrics. By that I mean a lyric that in any way condones or glorifies the use of drugs.

H.S.: Any kind of drugs? Do you differentiate between soft and hard drugs?

M.C.: We do not differentiate.

H.S.: You feel that any song about pot, for instance, would come under what you consider "promoting the use of drugs."

M.C.: I'll leave the drug definition up to the individual. In our company here we don't have a standard; we make a decision based on listening to the record—whether this would influence any non-drug user to use drugs.

H.S.: Okay, I can see it if there's a song that literally says, "smoke pot." But what about a song that just talks about it—it doesn't encourage it, it doesn't discourage it, it's just a commentary on the times.

M.C.: I'm certain that we would never try to stop social commentary, no matter what they were talking about. We're talking about glorifying a drug experience on records, as a number of groups do today, so as to make it attractive to a non-user. Basically, it's a sound business decision, because let's face it, the groups that are associated with hard drugs, and I'm sure you know who they are, are very undependable—they are difficult to work with, and they're hard on your sales and marketing people.

H.S.: I don't know any groups that promote the use of hard drugs, and I listen to a lot of music. Or do you mean groups who themselves are on hard drugs?

M.C.: I wonder if a group that is on hard drugs doesn't in effect exploit or to a certain degree glorify the usage. I wonder if a person who is a fan of a hard drug group isn't going to tend to be turned on by that drug. I'd like to be totally uninvolved with any form of drug-oriented rock music, and I believe our label can succeed without it.

H.S.: What I'm curious about, though, is the difference I have in my mind between soft and hard drugs. Are any of the eighteen groups you dropped just in the area of pot—I mean, maybe they glorify being high from smoking.

M.C.: For the most part, the groups we severed our relationships with were dealing with hard drugs.

H.S.: But glorifying it?

M.C.: To my mind, they were glorifying a hard-drug experience. I could be wrong, but in our opinion, and in the opinion of our marketing and sales people, I can say that we were exploiting hard drugs by selling this product.

H.S.: Do you feel this is going to hurt you in terms of sales?

M.C.: No, because we're going to devote more time to the substantial acts on our label, who are going to be around three to five years from now.

H.S.: I heard a rumor that this means MGM is going very middle-of-the-road music.

M.C.: That's not the case, although I believe that the middle-of-the-road music, properly recorded, will be much more important in the next few years than it currently is today.

H.S.: Were any of these eighteen groups that were dropped for promoting and glorifying drugs big-selling groups?

M.C.: Some were marginal; some were very profitable to the company.

H.S.: Because the thing that sounds so odd to me about the whole thing is that generally people in the position of putting out art, such as record companies and book publishers, are usually fending off people from the outside, people who are trying to censor things—it almost sounds like a book publisher burning his own books.

M.C.: That's not the case.

H.S.: That's the feeling I got from it. But also you are going to go further than this, from what I understand. You are going to try to convince radio stations not to play this kind of music, not just from your label, but from other labels. Is that right?

M.C.: Based on the response we've had to the campaign, large number of top radio programmers in the country are quite pleased about it. This could be of great value in straightening their relationships out with the FCC. The FCC is very concerned about drug lyrics. You are aware of the conference they had lately.

H.S.: Yes, definitely, but your move sounds just like you played into their hands.

M.C.: Those are the kinds of hands I would like to play into. The point I'm making is that I'd like to be sure that our organization is not selling drug lyrics.

H.S.: Was this in direct response to Agnew's speech about such lyrics?

M.C.: No, it wasn't.

H.S.: When did you get the idea to do this—based on what inspiration? Were you just sitting around listening to some of the groups and suddenly thought, "My God, that song glorifies heroin"—or something?

M.C.: No, I think it was in response to radio programmers who have statistical facts available to them that a number of young people have first started using drugs based on the direction that they thought was being given to them by one of their favorite recording artists.

H.S.: Even though almost every major group has come out against hard drugs in print? I can't recall any instance of a major performer saying that heroin was good, and that people should take it.

M.C.: Then we have no problem.

H.S.: What you're saying is that if it's in their music, it doesn't matter if they deny it publicly.

M.C.: Basically, it doesn't take much to shoot holes in this kind of thing. The point is that we're doing everything we can to do our part. It's been blown out of proportion.

H.S.: The reason why your move to do this has attracted so much attention is that this kind of pressure usually comes from governmental bodies like the FCC and some radio chains. I've never heard of the president of a record company deciding that—it was a kind of a precedent. And this could possibly follow through to something else. I don't know if this is just my paranoia, but I want to hear your opinion on it. What if certain groups that record for MGM have songs you might feel are against the administration, especially their policy in Vietnam. There have been a lot of political songs done—let's say that becomes an issue. Would you get rid of any groups that were "anti" the present administration in Washington?

M.C.: Well, first of all, we don't have any groups like that on the label, so we wouldn't have that problem.

H.S.: Well, you have Eric Burdon. What if he recorded a record like that?

M.C.: I'd just have to consider it at the time. I don't think I could make a decision right on the spot.

H.S.: But does that put you similarly uptight? Could you imagine not wanting to put that out?

M.C.: Yes, it could, as a matter of fact—but I'd have to hear it and see.

H.S.: You have a bunch of country groups on MGM. A lot of country music is involved with liquor and sex—a lot of their lyrics talk about cheating on your husband, on your wife, what it's like being drunk. Are you going to crack down on that?

M.C.: Liquor is not illegal.

H.S.: It is in a lot of places in the South.

M.C.: I've got to go to a meeting—is there another question about the drug situation?

H.S.: One more thing. Did you discuss this type of thing with the various groups and their managers before bouncing them from the label—such as, you can stay with our label if you want, but no more of these kind of songs.

M.C.: Yes, I did.

H.S.: Did any groups accept?

M.C.: Yes, they did.

H.S.: Did you discuss it with all the eighteen groups that were bounced?

M.C.: Yes, I did.

H.S.: And they all refused.

M.C.: Yes, they did.

TELE•POT•ATION

The ultimate in "dope smuggling" has finally become a reality. Dope is being brought into this country without risk of customs inspectors or narcotics agents: it is being brought in, regularly, by teleportation.

The dope in this case is hashish, and it is being sent over from Europe and the Middle East, through the powers of Yogi S————.

Yogi S———— was approached by some of his friends several years ago in his home city in India. These young men had had occasion to discover the yogi's metaphysical powers, and they asked if he would help them bring ganja or charas to the United States. At the time, he refused and gave no reason. Then, more recently, his friends approached him again. They told him about Operations Intercept and Cooperation, and the increasing demand for good cannabis in the United States by religious-minded people. They also explained to him that many very young teen-agers were using narcotics and dangerous drugs because they were unable to obtain cannabis readily.

The yogi looked over the situation, investigated the results of the enforcement operations on the Mexican border, and finally agreed that something had to be done. He tried to help the young men find some alternative to using his powers, but none that was acceptable could be agreed upon. So as a last resort, the yogi agreed to help the young people send hashish into the country to aid the many religious seekers here.

The mechanics are fairly simple: the dope is set on a table in a room in a small villa somewhere in Europe, and all but the yogi leave the room. Several minutes later, the yogi opens the door. The hash is no longer on the table—it has moved to a tabletop in an empty room in America.

The team works out of a country in Europe where hash smuggled from the Near and Middle East may be obtained at a fairly good price, and their friends in America operate a tight distribution network composed of their friends, all of them stoned freaks who can smell the heat a mile off. At times, it is not possible to obtain good-quality hash at the right price at their base city, and on a very few occasions two members of the group have gone to North Africa with the yogi and "shipped" it directly from there. However, the yogi prefers to stay in Europe, for undisclosed reasons, and will only make the trip to Africa when there is a great need to be filled.

In order to make the project work, the yogi receives no compensation for his work; he lives in the rented villa with his friends and works part-time at a local job to earn money for his few needs.

Approximately once a week, at a designated time, the American dealers are sitting around their apartment in an East Coast city. One of their members, the most "psychic," prepares the back room, adjusts the table, closes the door and goes back into the living room with his friends. They get high and sit around in meditation. An hour later they unlock the door to the back room and weigh out the hash and prepare to distribute it via close friends.

THE REAL DON STEELE

Don Steele is the number one disk jockey on L.A. top-40 radio. He has the afternoon slot on KHJ radio, which is the number one top-40 radio station. He is unmarried and his age is always seventeen. He has been with KHJ since 1965, when the station first went top-40 and knocked KRLA from the top spot. I met him first in the spring of that year, when I was a teen idol. We were photographed together on the set of *Hollywood A Go Go*, a syndicated rock 'n' roll show, with our arms around each other's shoulders. Since then I have not seen Don Steele, but I have heard him—wedged between commercials and records. I interviewed him in Nickodell's Bar, just around the corner from the KHJ studios on Melrose Avenue, between the old RKO lot and Paramount. Don had just come off his afternoon shift and we were drinking bourbons. He has hawk-like features, quite a bit of early-Beatle hair and shades.

IAN: How would you describe your thing?

DON: It's hard to verbalize. I'm a hard-sell announcer.

IAN: I know, it's obviously very hard to answer. I ask you that because talking to Ted just now [Ted is the program director], he said that KHJ may sound very improvised, but they're very aware of every detail. I was listening to your catch phrases, which were very good, but I didn't know what they meant. I thought, "Does Don prepare these?"

DON: I have a phonetic hang-up. Maybe why I'm liked is because I'm funny, but what makes me funny is not that I'm telling a joke per se. I dig sound. You don't have to know what they mean—preferably, if it has not a double meaning, but a quadruple meaning.

IAN: Can you give us an example?

DON: "It ain't that bad if you fry it right." I actually did hear it. I was sitting in a bar near some fellows and they were talking about catfish or something. He was the typical beer-drinking, scratching hard-hat and he said, "It ain't that bad if you fry it right." And I said, "Hey, I like that!"

IAN: Do they ever actually mean anything, though?

DON: I think it sounds go!

IAN: No, but what does it mean?

DON: I think it means a lot of things. How about *life?* How about having to *eat shit?* Having to *pay your dues?*

IAN: I see. Can you think of any more?

DON: Wait a minute . . . "If you got it—flaunt it!" And I use these for my IDs. The format requires you must give the time and I came up with "It ain't that bad if you fry it" at three-thirty, and "If you got it—flaunt it" at four o'clock. You know—"Spread your love at five-thirty."

IAN: [Excited] What you're doing is another art form! An oral art form, which is impossible to put down in words!

DON: [Warming to the theme] "Take that piece of meat, put it in your pan, and fry it, baby!" Now you tell me what that means!

IAN: Do you ever get trouble from the station authorities?

DON: No, because I'm a pro.

IAN: Do you ever feel repressed on the air? Would you like to express your opinion on world problems?

DON: [Very excited] No feckin' way! I think I'm still coming on as a human being. I like a little magic; I like a little show biz. The majority listening to me on radio—they don't see me. They just hear a zooooow coming at them out of that radio. There surely is a term for it—a "spoonerism" or something.

IAN: Could it be "aphorism"—a wise saying?

DON: O.K. . . . I said, once, on the air, after one of my IDs, "Hey, that's a spoonerism," after I'd been a bit disoriented and I was jerking along and I knew I had about eight more measures to do. So I said, "Wait, now wait! That's not a spoonerism." And I described what a spoonerism is: when you take something, turn it around and do it backwards. I said that at approximately three o'clock. At five-thirty-five some housewife with two children had been driving all the way since my remark to say that I was a dirty man. And I didn't even intend to be dirty, because I could get much dirtier, you know. With much more finesse.

IAN: I know you're a pro. I can hear you're a pro. I've known that for years. But still, it must be quite hard to keep that hard sell going.

DON: I feel I have done a day's work after only three hours on the air.

IAN: What do you do afterwards?

DON: I come in here, have a drink and come down.

IAN: So what sort of things do you do?

DON: I like girls.

IAN: You have the image of being a high-speed bang bang bang screamer disk jockey. Is that really you? Is that your personality?

DON: Yeah.

IAN: But that isn't the you I see now, Don. The you I see now is rather shy, in a very nice way—almost retiring . . .

DON: I'm afraid of your tape recorder. [He gives the mike to a passing director/producer] Tell it like it is . . .

IAN: Do you see what I'm getting at? I see a different person . . . I . . .

DON: Look, man! You're not singing—does that mean you're different now? Course, yeah, you're different—but you're not *fake*.

IAN: When *did* you start?

DON: Man, I don't even remember.

IAN: About ten years ago?

DON: I think about five years, in front of here [KHJ].

IAN: Where d'you come from?

DON: Here. Born and raised about two and a half miles from here.

IAN: And Don Steele's your real name?

DON: It is my real name.

IAN: Why are you called the "*real* Don Steele?"

DON: That's a radio story. In Omaha—working there as Don Steele—"Be aware, I'll be there" [he sings]. So, I'd been there pushing a year, which is a *looooong*, motherfuckin' time to be in Omaha, Nebraska, my friend.

IAN: I have toured there.

DON: A nice place to fly over. The program director—I'd like another of those: a tall Cutty and water—he called me up. By this time I'm totally disgusted; I want to get out of this goddamn town, was drugged with the station, drugged with the management, drugged with the city. By this time it had gotten to me. The P.D. calls up and says, "Why don't you call yourself the "*real* Don Steele?" I looked at the receiver and I thought, "You rotten, stupid, son-of-a-bitch, asshole motherfucker." He wasn't asking me if I *wanted* to call myself that. But I thought: "Right, I'll take your dumb order, you dummy!" Well, all of a sudden people on the street no longer called me "Bob Steele" [the B-picture Western star]. They called me "The REAL DON STEELE." A phonetic thing—people react to certain words.

IAN: Why did they like this phrase?

DON: Tell me why they liked "Tiny Delgado is ALIVE, ALIVE!!" [He singsongs the last two words, throwing his head back in the darkened bar, making the words have a Swiss valley dying fall]. I used that in Portland, Oregon, and soon it was all over town like "Kilroy was here." Dumb thing. I don't have any idea why. I knew it was a hit; I could feel it was a hit.

IAN: Have you ever thought about these things? About *why*? It's a sort of subculture, isn't it?

DON: [Over the last sentence and rightly so] I don't know if "Roberta Delgado is alive, alive" would have been as heavy. I just don't know.

IAN: D'you ever think, "Am I caught up in some kind of insanity?"

DON: [Tee-heeing in agreement] Oh, yeah! But it doesn't depress me, because I kind of enjoy it, you know, sitting there suddenly saying, "If it ain't that bad, fry it," looking through a glass and there is an engineer in his early forties—valley community, Little-League baseball coach, Mr. Legitimate—cuing in noises that'll go "woweee" rather than "chooo." And I think to myself: "What is this? A world situation like this and we're in here giggling like *did dad doo!*"

IAN: But Ted [the program director] told me tonight that he made sure his disk jockeys were politically aware of the Middle East situation. I asked him how they got this across on the air. What about all this giggling, then?

DON: But I don't feel ashamed of that. What a wonderful thing to have fun working! Not many people get that break.

IAN: You don't feel you'd like to be able to say what you feel about Ronald Reagan, the street scene, the campuses?

DON: Yes, I do. But then I think: "What can I say that hasn't already been said?"

IAN: Have you ever had the desire to write? Books?

DON: I've always thought it would be nice if I could write, if I had a flair for writing. But I don't . . .

IAN: Do you look upon the printed word with respect?

DON: Of course! And the printed word will always be there, because that's permanent. You can get aesthetic, but I look at it commercially: that's why advertisers prefer buying newspaper space—although radio time makes them more money—because they can hold it in their hands, whereas a radio spot is gone. You can keep your newspaper ad in your wallet and show your wife. Your name is spelled right.

IAN: Do you ever feel you'd like to be more permanent, too?

DON: [Jokingly] That's why I'm talking to you—so's you'll put my name in your book.

IAN: I will, I will . . .

DON: I don't know what you're going to do to me with this tape . . . but . . .

IAN: [Splutters some incomprehensible words.]

DON: I'll be very honest with you—and, hopefully, you will not destroy me . . .

IAN: [Clearer] . . . no intention . . . doing that . . .

DON: This is what print does. I like it, but it's so scary. What you say—sometimes—in print is *totally different*. Totally.

IAN: Has this happened to you?

DON: Many times. That's why I don't do interviews if the guy's . . .

IAN: But you're not frightened of me, are you?

DON: A little bit. Things change from audio to print; entire meanings change.

IAN: Do you look upon print as a higher form?

DON: Depends on who's the printer and who's the audio-er.

IAN: Do you read books at all?

DON: Very little, which is nothing I'm proud of.

IAN: Have you been to college?

DON: Four weeks at U.S.C. [University of Southern California—a private one].

IAN: What course?

DON: Are you ready? Journalism.

IAN: Why did you leave?

DON: I wouldn't have proved anything. The journalism course trains you for absolutely nothing.

IAN: Have you got any outside interests?

DON: None, unfortunately.

IAN: Fishing, perhaps?

DON: None.

IAN: Collect stamps?

DON: No, no, no. I guess I'm pretty shallow.

IAN: Oh, I don't know about that!

DON: [He speaks very slowly] You see, it's so hard to make it. I really think that my life is getting more narrow all the time. But my cop-out is that I couldn't allow any *side thing* because I had to be number one. I want a drink. . . . Give this man a . . . Are you set?

IAN: [To waiter] Could I have a shot of rye whiskey, in a glass?

DON: Take care. I had this fixation, or hangup—and I made it. But in doing so, I had to build up this armor. I'm thinking about gittin' where I'm gittin', gittin' where I'm gittin', gittin' where I'm gittin'. Now I'm looking back and I'm seeing what I've done to myself.

IAN: And what have you done to yourself?

DON: I'm like one little laser beam, cutting through a lot of shit. I'm very good at what I do. I am a specialist. I've honed it and polished it and soon I'll be out of it, like a moonshot man without moonshots.

IAN: Did you lose many friends on the way?

DON: No, but I didn't *make* any.

IAN: Do you have a lot of close friends?

DON: No. Do you?

IAN: A few. More than when I was a hot pop star.

DON: I got a guy I went to high school with, who's a cop, of all things.

IAN: You think it strange that you should know a cop?

DON: Yeah. Not only is he a cop, but he's one of the real heavy-weight narcotic agents. A very close friend—I can depend on him, no strings attached.

IAN: [As fresh drinks arrive] Cheers!

DON: Yes. Do it. Morgan [Robert W. Morgan, a fellow disk jockey on KHJ] is a friend because we grew up together in our careers. And I grew up with this cop in our youth. I worked with Morgan—we helped each other—for seven years, which is a super-long time in radio . . . like twenty-five years with the telephone company.

IAN: Have you looked into the future?

DON: I want to be successful. I've had to be narrow like that laser beam, but at least I can be giggly . . . unlike the people I grew up with. They're old. Now, I don't want to be a perennial youth freak but . . .

IAN: How old are you?

DON: I'm seventeen, baby, forever! I see them working there and, well, I'm glad I dropped out of college.

IAN: You wouldn't have liked to have a regular job? Wife and kids and settle down?

DON: I don't think I could have handled it. When I got out of the service there were two things open to me: I'd either rob banks or be a radio announcer.

IAN: Seriously?

DON: I'm talking seriously. I thought, "The work's easy—no sweat." I didn't know then how hard it is, how dedicated you have to be. But I'm glad I did it.

IAN: You might have been a "wild one?"

DON: Not a wild one. I wasn't gonna run around with machine guns. I wanted the easy money . . . easy [He stretches the word, through closed teeth], easy, baby. But now—it's the job, not the money.

IAN: Are you politically aligned? Are you left wing or right wing?

DON: I will tell you honestly: I am *for* things that are good for me, and *against* things that are bad for me.

IAN: So you're for yourself?

DON: See what I mean about print? That looks terrible. I'm not really that.

IAN: Perhaps you could put it some other way.

DON: I wish I could give some glib answer here, but . . . I usually . . . I . . . this is where I usually get fucked in interviews.

IAN: I get the impression you're very wary of the press, that you've been distorted by them. Why did you agree to this interview?

DON: You've got a little entertainment background. I figured you would understand what I'd try to say—unlike some guy who's had a journalism course and is going to report "the facts." I was totally destroyed by the *Herald-Examiner*. I wasn't that bad; I was just saying "I'm the best." I said I was the highest paid—in *this* tone of voice [quite normal and casual, but not flippant]. All right, here comes the spread. They got a picture of me looking like Hitler, very cocky, and a quote under the picture: "*I'm the highest-rated disk jockey in the city, bar none!*" You know, "bar none" isn't an expression I use. Made me look like Mr. Ego-Maniac . . . which I am, but not really. But the average journalist wants to *zing* me. They want a *story*. They come prepared to make me out as the trite, plastic music-machine . . . I say to them, "Be kind!"

IAN: Don't you think you're part of a machine?

DON: What's new? But the writers of these pieces are using me to get a hit, to get their ratings up.

IAN: Well, I suppose I'm using you, too! Do you ever get a desire to retire, to get out and into the countryside?

DON: I got that feeling this afternoon at about two o'clock. However, I'm driving a ten-thousand-dollar car, and I've got a wardrobe of dynamite suits. So I said, "Wait a minute!"

IAN: Where d'you go on your holidays?

DON: Vacation? Vegas.

IAN: Not the mountains?

DON: I'm thinking about it. But I get relaxation with *action!* I can watch other people perform, see them do their number, and relax. I went to Hawaii once—but never again. That's the place you're supposed to go to relax, right? I was on every island, stayed at the top hotels. I even stayed at the top *huts*—real remoters. All of a sudden, I'm sitting there in this top hut on this island, with a fistful of American twenty-dollar bills. It's six o'clock and *there ain't no fuckin' room service!* What good is this money? How can I be an Ugly American? The only way to see Hawaii would be to fall in love with a stunning broad, get married, jump on the plane and go there that night. Once you've seen the white sand and the water . . . I can't get that much involved with conch shells, and plastic pigs that they bury for the luau. After seeing every island, I was so glad to get back to Waikiki because at least they had a twenty-four-hour-a-day coffee shop.

IAN: You've no desire to get *back to the land,* as it were?

DON: I wouldn't mind a big estate with guards. With some trees and shit.

IAN: Ever want to go to England?

DON: I'd like to, but I haven't got the time because I'm trying to be number one. I may get there sometime, unless I "O.D." on nerves, or whatever . . .

IAN: Well, I've asked all my questions so . . .

DON: What are you going to do with this? [kindly tone]

IAN: I don't want to do anything with it. Maybe it's just too private. You see, I didn't like being a hot pop teen property either. I really wanted to make sure I didn't sell my soul. So I chickened out and went back to college. [Don nods in agreement throughout this speech.]

DON: So you know what it's like. I had to be stone-soul dedicated to getting to number one, but I think I *kept* myself.

IAN: For instance?

DON: Well, I've been working in some small market (the listening area covered by the radio station beam). I've been told, "You will do a remote—outside broadcast—for the So-and-so Tire Company, standing with bunny ears on your head because it's Easter." I've been on the Bowlathon—forty-eight-hour bowling sessions.

IAN: Why do people like that?

DON: I think the Romans had it together; they put on a hell of a show. Same thing.

IAN: Well, I could never understand why the public bought my "You Turn Me On" hit song, because I thought it was rubbish. But I had to sing it, just as you had to wear your bunny ears at Easter.

DON: I once had to wear an Uncle Sam suit. D'you remember when that was in, when the flag was together? [light chuckle] If I sat in an Uncle Sam suit now I'd blow all my young kid audience.

IAN: When did this suit affair happen?

DON: Seven years ago, in Portland, Oregon. During the election—I don't even know who was running—I decided to run for President. I sat on a bridge called "The Steele Bridge," in the rain, with my mike, saying I had the strongest platform of all—so strong you could drive a car over it. People honking at me and saying, "Hi." I'm saying to myself, "Is this insanity?" But is it more insane than some poor son of a bitch who works his nine hours, comes home and gets into his wash-and-wear apartment, talks to his Perma-Press old lady about visiting the Grand Canyon because he saw it on a cigarette ad on TV? Fuck that shit! I'm going up, up, up, and if I don't I'm gonna go down, down, down—but I'm going down in fuckin' flames with all guns shootin'. I wanted magic: either robbing a bank or . . . That other life doesn't interest me. Yet, looking back now I see that my thing is just as nine-to-five as theirs. But at least I don't have to look forward to a vacation. Everybody else plans their entire year around the cities they're going to hit with their camper.

IAN: Were you brought up in a middle-class home?

DON: My mother was a band booker and pianist. She used to take me on gigs—me and Judy Garland. My dad was a truckdriver. I used to play trumpet, but I was never that good. I had it here [he points to his stomach]—but I couldn't get it through my ax. I didn't want to play third trumpet all the time. I wanted to be number one—whatever ego-hangups that shows, I'm not afraid to say it.

IAN: There's nothing to be ashamed of. That's what drives me, too.

DON: Thank you. I've never seen more people rank disk jockeys than journalists.

IAN: I agree. But that's because they're unhappy because they're not writers; they're not in hardbound books.

DON: Right! I like the way you put that.

IAN: You know, I'm just as much of an egotist as you. I mean, it really bugs me that my record "You Turn Me On" isn't on your "oldies but goodies" list at KHJ. It's not your fault, of course . . . I want to kill all those buggers who are on the hit parade right now. You know, I have to go out and interview them for my book on pop—and be nice, polite, when all the while I'm thinking, "You untalented shit!" But right after I've done this book I'll get back into that scrum and beat them all! And I'm in a terrible position right now, as a fallen star.

DON: Right! What I'm going to have on my gravestone is this: "EGO IS NOT A FOUR-LETTER WORD."

IAN: And we're not harming anyone, are we? And yet, I don't really want to print this interview because I don't want to use you . . .

DON: You want to be number one. You want to have a hit.

IAN: Yes, but . . . you know, I'm covering the Manson trial tomorrow, and I feel guilty about using him, and all those killings . . .

DON: [Pause] I'm very glad you interviewed me because we had a chance to talk things over.

IAN: Was it like your other interviews?

DON: No. They never tap-danced.

IAN: I think you use art to say forbidden words. I think you get through; you're not part of that machine. But maybe you could say more on FM listener-sponsored radio? No. There aren't enough listeners. Well, I must go because I was supposed to be somewhere at eight P.M. and it's now twenty to nine. Good-by.

DON: Good-by, Ian. Be kind.

Daphne Davis

THE COP OF THE YEAR

This interview with Devon was done in Jimi Hendrix's apartment shortly after the Stones' United States tour. Part of it was published in *Rags*, June 1970, with the following introduction:

> How do you get Mick Jagger, when you're already living with Jimi Hendrix? Or as one green-eyed groupie put it, after Devon walked off with the cop of the year, "Mick usually goes for those scrawny blonde English birds. A lot of people didn't think Devon could cut it." Sitting in Jimi's West Village apartment, she was more than happy to share her experiences. Hendrix's place is decorated in contemporary Casbah, with Oriental rugs, canopied couches, tapestries, brass hookahs. It's moon over Marrakech as jasmine incense floats through soft blue lighting. Devon, Jimi and Colette (a beautiful Moroccan friend of Devon's and Jimi's personal couturière) are spending a normal afternoon at home. The ultimate rock *ménage à trois*: star musician/star groupie/star designer. Jimi is hanging around, unsure of whether he's wanted, maybe a little jealous that Devon is being interviewed. The doorbell rings. The groceries. Devon tells Colette to unload them and she disappears. Jimi splits to the bedroom. Posed on harem pillows in an Ossie Clark hostess gown, Devon's movie starts to roll.

How did you meet Mick?
Mick had my number. He got it from a friend and called to ask me to go to Philadelphia with him for the Stones' concert. I met the Stones a couple of years ago at a press party for them at the

Playboy Club, where I was working as a bunny. I went out with Brian first. I was closer to him than any of the others. He was the true Rolling Stone and he introduced me to Mick. When I heard the Stones were coming for a tour, I knew I would hear from Mick. After the Philadelphia gig, we spent the week together in New York. Six beautiful days and nights. He was great. I never had to sit by the phone and wait for him to call. He'd call when he said he would—very punctual. Then he would rap and rap, very intelligently. If I wanted to go to Boston with him I could, or I'd wait for him to come back. I just felt beautiful. Everyone was really happy for me. Colette used to help me get dressed before I'd go out with him. A lot of chicks were envious. But I'd get calls from my friends who'd congratulate me and say, "Hey, you did it!" Like heavy score, right?

What did Jimi think?

Oh, he loved it. Mick and Jimi like each other a lot. They were like two little boys. Mick's like a kid, man. I couldn't help saying to him, "You're beautiful, man." I thought I was going to see him with long black hair and he said, "You just missed it, Devon." He looked nineteen, really young, healthy and together. The night of the Stones' Madison Square Garden concert I gave a surprise birthday party for Jimi at the apartment. Mick came in an out-of-sight black-and-white checkered zoot suit. It was their big night out and everyone had a fantastic time.

What did you do the rest of the time?

Mick wanted to see a lot of Jimi. I'd go over to the Plaza, where the Stones were staying, or he would come down here. We'd visit friends of mine. Most of the time Mick and I didn't do much of anything. He didn't want to go to any clubs. He loved to order from room service—coffee, toast, honey and crepes. One night we watched an old, old Errol Flynn movie. It was a gas. You know, like Monkey Man grooves on the Swashbuckler.

Did you ever go to the movies?

Mick doesn't like movies. He told me he didn't like making them—not even the one with Godard or Ned Kelly.

How would you describe him?

He's beautiful. It's his mouth and his eyes. They're blue, blue, blue, blue . . . After all, he's the biggest sex symbol ever.

Do you think he's narcissistic, conceited and in love with himself?
No, not at all. He plays games. Little innocent games, to find out
where you're at. He did it with me after not seeing me for three
years. I wondered, in ways, if he'd changed. He's a typical Leo, my
exact opposite. I'm an Aquarius. Flatter them to death, right? He
loves flattery. Honest flattery. He dug it when I said, "I've always
been a Stones fan." "The concerts are fabulous." "The new album
is great." The group is really together—much tighter since Brian's
death. He didn't have too much to say about Brian.

Why do you think he never married Marianne?
I think she's too old for him, physically. I hope I'm not going to
get into trouble for this. He may never see me again—and I want
another date with him.

What are his good qualities?
He's very gentle. Mick has magnetism, you know. When he
walks into a room everyone knows he's there and it's beautiful to
watch. He comes over and talks to you. He doesn't have to know
you, he just talks. He's a fantastic dancer.

What are his bad qualities?
He doesn't like to get up early at all.

Is Mick interested in sports? Does he have any hobbies?
We really never discussed it.

*What does he think about teenyboppers, groupies? He told the
press he didn't come to the States to sleep with teenyboppers.*
I think he meant it when he said that. A lot of girls I know—who
are considered groupies—he's known for a long time. He com-
mented on how some hadn't changed. They were just taking
different drugs.

What kind of drugs does he take?
I don't think I should answer that.

What do you think of Keith?
Dynamite. Sagittarius. Very powerful. Just like Jimi . . .

How did he feel about Altamont?
Really uptight. I felt bad, too. Everything else had gone so well.
Mick said he was going to go on vacation to Morocco for a couple
of weeks when he got back. He asked me to meet him in the south
of France and we'd drive to Marrakech.

How did he feel about the U.S. tour?

Mick loved being on the road. The Stones liked the New York audience better than the California one. It seemed to them that the California kids had saved up all their heaviest drugs for the Stones concert and said, "let's freak out," and didn't get into the music. The Madison Square Garden crowd was much more responsive.

What do you think the words "Rolling Stones" have come to symbolize?

Each one of them. Their freedom. Their weirdness and their honesty. They are completely honest.

What's the difference between the Stones and the Beatles?

To me, the Beatles are like the British Supremes. The Stones are down. They're funky, man. They're hard. They're like that as people and their music is them. I like the Stones' early stuff as much as I like their latest album.

How does Mick feel about John and Yoko?

I think he thinks it's all pretty silly, what they're doing and everything. Not the cause itself, but the way they're going about it.

What do you think Mick's talking about in a song like "Let It Bleed"?

Exactly what it says—it's more a support thing than a balling song. Like "Gimme Shelter" is all about getting together with other people and helping each other out. You know the song "Stray Cat Blues"? Mick told me he wrote it about a certain chick. He said he usually doesn't write like that but he had this particular one in mind. When he was in California, the girl called him and said, "Thanks for writing that song about me." He was shocked because he felt there was no way she could have recognized herself. But she did and it freaked him. Mick understands blues so well because he's into spades. He digs Tina Turner, Taj Mahal and Robert Johnson. He wrote a song about me.

> Your mother she was a country girl
> Where's your father, he done left this world
> Every brown girl has to pay a due
> Every white boy he just sings the blues

Do you think he's a big influence on fashion?

Yes, both guys and chicks dress like him. I do. T-shirts, scarves, studded pants. The night of Jimi's birthday he had a ruby ring on his baby finger. It looked like a Mafia-type ring.

What do you think other girls would like to know about Mick?

Well, he definitely likes women. He has a great body. He's intelligent and wonderful to be with.

What would you like to do?

I'd like to be in movies, but that's really getting up early. I hate getting up early. That's the one thing Mick and I have in common. Neither one of us likes to get up any earlier than two in the afternoon. We're both night people.

What do you think Mick liked most about you?

I wasn't wearing a wig. He really liked being with me and was glad I was there. There were a couple of bad moments. He'd call and say, "Could you please come over and just talk to me." I'd get there and say, "What's wrong?" and he'd say, "It's all better." We'd talk a lot. He was leaning on me.

What are you going to do for an encore?

Oh, I don't know. Probably marry Jimi . . . Want to publish my wedding pictures?

LIBERACE

This fifty-year-old groupie was standing outside the stage door with three albums of clippings and pictures of her idol and super-hero packed moisture-free in a large plastic envelope and tied with a piece of red knitting yarn. Tucked at an angle under the bow of yarn was an envelope containing a letter of her most fervent words. It was addressed, simply, to "Liberace."

He barrels down the slanting aisle, the bluish-white spot shining not so much on him as from him. He bounds up the three steps to the round stage, in the center of which stand the gleaming black Baldwin beauty adorned with the inevitable candelabra—these days completely electric, as in staying abreast of the times.

But the piano is merely a prop, as the twelve-piece "orchestra" is a prop, as are the outrageous costumes changed six times during the course not of the concert, but of the act. For that matter, the star himself is a prop to a central idea, which is Cuddlyqueer-demonicmanship. Coupled with Aspiration-to-Culture. Liberace is Long Island's Leonard Bernstein, and the Westbury Music Fair, in which his act had settled for a week, is Long Island's Lincoln Center. Or reverse it a little on the edges and get Fillmore East. Or wherever experience never happens.

Liberace is making a comeback, though I don't think he ever went away. Like cornflakes and Nixon. They are back now in an effort, which, as far as I can tell, is succeeding admirably, to make us all forget that the 1960s ever existed.

He takes the ovational applause in his teeth, pasting his cheeks up to the sides of his face and leaving them there, intact, as he

does a 360-degree tour of his admirers. He is completely surrounded by warmth. He looks a little like Eisenhower, the guy
who supposedly started it all—even before the airline-stewardess
phenomenon. Celebrities think they have to look happy in a
crowd. It's probably a natural reaction based on instinctive fear of
the mob.

They love him. They love his suits and his patter and the way he
smiles and moves when he plays the piano and sings. He sings
about as well as he plays the piano. But he makes fun of his
singing, as he makes fun of his clothes, and he cracks innumerable
jokes about his money and having so much of it. But he never,
ever, ever says anything funny about his music—though it really is.
He takes everything from Beethoven to "Let the Sunshine In,"
feeds it into the famous Liberace music grinder and transforms it
into hamburger. He is the great synthesizer, and the people love
him for bringing real music down to them. He is not unlike
Prometheus. He raps with the front rows of the audience: "What
do they represent?" he asks about the pattern his diamonds make
on his coat. "Oh, nothing," he replies semi-casually, inflections of
wealth dripping from his tonalities. The man is a genius. Instanta-
neously, he has referred the question to the instinctive fear of
abstract art and potential mind-blows and has made himself the
comforter. His music is exactly the same. He never plays one piece
through entirely: he always plays a medley, whether show tunes,
ragtime, rock, semiclassical or classical. Each song blends into the
next, all of the same "genre." He punctuates each medley with an
Important Song, although that, too, he plays only about halfway
through.

One of these ("my favorites") was the "Moonlight Sonata." It
was the highlight of the first section of the show, and everything
was coordinated. Liberace—black sequined tuxedo and tails,
sparkling in the light bath which was dimmed for the appropriate
seriousness. He played the first movement only.

He showmanned their eyes out and the oldsters were impressed
with his piano playing, which, all things considered, was not at all
bad. He kept time most of the evening, and made only one "mistake" (he lost a beat in a particularly fast number). He played
from every corner. He moved his hands a lot and people thought

this was elegant. He talked about his command performance for the Queen of England. He was simply marvelous.

His secret? Intimacy. He is personal. He takes the audience, as a group, into his confidence. "I want to tell you something . . ." He speaks of himself as a real person. He even makes references to the money he makes "from you." "Why shouldn't I wear this?" he says about a particularly ostentatious garment. "After all, you bought it." Closeness is his act.

He is a master at whatever it is he is. He is superplasticman. We can love him. He is completely nonthreatening, the apotheosis of charm. He is the dying art of being so wonderfully yesterday. He is the epitome of both the traditional standards of Middleamerica and the flaunting of their excesses. He is music-made-democratic and a reassertion of the "excellence" of the middle. He may not be Rubinstein, but then he's a cut above the jukebox. We can feel better than him and be awed by him at the same moment. Additionally, he is an institution, like Presley and Coke and Louis Armstrong and the Kennedys. Women can cuddle him and coo (he is one of their own). Men can relax with him.

His show is not without a touch of the carny. No matter how much class he tries to accumulate, Liberace will always be strictly a traveling road show, which is why, ultimately, he is great. He is the last of the vaudevillians. And so he brings his troupe along—a ten-year-old juggler ("the world's youngest") and his father. The kid juggles hoops and disks and twirls things on his arms and one leg while balancing a balloon on his nose and then, yes folks—and the little devil can scarcely be more than ten and he's no midget, let me assure you—his old man lights up three torches with real fire.

No one in the audience is completely certain that he won't drop one of them and make charcoal of the lot of them as he starts juggling the torches to the incessant beat of a drum. The lights all go off and we are transported into the primordial jungle right there on Long Island, encircling this kid prodigy, who is playing with fire, something kids are not allowed to do. But this is a special kid, and not even the lights of the plastic dome and the vinyl seats can obscure the fact that this kid is one of the mutants. He is completely coordinated and developed. And he is mocking us as we gape at him.

Suddenly, the father, the grinning old man who cannot juggle so the kid must have picked it up naturally or at birth or from his infant beads, goes running in a heart-stopping panic from the stage and up the aisle, while the kid keeps the three balls of fire going above his head. The drum continues, so very few people realize that the old man has gone. Then, just as the lad is winding up his act, the father barrels down the aisle again, carrying the wet cloth to wrap the torches in. That fire we had tucked away in the pockets of our incipient fear. It might have happened.

Liberace knows that no matter how much the people "love" him and his music, they are easily bored. He knows the attention span of Middleamerica, and he knows the wisdom of added dashes of savagery, masochism and pederasty. It was the sexiest little kid I ever saw—a freak show for the straights.

Next came the fat lady. Her name was Fay Mackay. She weighed nearly three hundred pounds, and she shrieked and imitated Jimmy Durante. She wore a black dress with four-foot long glittering white fringe that thankfully hid everything but swift glimpses of her ankles. She wore black stockings. She thought she was a honky Pearl Bailey. She sang "Hello, Dolly," and strutted around the stage. She did one set with Liberace and one without him. They flung sly sexual innuendos at each other. It was unbelievable.

Her big number was "The Twelve Days of Christmas," with different kinds of booze substituted for the traditional gifts. On the tenth day, she pretended to barf her guts up into the microphone. The audience went wild.

By his last set Liberace had the audience eating out of his hand. He strolled around the stage dipping into the audience, letting them feast their eyes on his diamond rings and buttons. He bantered with them about their cost again. And then came the capper—yes, he played "The Impossible Dream." A spotlight reflected off of a multi-faceted mirror globe, and stars glittered around the people like little calls from heaven. It all ended as it began.

He encored the second time, not with a song, but with another outrageous suit. White at the end/as black at the beginning: the rush outward into greater increments of innocence. And then he unscrewed his candelabra, one bulb at a time, to flowing orchestral strains of farewell. When he reached the center candle, the one that stood tallest, he "blew" it out. *Poof!* and out it went. *Even though it was electric!* The last phallic touch.

Then, the surprise they had all been waiting for but had feared he had forgotten. The door prize. Grandma's candy at the end of the trip for being good. The lights went out and . . . his jacket, suddenly, *marvelously,* surprisingly flashed on in a thousand tiny bulbs, blinking on and off. And then he was back—not in the mystery of flicking bulbs, but "real," in the flesh. And so the last spotlight came on and shone down on the treat, who waved a hand and ran up the aisle, glistening with sweat and diamonds.

Michael Rossman

EVENING, ARTICLE FINISHED

Evening, article finished, at puzzled ends and seeking a touch. I drop in on Oglesby. He is tortured by dissonance and choice. The hard-line kids with their clumsy liberal smear, and his exclusion from the National Collective now forming, have stung his political conscience into a harsh self-examination. The crazies are calling apocalypse down on our heads in the street—but their flawed example, too, cannot be denied, is shared in his blood, and mine. Does he *want* a revolution? "The precondition is a nuclear war . . . " And where will his body be then, or his hands busy with fuses? And is there choice, in our time geared to the inexorable bloom of beauty and despair?

He sits with his guitar at the typewriter, pursuing his muse down vanishing deChirico perspectives, trying to ignore the loudspeakers of ideology, the noise of the traffic. "I had the misfortune of having the right words at the right time." He thinks of the years when he first entered the Movement, of learning hard politics aloud when many were growing ready to follow that lead. It made him a national spokesman. "But I'm an artist . . . "

His fingers are distracted on the strings, steady around a coffee cup as he points to the spiky brave first collage of balsa wood scraps—left over from building a model biplane, "not plastic"— that he and Caleb painted together, with mutual five-year-old gravity, and glued on the wall.

He wants to follow song where it leads, explore the wilderness of creation. Outside, a fledgling movement struggles for self-definition while the clouds of repression gather. On the desk, among fragments of paper airplane, lie pages eleven to twenty, rough draft gone over once with dark pencil, using a deft analysis of the inaccuracies of Davidson's current hard-line dismissal of the "student power" movement as liberal and co-optative, to punch home a reappraisal of the possibility that students do in fact constitute an emergent and hitherto unrecognized class compatible with classical analysis. Life is a sphere of (r)evolution and tension. "I don't want to talk about it." It hurts, and the words go round and round.

Be kind to yourself, I tell him, asking for help. Return to your source through those harmonies. Decisions are made with the whole being, not only with minds wielding shards of mirror-sharp ideology: you must make space for your parts without words to have their say. In period with the moon we pass through modes of feeling; the spirit is an animal with rhythms. "At nexus of large decision all aspects of the organism—whether touchable by reason or not—must move and be freely together, if there is to be Right Action."

Imperialists of the heart, we fight to defend and extend a space of freedom that lives in its occupancy, and from which we draw our life. The rock or bottle curve of fingers echoes in every plucked minor chord. The revolution is transformed, not lost, in a guitar among the trees—if it be not so secure, was it ever? True patriot's harmony is a cycle between being the eagle guardian and being in other ways the life in the nest defended and growing. The revolution dies which does not bring its singers down from the hills to the lines in their time, nor grant them space to learn their songs in its own. And the warrior fails who does not know his softness as a man, nor honor his self's fullness and the needs of its changes.

YOUNG HEART PATIENT, JOHN
BROWN, RECEIVES RUBBER DUCKIE
WATCH AND TOY FROM COLUMBIA

John Brown, nine-year-old youngster from Passippany, New Jersey, underwent major heart surgery at a Houston hospital, performed by one of the foremost heart surgeons. Born with a defect, John has undergone similar surgery seven times prior to his last surgery, at which time a pacesetter was placed in his body. With the pacesetter, John is expected to be able to live a normal life and enjoy the activities of a normal boy his age.

John heard the "Rubber Duckie" song on KPRC on the Buzz Lawrence Show during the Sesame Street promotion and asked his mother to call Buzz to see if he would send him a Rubber Duckie. Buzz contacted Bill Heard at Columbia, and the two of them presented John with a Sesame Street album, a Rubber Duckie watch and a Rubber Duckie duck.

As Buzz and Bill left the sixth floor, the sounds of the rubber duck could be heard momentarily fulfilling the dreams of a young lad.

Steve Sidorsky

TOPICAL INDEX TO
THE AESTHETICS OF ROCK

by R. Meltzer (*Something Else Press*)

Robert Levin

ROCK AND REGRESSION: THE RESPONSIBILITY OF THE ARTIST

A Universal Cure for Illness
don't go to bed
until you
fall
in
it
—Norman Mailer, *Cannibals and Christians*

When we were conscious—when we saw precisely where it was, what we had to get to—what did we mean by "revolution"? We meant that we wanted (and knew it was possible) to *turn the whole scene around*. We meant the construction of an environment which was free of preimposed standards, disciplines and moralities, and conducive to the existential, and thus uncircumscribed, growth of all of our creative capabilities. We meant that we wanted to get to the most profound levels of who and what we are and effect a revolution of *fundamentals*, of sensibility, of value systems, of the way we perceive and judge what is and what is not beautiful and real. We meant no less than the destruction of our "nature" and the resurrection of our Nature.

For many of us, rock, a phenomenon which embodied the energies and expressed some of the best perceptions generated by our awakening and which was uniquely accessible to an enormous audience, gave promise of implementing the vision. Like the new "free" jazz, rock reflected a new and dynamic passion for life.

"They wouldn't have this music at the White House," drummer Sunny Murray remarked to me in an interview. "If they did they would think they were being attacked. All of a sudden a rock or an avant-garde jazz musician jumps up and goes into his thing and the politicians would run and hide under tables . . . Now if Lawrence Welk plays there—doo-pee-doo—oh, they cool now, man. The submission in the music tells them that the people is submissioned. But if a musician is playing like a rock or avant-garde jazz musician does, then, dig it, what's going on with the people?"

By the beginning of the 1970s, however, rock could claim about as much revolutionary potency as the Teamsters' Union.

A major factor in the decline of rock as a subversive energy has, of course, been the Aquarian-age businessman. But this agent of illusory revolution in the service of the status quo could not have been successful in rendering rock innocuous without the complicity of a fifth column, i.e., a susceptibility within rock artists to the control and exploitation of their work. That susceptibility is not sufficiently explained by "ambition" or "avarice" per se. What is meant by "every man has his price" is that every man has his uncertainty about the validity and sanity of his perception of the truth. To "sell out" is to capitulate to that uncertainty.

It is uncertainty which ambushed rock's revolutionary thrust, and I think looking at certain simultaneous socio-political occurrences in the country in general may clarify what I mean.

If the notion of revolution is, for the majority of Americans, subconsciously very attractive and, in the absence of belief in themselves and in their infinite potentialities as human beings, an utterly untenable notion; and if the eruption in the last decade of mutinous energies on all levels and in all departments of the culture consequently produced so intolerable a havoc in the psyches of those Americans that, to repress those energies and restore "stability," they could elevate a Richard Nixon to the Presidency, a similar kind of conflict must have existed for rock artists in relation to developments in their music.

Departing from old and familiar realities, rock musicians, in the pursuit of a new reality, had first to negotiate the labyrinthine antechambers of that new reality. The difficult new complexities—

self-conscious cerebrations, disjointed connections, etc.—which necessarily cropped up in their work as they sought to find entrance into that new reality and which were embodied in "heavy" forms like "psychedelic" rock, not only created confusions and opacities for rock artists in their own perception of their work, but also threatened to lose them the support and encouragement of their audiences and to disconnect them from their audiences— e.g., "We can't dance to rock any more." When an artist, through recognition and acclaim, regains the love he lost when he announced that he was going to be an artist, the prospect that he will lose that love again by taking the next step and altering the content and style of his work presents an excruciating dilemma. I think that ordinary doubts which rock artists had about the sanity of their pursuit were exacerbated by these circumstances into unbelief. Disease, madness and death, not the millennium, came to loom at the horizon. Rather than ride through the anxiety that grew out of this situation, which, like the hysteria of the electorate, was an indication that they were moving from one reality to another and was symptomatic of growth, rock artists aborted the mission and retreated, in multiple ways, into a glib, deceptive radicalism, an Aquarian-passive reaffirmation of "simplicity" and the "basics": to wit, the Beatles' "Revolution," "Get Back" and "Let It Be"; the increasing pervasiveness, as encouraged by Bob Dylan and Nashville Skyline, of country music—which music actually represents the quintessence of the pathological sensibility that has created the necessity for revolution; and the return to the songs and styles of 1950s rock and roll—a nascent stage of rock which belongs to a comparatively limited consciousness, a time when, say, street gang kids were still battling each other, before they got hip to who the real enemy was.

(Similar regressive developments in the name of "love" and "communication," it has to be pointed out, have occurred in the music of certain "New Thing" jazz musicians. The quasi-spiritualism which Pharaoh Sanders has settled for in albums like Karma and Jewels of Thought, and which, as one observer has remarked, has moved him dangerously close to Martin Denny, is the most glaring example. Albums like Ornette Coleman's Friends and Neighbors and Archie Shepp's For Losers are other examples. Still,

I think new jazz players have, by and large, done better at repelling the enemies within and without, and at sustaining the revolutionary integrity of their music, than have rock musicians, and I think this is because the black musician arrived at his present consciousness without the assistance of chemists or the local power company. He did not ascend via an air-conditioned express elevator, but up the stairs and through the ambush-ridden corridors of the stultifying superstructures which define our culture. The dangers he risked were far greater than a night at Bellevue. They involved his total being, the placing in jeopardy of his soul (of "soul"). And the natural, as opposed to artificial or vicarious, quality of his trip has given him a certain conviction in the consciousness he has reached, which makes that consciousness strong, dense and certain, makes it less revocable and not so vulnerable to control, exploitation and vitiation by the businessman, as is the consciousness of rock artists.)

But if it is a close to herculean task for artists of revolutionary persuasion to keep their work alive and audacious in this society, it is also imperative. America writhes in malignancy, and artists (because it is their profession, their raison d'être, to be in touch with truths beyond the collective consciousness) constitute the only force that might effect remission and reversal. The artist by definition is supposed to be aware and in the pursuit of an alternative to madness, and if he does not continue to chase that alternative, no matter how difficult social and personal circumstances may make such an endeavor, he is an accomplice to his own destruction. But there are very few artists left who haven't succumbed, in one manner or another, to ambivalences within themselves which have weakened their resistance to the poisons in the air—poisons which have debilitated their energies, dimmed their passion, eroded their belief in the sureness and accuracy of their visions, disengaged their concentration and focus from where they knew the truth really was, and diminished their revolutionary ardor to, at best, a sexless reformism.

A recent posthumous release of a Lenny Bruce record (*To Is a Preposition; Come Is a Verb*) reminds me of an artist who provides a good example of what I mean. The actual demise of Lenny Bruce, who was cornered by the mad guardians of the pathological American sensibility into a terminal depression, was anticlimactic. Bruce entered death on the day he stood before the censorship court and, rather than tear off his clothes, chose to ask the court for its "understanding." (There must have been a scent of the grave on Lenny's breath as he uttered that request.) Continually harassed in the last few years of his life by the police and the courts, Bruce was finally reduced to the level of his doubt. Too conflicted to say "fuck you" to his adversaries, and too hip to surrender completely, Bruce allowed himself to be seduced into the cul-de-sac of doing combat with American censorship law on the law's terms. Once he had done that, Bruce was no longer a figure of any serious consequence. He was into reform (which is to say, the liberalization and perpetuation of a murderous institution), not revolution. And he no longer had any place to take us that we had not already been.

(To be sure, one demands a great deal. Had Bruce told the court to "fuck off" he may well have been assassinated. But there are deaths which open love and promise conception to the seed, and deaths which inspire nothing more than an onanistic tension and leave the seed to expire in the plumbing. Is it foolish to speculate that if Galileo had not renounced his discoveries in order to save his neck we may have been blessed with the inspiration to put them to better use?)

But our vision was not reform, it was revolution. Indeed, when we were conscious, we were not talking about civilizing insanity. We wanted to abolish the police, not "humanize" them. Nor, when we were conscious, were we talking about hipping up mediocrity or changing shallow mores and conventions per se. Ad men and accountants smoking grass and growing hair. And we were not talking about saving malignant infrastructures and renovating superstructures. Like, we wanted to eliminate money, not spread it more equitably.

Ultimately, the only revolutionary artists worthy of the name are those who can trust and accept what they see, and who are prepared to will their way through and past their misgivings and the various stages of their anxiety, the subtle and blatant ambushes of fever, pain, strain, illness, anger, depression, confusion, listlessness, that are the road signs and the cruel, but necessary, hazards of the trip. To do anything else is to become the lie they originally stood against and to create, at best, nothing more than another hip commodity.

Nashville Skyline is a compromise, not an achievement—a withdrawal from anxiety, not a transcendence of it. It is the artist bringing it all back to the home which he did not, finally, have the courage to leave, and saying that, after all, the established order is correct.

Rock began as a visceral music, a body music, and, for sure, it must always be a music that calls the body to dance. But the dance must now have a new dynamic. And it must incorporate touch again. To return to simplicity—to the fox trot and lindy which issued from an uptight, emotional order whose cowardly puritanism eventually cornered us into the onanistic twist—is to deny and waste all that has been accomplished in the last decade. Rock must choose to pursue a new simplicity, a new reality on *the other side of anxiety*, which can be reached only by going *through* the anxiety which constitutes the price of the journey.

A new dance, a dance which belongs to a profoundly new sensibility, is what we mean.

About the Author

JONATHAN EISEN was born and raised in the City of New York, hereafter known merely as New York. He helped edit *The New Student Left* a long time ago. He helped found *The Activist*. He worked for *Commonweal* magazine and some others, for Pantheon Books and some others, and oh so briefly for *The New American Review*. He edited *Altamont, Age of Rock* and *Age of Rock 2*, the title for which came to him one day while humming "Rock of Ages." He wrote a book to be published by Random House in 1971. Please send title suggestions to the author c/o Random House, 201 East 50th St., New York City. All entries become the property of R. Meltzer. The winning entry gets a kiss from the author. He now makes his home in Thule, Greenland, ever since rock music got him into geology.

Twenty-Minute Fandangos and Forever Changes

Edited by Jonathan Eisen

A second cousin of Jon Eisen's The Age of Rock and The Age of Rock 2, Twenty-Minute Fandangos is a book of original writings that take off from music and rock. It is contemporary satire at its best—a serious spoof on today's rock culture, a parody on academic styles, and criticism generally. This new criticism is written in forms as up-to-date as the styles and music and lives it describes.

Twenty-Minute Fandangos is less an anthology than a collage of these different forms and it covers the scene with articles by the best writers writing.

Writers: Richard Meltzer, Robert Abrams, Nick Tosches, Sandy Pearlman, Ian Whitcomb, Michael Rossman, Susan Lewis, and Jonathan Eisen.

On: Rock, drugs, the Doors, Iggy Stooge, Andy Warhol, Jim Morrison, Janis, the Byrds, Elvis, sex and the world, N.Y., L.A., S.F., etc., business, fans, secrets.

Jonathan Eisen was born and raised in New York City. He was going to be an actor in high school but decided to work for political change instead during the 1960's. He helped edit The New Student Left (Beacon) and helped found The Activist at Oberlin College. He worked for Commonweal, Pantheon Books, and briefly for The New American Review. Eisen is editor of The Age of Rock and The Age of Rock 2, published by Random House, and co-editor (with Dennis Hale) of The California Dream, and the editor of Altamont. He is a contributor to many journals, and is at work on a novel.

JACKET DESIGN BY TED BERNSTEIN

Also available in a hardcover edition from Random House

A VINTAGE BOOK   V-120   394-71120-3